Lawyers Crossing Lines

Lawyers Crossing Lines

Ten Stories

Second Edition

Michael L. Seigel

James L. Kelley

CAROLINA ACADEMIC PRESS

Durham, North Carolina

Library of Congress Cataloging-in-Publication Data

Seigel, Michael L.
  Lawyers crossing lines : ten stories / Michael L. Seigel, James L. Kelley. -- 2nd
ed.
    p. cm.
  Rev. ed. of: Lawyers crossing lines / James L. Kelley. 2001.
  ISBN 978-1-59460-684-7 (alk. paper)
  1. Practice of law--United States--History. 2. Lawyers--Malpractice--United
States--History. 3. Lawyers--United States--Discipline--History. 4. Legal
ethics--United States--History. I. Kelley, James L. II. Kelley, James L. Lawyers
crossing lines. III. Title.

  KF306.S45 2009
  174'.30973--dc22

                                2009034811

                  CAROLINA ACADEMIC PRESS
                         700 Kent Street
                  Durham, North Carolina 27701
                   Telephone (919) 489-7486
                     Fax (919) 493-5668
                      www.cap-press.com

              Printed in the United States of America
                        2021 Printing

*To the lawyers in my life, including Professor Phillip Heymann,
the Honorable Edward R. Becker, and Philadelphia Organized Crime
Strike Force Chief Joel Friedman, who taught me early on that certain
lines are never to be crossed.*

—M.L.S.

Contents

Preface to the Second Edition

As the oft-repeated adage tells us, we typically learn more from our mistakes than our successes. In some realms, however, personal mistakes can be extremely costly, so it is best if we learn from the unfortunate miscues of others. That is the premise of this book.

Lawyers Crossing Lines is a collection of true stories about lawyers from all segments of the legal profession who transgressed ethical boundaries. Most of them ended up being sanctioned by their state Bar, sued for malpractice, prosecuted, or some combination of all three. In one case, however, a lawyer made the very difficult and potentially laudatory decision to follow his conscience and risk disciplinary action, which was instituted but ultimately came out in his favor. All of the cases are rich in detail, many are bizarre, and a few feature conduct so outrageous as to stretch the reader's credulity. Each tale is followed by comments and questions designed to explore the issues in greater depth.

This modest volume is intended as a supplemental text for students in Professional Responsibility courses at American law schools. It can also be used as the foundation for an advanced seminar in ethics. It is based on the proposition that, although the rules of professional responsibility are, of course, of supreme importance, sometimes the study of them can be monotonous and dry. More important, students—none of whom have been in law practice and most of whom have never been out in the working world— often find it hard to believe that the rules can be so easily and egregiously broken. Real world scenarios bring the ethical quandaries faced in everyday legal practice to life.

The chapters in the book include an in-depth look at the behavior of (1) Mike Nifong, the prosecutor in the infamous Duke rape case; (2) a family law attorney who had sexual relationships with six of his clients; (3) a criminal defense attorney and his prosecutor-friend who got in trouble over an autographed baseball; (4) an out-of-control judge whose outrageous conduct resulted in her removal from the bench; (5) class action lawyers at the prestigious firm of Milberg Weiss who for years illegally paid individuals to be lead plaintiffs; (6) a criminal defense attorney whose deliberate ineffective assistance aided his client in receiving the death penalty; and (7) a major but now defunct law firm that violated its duty of loyalty to a client by breaching a Chinese wall. There is also a chapter examining the conduct of lawyers who "went undercover" against a judge's law clerk to get information that would lead to the recusal of the judge, and one confronting the issue of whether it is ever proper to breach one's duty of confidentiality to overturn a wrongful conviction.

The information in the chapters comes from a variety of sources. Whenever possible, original records, including those from courts and disciplinary tribunals, were employed. In some cases, participants in the events were interviewed to gain additional detail and a present-day perspective on what transpired. Many chapters also rely on a whole variety of secondary sources, such as books, magazines, newspapers, and Internet sites. The book employs the ABA Model Rules on Professional Conduct (2008) as its primary source of law, although from time to time it also makes reference to the ethical rules of specific jurisdictions as well as some state and federal criminal and civil statutes and regulations. The authors assume that students will have a copy of the ABA Model Rules available to them as they engage the text.

By its very nature, *Lawyers Crossing Lines* creates a pretty dismal picture of the ethical standards of the legal profession. Not only does it pick out the bleakest cases for discussion, but it often reveals that lawyers situated on the periphery of these cases who became aware of gross ethical violations by other lawyers simply looked the other way. Nevertheless, we do not intend to suggest that the book is a portrait of how the profession as a whole behaves. There is, of course, no objective way to measure levels of ethical conduct among lawyers; informed judgments about the seriousness and scope of misconduct come from practitioners, disciplinary authorities, malpractice insurers, and students of the problem. Nevertheless, we believe firmly that the great majority of lawyers play by the rules—most of them scrupulously, others in their fashion. Very few lawyers give in to temptation and fewer still plainly flout their ethical responsibilities. These, then, are cautionary tales.

We are hopeful that this work will help create an atmosphere in the classroom in which lively discussion and debate take place. The more robust the discussion of ethics occurring in our law schools, the more likely we are to turn out future generations of lawyers who understand, respect, and obey ethical lines. That is our goal.

Michael L. Seigel
Tampa, Florida
August 2009

Acknowledgments

The creation of this book was a truly collaborative effort that crossed generational lines. First and foremost, recognition must be given to the late Judge James L. Kelley, who conceived of this project and carried it through to fruition in the first edition. Though I never met Judge Kelley, I have come to appreciate the wisdom he developed through his years on the bench, and I have done my best to remain faithful to his vision. Two of his original chapters remain a part of this edition, and they are remarkable for their research depth, lucid writing, and cogent analysis.

I am, of course, indebted to Publisher Keith Sipe and Senior Editor Linda Lacy of Carolina Academic Press for inviting me to write this second edition of *Lawyers Crossing Lines*. I honestly don't know why they thought I was right for the job because, at the time they asked, they had not yet seen the manuscript for the first book that I wrote for them, though I flatter myself to think that they were aware of my mystery novel and figured that my experience as a fiction writer would serve me well in this endeavor. In any event, I am grateful for the opportunity, and I hope I have lived up to their very high professional expectations.

The process by which this second edition was created was one of the most enjoyable experiences of my teaching career. Early on, I realized that, to meet a tight production schedule, I would need an extraordinary amount of assistance. After some brainstorming, I scheduled a seminar at the University of Florida Frederic G. Levin College of Law based on the first edition of the book. After collectively reading and analyzing that work, each student selected a new ethical scandal about which to research and write. The eight best seminar papers became the foundation for eight new chapters in this edition.

Therefore, I am grateful for the enthusiasm, diligence, and research and writing abilities of the following students, listed in the order of the chapters for which they provided help: Andres Healy, Susan Malove, Elizabeth Manno, Emily Banks Jahr, Stephanie L. Varela, Mindy Yergin, Loren J. Beer, and Ann Hove. I could not have accomplished this project in the time allotted without their superb contribution to the effort. They made me proud of the University of Florida, and I'm confident that they will each continue to make me proud as successful practicing attorneys who understand where the ethical lines are drawn.

I also want to acknowledge the contribution of Robert J. Luck, who graciously agreed to serve as my copy editor and proofreader for this endeavor. A former stellar student of mine, Robert has lent a helping hand on nearly every project I have undertaken since his graduation. It is relationships like ours that makes teaching such a rewarding endeavor.

Finally, I must thank the University of Florida Levin College of Law, and the University of Florida Foundation, for their financial support of this project. I could not conceive of a more supportive environment in which to carry out my work.

Michael L. Seigel
Tampa, Florida
August 2009

Lawyers Crossing Lines

Chapter 1

Breaking Up Is Hard to Do[*]

*"Were you aware that on or about July 16, 1992 your company's law firm
was considering whether Admiral Murphy could divert business to a new
company, allowing your company to wither?*

No. Why would I think that? They were our lawyers."

  —Colloquy between examining attorney and Margot Bester of Murphy
  & Demory, in *Murphy & Demory v. Admiral Murphy.*

Murphy & Demory, Ltd., a Washington, D.C., public relations firm, was
founded in 1987 by Daniel Murphy, a former Admiral and Deputy Director
of the Central Intelligence Agency, and Will Demory, a lawyer and econo-
mist. The firm prospered, generating $2.5 million in revenues in 1991, from
which the Admiral (as he was called) and Demory took home $340,000
apiece. The Admiral as the rainmaker and Demory as the office manager
seemed to be a winning formula. Unfortunately, the firm's success was accompanied by growing tensions between the two owners over the kinds of
business they should cultivate, over their respective roles, and—from the
Admiral's perspective—over Demory's performance. With each owning fifty
percent of the company's stock, neither was in a position to assert control.
Power was also shared through corporate offices, with the Admiral as chairman of the board and Demory the CEO.

Demory responded to a worsening situation by standing apart and
keeping his own counsel. The Admiral took a more aggressive approach.
Without consulting Demory, he began to explore ways he might take over
the firm, or, failing that, start his own firm, taking along the clients he had
brought in. This chapter tells the story of how Murphy & Demory, Ltd.
(M&D) was broken up, leading to court judgments against the Admiral and
Pillsbury, Madison & Sutro—M&D's corporate counsel which took sides
with the Admiral.

---

[*] This chapter is based on the original research and writing of James L. Kelley. Because
Judge Kelley used only original court records in composing his narrative, the chapter is without
footnotes.

In June 1992, the Admiral met with Deanne Siemer, a partner in the Washington office of Pillsbury, Madison & Sutro, a national law firm based in San Francisco. The Admiral's relationship with Siemer went back to 1977 when he was Deputy Undersecretary of Defense for Policy and Siemer, not yet forty, was General Counsel of the Defense Department. He had continued to seek her advice from time to time after leaving Defense. Seimer's work for M&D had begun shortly after the firm was founded in 1987 and Siemer was a partner at Wilmer, Cutler & Pickering. She continued to represent M&D on a variety of matters after she moved to the Pillsbury firm in 1990. She also worked for the Admiral on personal matters, like his will, and on matters involving both personal and firm interests which were not readily separable. However, all Pillsbury bills, whether related to M&D or the Admiral, were sent to and paid by M&D.

After their meeting, Siemer directed Frazer Fiveash, an associate, to do research and write a memorandum on the law governing dissolution of Virginia corporations, the state in which M&D was incorporated. In July, Siemer asked Fiveash for a memorandum concerning whether the Admiral would have the right to divert business from M&D to a new company to be controlled by him alone, allowing M&D to "wither." Fiveash expressed concern about a conflict of interest, but did as she was told. Siemer reviewed the Fiveash memoranda and conveyed their substance to the Admiral by phone. In August, another young associate was assigned to draft a complaint for the judicial dissolution of M&D, with the Admiral as plaintiff and M&D as defendant. Demory was to learn of the memoranda and complaint only after M&D sued the Admiral.

The Admiral and Demory had always operated their firm informally, more like a partnership than a corporation. Board meetings had been viewed as a formality, with no real business transacted. By this time, however, the Admiral had learned enough corporate law from Deanne Siemer to know that a vote of the board of directors could shift control to him, despite the equal shareholdings of himself and Demory. There were three board members: the Admiral, Demory, and Margot Bester, a lawyer who had been with the firm from the beginning. The Admiral believed that if he could persuade Bester to join forces with him, together they could activate a dormant board and vote effective control to him.

Apparently assuming that the husband could control the wife, in late August the Admiral directed Jeff Grieco, an M&D employee, to meet with Bester's husband, Bruce Markowitz. Grieco immediately phoned Markowitz and arranged an appointment at his law office for later that day. As Grieco described his mission: "The Admiral asked me to get a pulse from Bruce as to what Bruce thought Margot would want to do" if the Admiral "had to restructure the firm or start a new company."

Grieco and Markowitz knew one another socially. Both were avid Buffalo Bills fans, the kind who debate the merits of draft choices. Following pleasantries of the "how 'bout them Bills" sort, Grieco outlined the Admiral's concerns about M&D and his plans for either taking control or leaving. Grieco charged Demory with various faults and transgressions, personal and professional: Demory was involved in illegal transactions with Libya and Iraq; he had opened foreign bank accounts to evade income taxes; he wasn't developing business for M&D and was undermining clients of others to win them over to himself. As if that weren't enough, Grieco claimed that Demory was on anti-depressant medication.

Markowitz thought Grieco had come to him "to convince me to persuade Margot to leave Will [Demory] and join the Admiral in a new firm and to poison my mind against Demory." Markowitz was "extremely concerned and upset" by Grieco's statements and, believing his wife might be in professional jeopardy, phoned her right after Grieco left. She told him Grieco's charges were baseless and that she would side with Demory in any struggle for control. In hindsight, Markowitz found it "rather humorous that [Grieco] thought I would have that kind of influence over her. She's a lawyer and her office was two doors down from the Admiral's. All he had to do was ask her himself."

Frances Gray was the office manager at M&D during the breakup. Several days before the Admiral resigned, Grieco asked Gray to copy the contents of the safe. Gray made the requested copies—including client contracts, income tax returns, balance sheets, income statements, and current bank and money market balances—and sent them by messenger to the Pillsbury firm, as Grieco had requested. After the breakup, Gray had to decide whether to stay with M&D or join the Admiral's new company. It was "one of the hardest decisions I've ever had to make, but I just didn't think Will was going to be viable."

As the break-up became imminent, the legal work involved in making it happen fell primarily to Keith Mendelson. Mendelson had come to Pillsbury, Madison & Sutro as an associate in 1984. He was promoted to "senior counsel" in 1991 and was under consideration for partner in August 1992 when Siemer drew him into the problems at M&D. Mendelson first became involved on Friday, August 28, when he was called into meetings with other Pillsbury lawyers, Grieco and another M&D employee, ostensibly for his expertise in corporate law. Mendelson's notes included the statement that he was "uncomfortable that what we were trying to do was find out information about a client of ours," but he was not uncomfortable enough to decline becoming involved. After that meeting, Siemer asked Mendelson to accompany her to talk with Demory the next day in response to the Admiral's request.

Siemer and Mendelson met with Demory at M&D the next morning, a Saturday. As Mendelson recalled the meeting, Siemer opened on a concilia-tory note, saying they were there to "help you guys work out your problems." At that point, Mendelson recalled that Demory "looked like he was going to cry" as he said: "Deanne, I can't tell you how happy I am that you are taking that approach." But as the meeting progressed, Demory's answers to Siemer's questions (according to Mendelson) became evasive and defensive. Siemer closed the meeting by urging Demory to meet with the Admiral over the weekend to "see if they could sort things out."

Demory remembered the meeting with Siemer and Mendelson some-what differently. Siemer had begun by saying that she was representing M&D, neither Demory nor the Admiral individually. The meeting proceeded on a cordial note with general discussion of company business and prospects. Siemer went on to comment, however, that she had met with the Admiral several times in the past year to discuss "restructuring" or breaking up M&D, a disclosure which "came as pretty much of a shock" to Demory. After that, the tone of the meeting changed. Demory sensed that he was being interro-gated, that Siemer was becoming accusatory and implying he might be in-volved in illegal dealings.

After Siemer and Mendelson left his office, Demory phoned Margot Bester to report what had been said and his impression that Siemer was acting at the Admiral's direction. Putting that meeting together with what Grieco, the Ad-miral's agent, had said to Bester's husband earlier that week, Demory and Bester decided to fire the Pillsbury firm and hire new corporate counsel. They called John Dowd of the Washington firm of Akin, Gump, Strauss, Hauer & Feld, still on Saturday morning. Dowd then called Siemer's office and left a message informing her of his firm's representation and that Demory would not meet with the Admiral over the weekend. Siemer interpreted Dowd's message to mean that he was representing Demory individually. As far as she was con-cerned, the Pillsbury firm still represented both M&D and the Admiral.

That afternoon, Mendelson helped the Admiral draft a letter to Demory proposing that he be given control of M&D. The letter was delivered by mes-senger and Demory found it on his front stoop on Sunday morning. In the meantime, the Admiral renewed his efforts to gain the support of Margot Bester for his takeover proposal. He phoned her and she agreed, reluctantly, to meet with Mendelson at her home. Mendelson went to Bester's home in Potomac, Maryland, on Sunday around noon. Bester's husband, Bruce Markowitz, joined the discussion. Mendelson began by saying he was there as counsel for M&D, not for the Admiral personally. That got him a cool recep-tion. Bester told him that, in her view, the Pillsbury firm had a conflict of interest and that, as a director of M&D, she did not acquiesce to his presence in their home as counsel for the firm. Markowitz, an experienced corporate bankruptcy lawyer who dealt with conflict of interest problems routinely, added his opinion that the Pillsbury firm "had a blatant conflict." Markowitz later testified: "I found that outrageous. I couldn't believe that this was happening in my living room. It was something you learn about in law school, Ethics 101." The meeting went nowhere, and Mendelson departed.

Mendelson had expressed concerns about a conflict of interest to Siemer before his Sunday meeting with Bester. Demory was strongly opposed to the Admiral's takeover plan, and he did own half of M&D and was its CEO. Immediately after leaving Bester's home, Mendelson called Siemer from a phone booth to restate his concerns. She reassured him that they didn't have a conflict. Siemer flew to California that afternoon on other business and later to Europe, leaving Mendelson to cope with a rapidly unraveling situation.

That Sunday afternoon, Demory drove to the Admiral's home and handed him a letter rejecting the Admiral's restructuring proposal. The two sat at the kitchen table while the Admiral read the letter. There was no discussion and Demory departed to fax a letter to Siemer firing the Pillsbury firm as counsel to M&D. When the Admiral learned of that the next day, he purported to rehire the firm, even though that authority was vested in Demory as CEO.

The Admiral, a former commander of the Sixth Fleet, would later refer to that Monday as "D Day." In the morning, accompanied by Mendelson and armed with a statement Mendelson had written for him, he met with the M&D employees. He stated that he and Demory "have drifted apart over the last three months." The Admiral expressed regret for having "delegated too much of the management" but asserted that he "cannot accept this situation any longer." He outlined his proposal to transfer a controlling stock interest and management authority to himself, the proposal Demory had rejected the day before. The Admiral expressed his willingness to "try to work things out" with Demory. Failing that, however, he would "seek to dissolve M&D and form a new company of my own." And if that were to happen, all the employees would be invited to join his new company.

Over the next three days, the Admiral and Demory met several times in fruitless attempts to resolve their differences. Then on September 4, Demory fired Grieco, the Admiral's factotum, without consulting the Admiral. Grieco went directly to the Admiral who rehired him on the spot. Demory took the position that "in light of what Mr. Grieco has done over the preceding week or so," it was necessary to fire him before there could be "constructive discussions." But as the Admiral saw the firing of Grieco: "That's a deal breaker; that's the end of it."

The board of directors was to meet on the afternoon of September 9. Mendelson met with the Admiral, Grieco, and several other employees in the morning to review their resignations and letters to M&D clients soliciting their business for the new company. Mendelson also drafted a resignation letter and a statement for the Admiral to deliver at the board meeting. Before the meeting, Mendelson discussed his conflict-of-interest concerns once again with another Pillsbury lawyer. As he recalled: "I wanted to be sure in my own mind what capacity I was going in. It was pretty clear by that time that Admiral Murphy was our client and our only client."

The board meeting was brief, its outcome foreordained. The Admiral brought the meeting to order and moved that M&D be "voluntarily dissolved." As expected, that motion failed for want of a second. The Admiral then submitted his letter of resignation, along with the resignations of several employees who moved out that afternoon to new office space in the same building. The next day, articles of incorporation for Murphy & Associates were duly filed in Richmond.

Margot Bester stayed with M&D. She described the breakup as "devastating." Within a short time, "the employees left, the majority of the clients left, which really affected our income stream. That in turn affected our ability to hire new people who could bring in new business."

Making a bad situation worse, M&D had recently entered into a lease for new space which called for payments of $1.5 million over seven years. The Admiral's new firm could have made effective use of that space, but the Admiral declined to assume the lease.

A few months after the breakup, M&D sued the Admiral, Siemer, Mendelson, and Pillsbury, Madison & Sutro in the Circuit Court for Fairfax County, Virginia. The complaint alleged breach of contract and violation of fiduciary duty by the Admiral and legal malpractice by Siemer, Mendelson, and the Pillsbury firm. The Akin, Gump firm represented M&D. The Pillsbury firm hired another firm to defend it against the malpractice claim. The Admiral opted for local representation, possibly on the theory—mistaken, as it turned out—that Fairfax lawyers would connect better with a Fairfax County judge. Following a period of discovery, the case went to trial on April 25, 1994, before Judge Jane Roush, sitting without a jury. The trial lasted six days; fifteen witnesses testified; some four hundred exhibits were offered in evidence.

Winston Churchill once summoned a waiter, saying: "Pray remove this pudding. It has no theme." A court case, like a pudding, needs a theme, a compelling message to shape the facts and impress the judge with the justice of your cause. The plaintiffs would speak of betrayal. They were the innocent victims of a treacherous scheme. The Admiral, assisted by the Pillsbury lawyers, destroyed the firm he and Demory had worked so hard to build. For their part, the Admiral's lawyers would portray him as the practical business-man, the one who had sought a constructive compromise, the reasonable one. It was Demory, they said, who had shown a "remarkable lack of com-mon sense," who had "dropped a bomb on himself" and M&D.

As the plaintiff, M&D had the burden of proving that the Pillsbury firm had deviated from the standard of care—the basis of a legal malpractice claim. Stated another way, the issue was whether the firm had acted like hy-pothetical "reasonable lawyers" would have acted under similar circum-stances? And in a case like this, where rules of legal ethics prescribe conduct in some detail, those rules may go far in determining the standard of care.

M&D relied on its expert witness, David Epstein, to establish the standard of care and to prove that Siemer and Mendelson had breached it. Epstein's qualifications were impressive. A graduate of Harvard Law School, he was a founding member of the District of Columbia's Board of Professional Respon-sibility. He had taught professional responsibility at the Georgetown University Law Center and had served as an Assistant United States Attorney before enter-ing private practice. He had represented lawyers charged with ethics violations and served as an expert witness in cases involving professional misconduct.

Epstein's testimony was elicited by hypothetical questions incorporating the basic facts of the plaintiff's case. He was asked to assume that the Pillsbury firm had an attorney-client relationship with M&D when the Admiral went to Siemer for advice on restructuring or leaving the firm; that the Pillsbury lawyers provided the Admiral with the requested advice; that neither the Admiral nor the lawyers disclosed to M&D that the Pillsbury firm was working for the Ad-miral; and that they assisted him in carrying out a strategy to break up the firm.

The principle is embedded in Western culture: "No man can serve two masters" (*Matthew* 6:24). "Whose bread I eat, his song I sing" (German proverb). Conflicts of interest are among the most pervasive, difficult, and consequential problems faced by lawyers. The Model Rules of Professional Conduct, in force in the District of Columbia and over forty other jurisdic-tions, contain no fewer than eight conflict-of-interest rules, far more atten-tion than the Model Rules devote to any other topic.

All parties agreed that the law of the District of Columbia, where most of Pillsbury's work for the Admiral had been done, would govern the malprac-tice issue. Epstein cited Rule 1.7 of the District of Columbia's Rules of Profes-sional Conduct—adapted from the ABA's Model Rule—as the best evidence of the applicable standard of care. That rule prohibits simultaneous represen-tation of two clients whose interests are "adverse"—the classic, direct conflict of interest. Textbook examples include the lawyer who represents both husband and wife in a divorce, or both buyer and seller in a real estate sale—situations where it's impossible to fully represent one side without compromising the other.

In Epstein's opinion, when Admiral Murphy set out to explore a takeover his objective was adverse to M&D—a corporate entity represented by its CEO and its board of directors. Epstein reasoned: "Once the third party [the Admiral] starts moving off in a direction that is serving only his interests, and the CEO of the corporation [Demory] and the board are not kept informed of that divergence, the law firm should advise the president and the board that there's a conflict." Unless both sides then consent to its continued participation, the law firm should then withdraw from the matter altogether, leaving both sides free to retain separate counsel.

Here, the conflict should have been apparent back in June, when Siemer assigned Fiveash to research the Admiral's options without telling Demory. According to Epstein, the Pillsbury firm's failure to withdraw at that point began a continuing violation of the rule, until the firm was fired in late August. And even if the situation in June were viewed as not involving a present conflict, the lawyer is expected to look ahead and see that—as Judge Roush expressed it—"this situation is fraught with potential adversity."

After Demory fired the Pillsbury firm and hired Akin, Gump, Pillsbury ceased to be in violation of Rule 1.7 because that rule applies only to *present* clients. However, Pillsbury went on to violate a separate conflict-of-interest rule by continuing to represent the Admiral against its *former* client, M&D. The District of Columbia's ethics rules prohibit a lawyer from switching sides during a controversy, unless the former client consents. According to Epstein, the rule is aimed at the law firm that switches clients after learning confidential information from the former client—information that may now be used against it. Pillsbury had obtained a wealth of inside information about the company while claiming to represent M&D and secretly helping the Admiral to break it up. In addition to violating the Rules of Professional Conduct, Epstein pointed to the common-law principle—a precursor of more recent rules of ethics—that a fiduciary (a lawyer or a trustee, for example) owes a duty of "undivided devotion and attention" to the client. In Epstein's opinion, the Pillsbury firm had violated that principle by covertly assisting the Admiral against its own client.

Counsel for the Pillsbury lawyers didn't call an expert witness of their own to controvert Epstein's opinions. It fell to Deanne Siemer to convince the judge that the Pillsbury lawyers, following her lead, had not committed malpractice. Siemer was a veteran trial lawyer with an abrasive manner. During

her years at Wilmer, Cutler & Pickering and later at the Pillsbury firm, she
was widely respected but disliked by some opposing counsel. Exceptionally
gifted, energetic and ambitious, she had written a book, *Understanding Modern Ethical Standards*, for the National Institute of Trial Advocacy, of which
she was chair-elect at the time of trial. Siemer might well have qualified as an
expert on legal ethics in a case in which she wasn't herself a defendant.

Siemer began by describing herself as the Admiral's long-time lawyer,
downplaying her work for M&D as "discrete matters" and suggesting that
there was no lawyer-client relationship between the Pillsbury firm and M&D
when the Admiral began to explore abandoning ship. It was shown, however,
that Siemer had done significant work for M&D on numerous occasions and
that Demory and Bester considered the Pillsbury firm to be counsel for their
company. In any event, Epstein laid that question to rest when he testified
that the comparative duration of two concurrent representations was irrelevant—a conflict would remain "if you've been representing one client for
fifty years and a second one for three weeks."

Siemer testified that she had become aware of a possible conflict of interest problem when the Admiral had asked her about restructuring M&D in
June 1992, and again in July when she asked Fiveash to look at diverting business to a new corporation, allowing M&D, in Siemer's words, "to wither." As
Siemer had seen it then: "I had been asked to provide information. It was my
judgment that [it was] in Admiral Murphy's interest he should receive correct
information, then he knows what to do, and he'll act correctly. It was [also]
in the corporation's interest that he receive accurate information.... They had
the same interest." Seemingly incredulous, counsel asked Siemer: "You didn't
possibly think, did you, that the corporation had an interest in having its
business diverted elsewhere and it withering up?" Unfazed, Siemer responded: "That wasn't the question that was asked. Whatever information
needed to be delivered to Dan Murphy so that he could make a decision, that
was in the corporation's interest." As long as the Admiral hadn't made a final
decision to leave, she thought it proper to assist him, without informing Demory—even to the point of preparing a formal complaint for dissolution of
M&D which she termed "a housekeeping matter."

Siemer didn't recall considering the conflict of interest issue again until
after her somewhat confrontational meeting with Demory on August 28—a
meeting she had arranged at the Admiral's request but in which she claimed
to be representing M&D. By that time the Admiral, with Mendelson's help,
was drafting his restructuring proposal and Grieco was meeting with Pillsbury lawyers to work out the details of setting up a new firm. In this advanced stage of the Admiral's plans, Siemer discussed the conflicts issue with

Mendelson and other Pillsbury lawyers. Nothing had happened to that point to change her mind. "We thought it was really quite clear there was not a conflict," adding, however: "I made the judgment."

Mendelson hadn't found Siemer's judgment completely reassuring. On September 1, after Demory had fired the Pillsbury firm but it was still representing the Admiral, Mendelson telephoned Ben Vandegrift in Sweden. Vandegrift was Mendelson's supervisor and head of the corporate group in the Washington office. Mendelson had come to recognize that they were dealing with "a thorny, hard issue" and he wanted to get Vandegrift's judgment on it. Mendelson described the facts to Vandegrift who concluded that they didn't present a problem. Vandegrift added that "ultimately, the partner in charge [Siemer] has to make that decision." Mendelson also sought out George Sugiyama, a member of the firm's professional responsibility committee. Sugiyama had acknowledged that it was a "tough call" but he, too, saw it as Siemer's decision.

Judge Roush asked Epstein whether there are distinctions in the potential malpractice liability of a partner like Siemer, compared to Mendelson, the senior counsel, and to associates. The judge expressed particular concern about the exposure of a young associate like Fraser Fiveash. "She's raised the issue and she's been overruled and she's a year and a half out of law school." Under the District's Rule 5.2 subordinate lawyers are bound by the rules "notwithstanding that the lawyer acted at the direction of another person." Epstein responded: "Today is the funeral of former President Nixon [which recalls] a situation where many people were doing what they were asked to do, but knew that it was wrong, and they got into a lot of difficulty and were disbarred for following orders." Subordinate lawyers may avoid responsibility only if they acted in accordance with a supervisory lawyer's "reasonable" resolution of an "arguable" question of professional duty. In Epstein's opinion, Siemer's resolution of the question had not been reasonable, nor had the question itself been arguable.

The plaintiffs called a certified public accountant with extensive experience in business valuations in support of their claim of damages. Using alternative methods, the accountant came up with pre-breakup values ranging between $1.5 and $2.5 million. He testified that after the break-up M&D's liabilities exceeded its assets and therefore its worth was $0.

Judge Roush rendered her decision from the bench in June 1994, about a month after the trial ended. She found that, prior to his resignation on September 9, the Admiral had breached his employment contract with M&D "by devoting his energies to activities other than those in the corporation's best interest." Among other things, the Admiral had formed a new company "whose primary purpose is to offer consulting services in direct competition with M&D" and induced its employees to leave and join his new company. She assessed compensatory damages of $1 million against the Admiral for breach of contract.

The judge also found that the Admiral had breached his fiduciary duty as an officer and director of M&D. She acknowledged that "some amount of predeparture planning is permissible. A fiduciary need not wait until he is out in the street until he looks for other work." She concluded, however, that Admiral Murphy's "preresignation planning crossed the line by a considerable amount into impermissible acts of disloyalty to M&D." Before embarking on that course, he "should have disclosed his intentions or resigned to form his new company."

Judge Roush turned to the malpractice claim against Siemer, Mendelson, and the Pillsbury firm. She ruled that the Pillsbury defendants had committed malpractice at every stage of their involvement with the Admiral in the breakup of M&D, listing numerous specifics, among them:

- by accepting representation of the Admiral in his efforts to take control of M&D or to form a new corporation, before resigning from M&D;
- by simultaneously representing the Admiral in matters adverse to their client M&D without disclosing the dual representation;
- by meeting with director Margot Bester to enlist her support in the Admiral's takeover plans;
- by inducing M&D employees to resign and to join Murphy & Associates;
- by drafting the Admiral's restructuring proposal;
- by drafting letters for M&D clients terminating their relationships and directing that their files be sent to Murphy & Associates;
- by filing a lawsuit seeking judicial dissolution of their then-former client, based in part on confidential information obtained from M&D employees during their representation of M&D.

Judge Roush found that Deanne Siemer's testimony—that the interests of the Admiral and M&D had been the same—"lacked credibility." She expressed agreement with Epstein that M&D "had no interest in Admiral Murphy's knowledge of how to undermine the company." She concluded that "Ms. Siemer willfully ignored the District of Columbia Rules of Professional Conduct with which she was well familiar, having written a treatise on legal ethics.

Judge Roush was disturbed that "the Pillsbury defendants ignored the warnings of associates at the law firm that the dual representation of Admiral Murphy was rife with conflicts of interest. Every inquiry by an associate into the propriety of the firm's actions had been referred back to Ms. Siemer for resolution. Clearly, Pillsbury, Madison & Sutro's internal mechanisms for resolution of ethical issues are seriously deficient. The partner in charge of the client relationship who is least likely to be objective is the ultimate arbiter of whether the firm has a conflict of interest."

That left the question whether Keith Mendelson, a senior counsel at the time, was liable for malpractice equally with Siemer and the firm. Siemer had been in charge and had, as she put it, "made the call." Normally, Mendelson would be expected to take directions from Siemer, the responsible partner. Should he refuse to take orders, he might jeopardize his chances for partnership for which he was under consideration at the time. Such pressures are not always subtle. Mendelson recalled Siemer saying to him as she was getting on an elevator: "Keep in mind you are a senior counsel, sort of pushing partner on this." Judge Roush noted that she was "not unsympathetic to Mr. Mendelson's difficult position," but found that "he was equally responsible for the legal malpractice. Simply put, Mr. Mendelson was senior enough that he should have put a stop to the undisclosed dual representation by disclosing it to the board in obtaining their consent of, failing that, by withdrawing from the representation."

Judge Roush found that the Pillsbury defendants' malpractice had damaged M&D in the amount of $500,000. How she arrived at that figure (or, for that matter, the $1 million damage awards against the Admiral) she did not explain. Some forms of damage, such as hospital bills, can be calculated to the dollar. In a case like this, however, damage awards are often highly judgmental. A few weeks after the trial, the parties settled all claims in the lawsuit for undisclosed amounts, foreclosing any appeals.

Keith Mendelson made partner at Pillsbury, Madison & Sutro in January 1995. Deanne Siemer and her lawyer husband had worked in the Trust Territory of the Pacific Islands in the 1970s. She left the Pillsbury firm and they returned to establish Siemer & Willens, a civil practice firm, on Saipan, the Mariana Islands.

Comments and Questions

1. This chapter introduces the subject of conflicts of interest with a direct and blatant conflict in violation of Model Rule 1.7(a), which states the general conflicts rule. (The substance of the District of Columbia rule, as relevant here, is the same.) Note that Judge Roush found multiple acts of malpractice, based on conflict-of-interest violations, from the time the Admiral

first sought Siemer's advice about his "options" until he resigned to form his own firm. According to an article in *Of Counsel* (August 15, 1994, p.20) "some observers have publicly marveled at the obviousness" of the conflict. The article cites Professor Stephen Gillers's suggestion that "there doesn't seem to have been anything subtle, much less waivable, about this particular conflicts charge."

One can only speculate why Deanne Siemer, a veteran litigator and author of a book on lawyer ethics, could have gotten into this conflict, and stayed in it, especially after an experienced lawyer like Keith Mendelson kept questioning her decision. Could she have convinced herself, as she claimed, that her services were beneficial to M&D as well as to the Admiral? Judge Roush flatly rejected that explanation, finding that it "lacked credibility." Did her long-term professional relationship with the Admiral divert her loyalty in his direction at M&D's expense? Or did she commit a deliberate violation of Rule 1.7, as Judge Roush found? If the judge was right, why might a lawyer in Siemer's position commit such a violation?

2. Since this case was decided, Model Rule 1.13 has been enacted to give specific guidance to lawyers who represent organizations. Section (a) of the rule makes it clear that a lawyer retained by an organization represents the organization, not any one of its constituents. Section (b) provides that, "[i]f a lawyer for an organization knows that an officer, employee or other person associated with the organization is engaged in action … that is a violation of a legal obligation to the organization, and that is likely to result in substantial injury to the organization, then the lawyer shall proceed as is reasonably necessary in the best interests of the organization." Why do you think the drafters of the model rules thought that this provision was necessary?

3. Keith Mendelson, the senior associate up for partner, was in a bind. He was uncomfortable helping the Admiral dismantle M&D, a client of the firm, and he expressed conflict-of-interest concerns to Deanne Siemer, the partner in charge of the matter. She kept telling Mendelson that there was no conflict. She also implied that his performance on the matter would be considered in his bid for partnership. Not reassured, Mendelson voiced his concerns to a member of the firm's ethics committee and to his regular supervisor, then in Sweden. Both deferred to Siemer. His concerns thrice rejected, Mendelson soldiered on and eventually had a malpractice judgment entered against him. Under the circumstances, what should Mendelson have done?

Judge Roush identified part of the problem: "Pillsbury, Madison & Sutro's internal mechanisms for resolution of ethical issues are seriously deficient. The partner in charge of the client relationship who is least likely to be objective is the ultimate arbiter of whether the firm has a conflict of interest."

How might a firm like Pillsbury structure "internal mechanisms for resolution of ethical disputes?" Pillsbury, like most big firms, has an ethics committee to which problems are sometimes referred. Here, the committee member apparently chose not to refer Mendelson's concern to the full committee. Should all concerns from associates be referred to committee? Should a lawyer concerned about a conflict be permitted to report to the ethics committee anonymously? If so, how long do you think it would take for the lawyer's supervisor to figure out who raised the concern? Should a lawyer be free to decline to work on a matter because of conflicts (or other ethical) concerns if the lawyer's supervisor believes that the concerns are unfounded? If an associate were to exercise that option, would it be likely to affect salary increases or chances for partnership?

4. It was one thing to hold Keith Mendelson responsible for malpractice, despite his "difficult position," as Judge Roush termed it. "He was senior enough that he should have put a stop to the dual representation ... or by withdrawing from the representation." But what about Fraser Fiveash, the associate less than two years out of law school? She had raised the conflicts issue with Siemer, had been reassured, and wrote memoranda on legal questions. Assuming Fiveash knew about the firm's relationship with M&D, she would be held responsible for violating Rule 1.7(a). That conclusion follows from Model Rule 5.2, under which a lawyer is held responsible for a rule violation "notwithstanding that the lawyer acted at the direction of another person," unless she acted in accordance with her supervisor's "reasonable resolution of an arguable question." David Epstein, the plaintiff's expert stated, correctly, that Siemer's position was neither reasonable nor arguable. But was it fair of Epstein to compare Fiveash to the co-conspirators in Watergate? Might someone in Fiveash's position be found in violation of the ethical rule but not guilty of malpractice? If so, on what theory?

5. Counsel for the defendants did not call an expert witness to counter the opinions of Epstein that they knew from depositions were forthcoming. Their only testimony on those issues came from Siemer whose conduct was being challenged. Can you explain that strategy, if strategy it was?

Chapter 2

From White Knight to Rogue: The Unraveling of a Veteran Prosecutor[1]

"I am innocent, Reade Seligman is innocent, Collin Finnerty is innocent —every member of the Duke University lacrosse team is innocent. You have all been told some fantastic lies, and I look forward to watching them unravel in the weeks to come, as they already have in weeks past.... The truth will come out."

> —David Evans, speaking from the courthouse steps after being indicted for first-degree rape, first-degree sexual offense, and first-degree kidnapping[2]

Durham District Attorney Mike Nifong was not a man who could be summed up easily. The twenty-seven-year veteran of the D.A.'s office had a reputation as "a no-nonsense, by-the-book litigator, who was tough on criminals and sensitive to crime victims"[3]—always well prepared, organized, and fair-minded.[4] He also had a reputation for a volcanic temperament.[5]

Though friends would kindly describe him as a "subdued, behind-the-scenes kind of prosecutor" who could at times admittedly get "aggressive,"[6] others were not so circumspect. They remembered how Nifong's demeanor

---

1. Based on the original research and writing of **Andres Healy**.

2. Richard Fausset & Jenny Jarvie, *Third Duke Student Indicted in Rape Case*, L.A. Times, May 16, 2006, at A4.

3. Cash Michaels, *Ethical Questions About Duke Case Prosecution*, N.Y. Amsterdam News, Sept. 14, 2006, at 4.

4. Oren Dorell, *Duke Case Prosecutor's Media Whirl Raises Eyebrows*, USA Today, May 2, 2006, at A2.

5. Stuart Taylor, Jr., & KC Johnson, Until Proven Innocent: Political Correctness and the Shameful Injustices of the Duke Lacrosse Rape Case 81 (2007).

6. Dorell, *supra* note 4.

in and out of the courtroom could quickly change from "low key" to "vicious."[7] "Working with Mike, you never knew from one day to the other who you'd be dealing with. He would curse you, scream [at] you, call you names over nothing."[8] Rather than being a point of shame for him, Nifong seemingly relished his reputation. After a particularly bitter argument, he once proclaimed, "My name is Mike Nifong and I'm the chief asshole of the Durham County District Attorney's Office."[9]

Regardless of his flaws, Nifong maintained the across-the-board respect and regard of his colleagues. He had an unparalleled reputation for being ethical and fair.[10] Indeed, in 1999, Nifong was tapped by then-district attorney Jim Hardin as the white knight to be put in charge of negotiating traffic court pleas—a position previously ravaged by scandal.[11] Given this fact, it's hard to believe that Nifong would eventually be summed up by the Attorney General of North Carolina, Roy A. Cooper, III, in two ugly words: "rogue prosecutor."[12]

Nifong's fall from grace began in early to mid March of 2006. At the time, he was campaigning to keep his job. Durham residents would be casting their votes in the Democratic mayoral primary on May 2, 2006, slightly more than a month away. They would also be electing their candidate for district attorney. Because Democrat voters outnumbered Republicans four to one, that candidate would be a shoo-in to win the position—the primary election was the only race that mattered.[13]

Unfortunately for Nifong, he was not the favorite. He was not even the second favorite. In a three-horse race, Nifong was bringing up the rear—and it was a distant rear at that. Barring some sort of miracle, a surge in the polls looked impossible. Although he had initially out-fundraised his competitors by relying heavily on contributions from local lawyers, his campaign coffers quickly dried up when it became apparent that his stock was plummeting. Funds eventually got so tight that Nifong had to loan himself nearly $30,000 just to stay in the race—a sum the long-time government employee could ill

---

7. *Id.*

8. TAYLOR & JOHNSON, *supra* note 5, at 81.

9. Richard Fausset, *Duke Student's Lawyers Want D.A. Off Case*, L.A. TIMES, May 2, 2006, at A5.

10. *Id.*

11. TAYLOR & JOHNSON, *supra* note 5, at 80.

12. Evan R. Goldstein, *The Power of the Prosecutor*, CHRON. OF HIGHER EDUC., May 11, 2007, at 59.

13. TAYLOR & JOHNSON, *supra* note 5, at 82.

afford to squander. Worse yet, he was the first person to concede that most Durham voters simply had no idea who he was. Though he had served as the interim district attorney for nearly a year,[14] Nifong's name recognition was near nil.

In contrast, the smart money was on Freda Black. The fourteen-year veteran prosecutor had been a former co-worker of Nifong's and could match his prosecutorial pedigree conviction-for-conviction.[15] She also had attributes Nifong lacked. Thanks to her high profile prosecution of acclaimed novelist and local resident Michael Peterson for the murder of his wife, Black had a name voters knew. She also appeared to have the backing of the business community—eventually out-fundraising Nifong by a margin of four to one. Her status as a front runner was not just a matter of speculation—the proof was in the numbers. A March 27 poll found that Black enjoyed a comfortable seventeen-point lead over Nifong with only thirty-six days left before the primary election.[16]

If that were not bad enough, Nifong also had to contend with candidate Keith Bishop. On paper, Bishop, a defense attorney who had never prosecuted a single case, should not have been a contender. In addition to his inexperience, he had recently been sanctioned by the North Carolina Bar for unethical conduct—not a good selling point during campaign rallies or debates. However, Bishop did have a major advantage over Nifong and Black: he was the lone African American candidate in a community that was about forty percent Black.[17] Even better, he had the support of the influential Durham Committee on the Affairs of Black People.[18]

To fully understand this advantage, and Nifong's predicament, it is necessary to understand Durham itself—a city defined by extremes: black and white; rich and poor. Home to the prestigious Duke University, Durham also wore the nefarious crown of "murder capital" of North Carolina. Once supported by thriving tobacco and textile industries, in recent years the city had fallen on hard times. Both industries had faded, taking most of the area's paychecks with them. Now, Duke University was the city's largest single em-

---

14. John Stevenson, *Foes Try DA on Rape Case*, HERALD-SUN (Durham, N.C.), April 26, 2006, at A1.

15. *Id.*

16. TAYLOR & JOHNSON, *supra* note 5, at 81.

17. Reports on the exact demographics of the community vary; however, most describe Durham as being comprised from 38 percent to 44 percent African American. *Compare* Fausset & Jarvie, *supra* note 2, *with* Fausset, *supra* note 9.

18. Fausset, *supra* note 9.

ployer. Nearly 19,000 residents worked on the university's payroll. Unfortunately, this did little to pad residents' bank accounts. Locals' common complaint was that Duke only offered jobs in low- or unskilled positions. They called Duke "the plantation." Because of the employment void, the per-capita income of the area plummeted to $23,000—a little more than half of what the average Duke student paid in annual tuition.[19]

Further exacerbating community tensions, strict Duke housing rules began pushing students off-campus. Long-time residents quickly tired of their student-neighbors' wild late-night parties.[20] Resentment soon built between the perceived "haves" and "have-nots"—a division that largely fell along racial lines.

Thus, it was widely understood that a candidate looking to be Durham's next district attorney needed to appeal to at least one of two distinct groups: the business community or the African American one. Nifong was appealing to neither—and it didn't appear that this was going to change.[21]

Of course, Nifong was not supposed to be in the race in the first place. That was the promise he made to North Carolina Governor Mike Easley when Easley chose Nifong to be Durham's interim district attorney in April 2005. Following his stint as the interim district attorney, he was supposed to return to his job as a prosecutor and not run for a full term. It made the governor's choice an apolitical one. Nifong, however, could not keep that promise. After assuming the mantle of district attorney, he had made his first order of business the firing of his longtime rival, Freda Black. No one doubted that Black, once elected, would return the favor. If that happened, Nifong would not only be out of a job, but would also take a $15,000 annual hit to his pension, which would otherwise max out in only three-and-a-half years.[22] He could not let this happen.

What Nifong needed was a game-changer—something that would catapult him into the public eye and allow him to make serious inroads into the voting blocs of Black and Bishop. He needed something that would give him the name recognition he needed to usurp Black's prominence and at the same time show the African American community that he could be their cham-

---

19. TAYLOR & JOHNSON, *supra* note 5, at 18.

20. *Id.* at 21–22.

21. Dan Seligman, *Frame-Up*, COMMENTARY, Feb. 2008, at 58 (reviewing the Taylor and Johnson book).

22. Robert J. Luck & Michael L. Seigel, *The Facts, and Only the Facts, in* RACE TO INJUSTICE: LESSONS LEARNED FROM THE DUKE LACROSSE RAPE CASE 13 (Michael Seigel ed., Carolina Academic Press 2009).

pion. With the election looming, he also needed these changes fast. On March 13, 2006, Nifong got what he needed.

It Begins: "Money to Be Made"

Unlike most Duke students, members of Duke's widely acclaimed lacrosse team did not enjoy spring break in Mexico or at home with their families. Instead, they were required to remain on campus and practice for their upcoming run at another appearance in the national championship game. Of course, spring break would not be entirely without its fun—after all, Duke's unofficial motto was "work hard, play hard." Having "worked hard" at practice all week, the team was getting set to "play hard." Usually that involved copious amounts of alcohol. It also meant a traditional "bonding party" at a local strip club. This year, though, things would be a little different. Because the team's usual spot had begun cracking down on fake IDs, the seniors decided to bring the party home. Rather than going to the strippers, the team would bring the strippers to them. Dan Flannery, a senior co-captain on the team, made the arrangements. Calling the number of an escort service he found on the Internet, Flannery arranged for "two white women" to arrive at the co-captains' house at 11 p.m. that night to put on a show.[23]

In keeping with their unofficial motto, the partygoers got an early start. Most started arriving at the house around two o'clock that afternoon. They drank beer, played beer pong, and drank more beer—all in anticipation of the evening's main event. Shortly after 11 p.m., dancer Kim Roberts arrived. Though African-American, Roberts had extremely light skin. Partygoers would later refer to her as Hispanic. She collected her $400 fee, had a drink, smoked a cigarette, and chatted with players while waiting for the second dancer to arrive. Crystal Mangum was not dropped off until 11:40 p.m. Unlike Roberts, she arrived already attired in her skimpy dancing outfit—a white teddy, a see-through red sparkling top over a white bra, white underwear, and white stiletto high heels. The team was surprised that neither woman had a bodyguard with her, as dancers usually do. They were also dismayed that neither woman was white, as had been requested. Though some suggested canceling the affair, the consensus was to make the best of it and carry on. After Mangum received her $400, both women entered a bathroom

---

23. Taylor & Johnson, *supra* note 5, at 18; Luck & Seigel, *supra* note 22, at 3–4.

shared by co-captain David Evans and a teammate to discuss their plan for the dance. Roberts also had to change into her dancing attire.[24]

The women's show started promptly at midnight. More than twenty time-stamped photos attest to that. The photographs also show the team and partygoers, seated on couches on the floor, smiling and cheering as the women began dancing and taking off their clothes. Their pleasure, however, was short-lived. Mangum could not dance or speak coherently. She had apparently taken a powerful muscle relaxant and was drunk as well. She "repeatedly tripped and stumbled over Roberts," and eventually "tumbled to the floor."[25] She did not bother getting up. Apparently, this surprised even Roberts who would later comment to the late Ed Bradley on CBS News' *60 Minutes*, "Something was going on, you know, where we were stumbling over each other, falling against each other, maybe almost tripping each other. So it started to get a little uncomfortable."[26]

That feeling was mutual. Pictures taken at the time seemed to indicate that the partygoers were not happy. Most were simply not paying attention. Others appeared to be leaving. Perhaps seeking to make up for Mangum's "condition," Roberts allegedly asked if any of the players were willing to take off their pants so the women could "play with it." No one took her up on the offer. One player countered by asking her if she had brought any "toys." When she replied that she had not, he picked up a broom and asked her, "Why don't you use this?" Roberts was not amused, and the performance was over. She stormed through the house toward the back door with Mangum "tripping, stumbling, and banging into walls along the way."[27] According to time-stamped photos, the main event had lasted a mere four minutes.[28]

For their part, Flannery and Evans tried to mollify the women. "We tried to apologize and reason with the Hispanic stripper," Flannery later told police, referring to Roberts. By this time, the conversation between the co-captains and the dancers had spilled outside. Fearing a noise violation or worse—the women were still topless—the co-captains persuaded the women to return to the house by promising apologies from the team. The women relented.[29]

As the captains were having their discussion with the women outside, the team was having its own discussion. "Guys thought that we might have been

---

24. TAYLOR & JOHNSON, *supra* note 5, at 23–24; Luck & Seigel, *supra* note 22, at 4–6.
25. TAYLOR & JOHNSON, *supra* note 5, at 18; Luck & Seigel, *supra* note 22, at 6–7.
26. TAYLOR & JOHNSON, *supra* note 5, at 24.
27. *Id.* at 24–25; Luck & Seigel, *supra* note 22, at 6.
28. TAYLOR & JOHNSON, *supra* note 5, at 25.
29. *Id.* at 26.

hustled when they said that they were leaving," Evans said later. "We paid $800 and they were there for five minutes, and naturally guys got upset." Though most of the players shrugged it off, one went into Mangum's purse, which she had left behind, and removed the $400 they had paid her. The money eventually made it into the hands of Evans and Flannery.[30]

At this point, the women had locked themselves in the bathroom. According to a statement Roberts gave to the police, she told Mangum that she wanted to leave. Mangum, on the other hand, wanted to stay. The team, allegedly worried that the women were doing drugs, began slipping money under the door to coax them to leave. Finally, around 12:20 a.m., both women left the bathroom and headed for Roberts's car, taking all of their belongings except for the unreturned money and Mangum's purse and shoe, which she had left in the living room. According to a statement Roberts gave police, "both women were close together every minute until both left the house." Roberts would later deny making that statement.[31]

Still apologizing for what happened, one player approached the window of Roberts's car and asked Mangum to come back into the house to retrieve her belongings.[32] A neighbor, Jason Bissey, later told police that he watched from his porch as a "skimpily dressed woman" exited the car and went back into the lacrosse player's house, "saying something to the effect that she would go back into 610 to retrieve her shoe." Roberts, too, verified that Mangum returned to the house of her own accord. "She obviously wasn't hurt or—because, you know, she was fine.... She wouldn't have went back in the house if she was hurt. She was fine." According to Roberts, Mangum gave another reason for returning. "There's more money to be made."[33]

Mangum's report of what happened next would catapult Durham into the national spotlight. According to Mangum, after returning to the house, she and Roberts were separated and two males, whom she identified as "Adam" and "Matt," pulled her into the bathroom. "Someone closed the door to the bathroom where she was, and said, 'Sweetheart you can't leave.'" For the next thirty minutes, the two men and a third named "Brett" "forcefully held her legs and arms and raped and sexually assaulted her anally, vaginally and orally," while hitting, kicking, and strangling her. Mangum later told police that at times she was not able to breathe. Struggling, she broke several fingernails while "clawing at one of the suspect's arms in an attempt to

---

30. *Id.* at 26–27.
31. *Id.*
32. Luck & Seigel, *supra* note 22, at 6.
33. Taylor & Johnson, *supra* note 5, at 27–28.

breathe while being strangled."[34] Mangum told police that, when the three were finally through, "Nikki" helped the players clean her up and then took her to her car where Nikki robbed Mangum of her phone, her ID, and $2000 cash.[35]

A Terrible Tale, But Was It True?

If true, Mangum's ordeal had the makings of being the game changer that Nifong could use to catapult himself ahead of Black and Bishop. The Black community was understandably outraged at the lurid, initially uncontested story of a local woman being brutally gang raped by white Duke lacrosse players "barking racial slurs," as the *News & Observer* described them on March 25. Suddenly the African American vote was in play. Nifong's best hope was to make the rape case the campaign's main event. At the least, he could garner publicity and match Freda Black's name recognition. At best, he could use the case to inflame the African American community and win over minority voters who would otherwise support Bishop.[36]

The caveat was *whether Mangum's story was true.* Plenty of evidence pointed to the contrary. Certainly, the lacrosse team painted a different picture of the happenings of that evening. They told police that no assault had occurred—better yet, they had evidence they said proved it. According to partygoers, after returning to the house to retrieve her belongings, Mangum stepped outside to make a phone call. That call was later determined to have been made to another escort service for which Mangum worked. It was made at 12:26 a.m., just six minutes after a neighbor had seen Mangum freely returning to the house.

Furthermore, it seemed apparent that the team wanted Mangum gone. When she stepped out to make her phone call, someone locked the door behind her.[37] "It seemed that the fellas may have been ready for the evening to be over," Roberts later said. But Magnum was in no hurry to go. A series of five photographs taken by partygoers and time-stamped from 12:30 a.m. to 12:31 a.m. show Mangum "standing on the back stoop with one shoe on, her

---

34. Probable Cause Affidavit, *In re* 610 N. Buchanan Blvd. Durham, N.C. 27701, (March 27, 2006), *available at* http://www.newsobserver.com/content/news/crime_safety/duke_lacrosse/story_graphics/20060405_warrant.pdf.

35. Luck & Seigel, *supra* note 22, at 7–8.

36. *Id.* at 14.

37. Taylor & Johnson, *supra* note 5, at 27–29.

clothes still skimpy but unmussed," smiling for the camera. They also show Magnum violently pounding on the door—trying not to get out, but in.[38]

The team's next piece of evidence was a 12:37 a.m. time-stamped photograph of Mangum sprawled out on the porch, apparently out cold. In this photograph, the team's accuser had fresh cuts on her right leg, which team supporters would later state matched the pattern of two jagged edges on the screen door that Mangum had leaned against and was not the result of an assault. According to team members, Roberts told Flannery that if he would carry Magnum to her car, Roberts would take her home. A 12:41 a.m. photograph shows Flannery doing just that.[39]

Additionally, Roberts, at least at first, verified the lacrosse team's account. Though she would later change her story several times after being arrested by Durham police on an outstanding warrant, her original statements to police ran contrary to nearly all of Mangum's most damning allegations. Roberts stated that she and Mangum had been apart for no more than five minutes the entire evening, that the women had freely lingered about the house even after the abbreviated "show," and that Mangum had never even hinted that she'd been assaulted in any way.[40] Roberts called Mangum's tale a "crock."[41]

Though the lacrosse players had finally rid themselves of Mangum, Roberts had not. Worse yet, she didn't know what to do with her. Roberts didn't know where Mangum lived, and Mangum wouldn't tell her. She also would not respond when Roberts asked for her share of the money. At this point, Roberts was suspicious of Magnum's condition. Responsible for the money, she suspected that Mangum was hustling her.[42] She wanted her out of the car. "I ... push on her leg. I kind of push on her arm," Roberts reported months later. "And clear as a bell, it's the only thing I heard clear as a bell out of her was, she said—she pretty much had her head down, but she said plain as day, 'go ahead, put marks on me. That's what I want. Go ahead.'"[43]

Frustrated and suspicious, Roberts eventually stopped at a Kroger twenty-four-hour grocery store and asked the security guard to help her get Roberts out of her car. He called the police. At 1:22 a.m., Durham Sgt. John

38. *Id.* at 28–29.

39. *Id.*

40. *Id.* at 57.

41. *Id.* at 30; Luck & Seigel, *supra* note 22, at 11.

42. Susannah Meadows et al., *What Happened at Duke?*, NEWSWEEK, May 1, 2006, at 40–51.

43. TAYLOR & JOHNSON, *supra* note 5, at 30.

C. Shelton arrived at the store. His conclusion was simple: Mangum was "just passed-out drunk." Based on Mangum's condition, Shelton decided that she was a danger to herself and others and had her transported to the Durham Access Center for observation.[44]

This wouldn't have been the first time that Mangum had been involuntarily committed. Just the summer before, she'd spent a week in the Holly Hill Hospital in Raleigh. Ostensibly, a stay at the Durham Center may have been in Mangum's best interest. However, a stay would have had other ramifications as well. Besides the obvious impact on her income, authorities alerted her that they would be checking on her children. Clearly, if Mangum could not care for herself, she could not care for them. Perhaps with these thoughts in mind, Mangum dropped the bombshell. She claimed that she had been raped.[45]

In the entire period following the women's departure from the lacrosse house, Mangum had never even insinuated that she had been assaulted. She made no mention of it to Roberts or the Kroger security guard. More importantly, she made no such claim to any of the three different officers who had interviewed her after taking her into custody at Kroger's. Now, however, she nodded yes when a nurse asked her point blank if she'd been raped—a question in direct violation of the center's policies. Mangum, who had identified herself as "Honey," also told the nurse that someone named "Nikki" had taken her phone, her ID, and $2000 cash—an allegation that would later appear in the probable cause affidavit, though no action was ever taken against Roberts, the only person who could have been "Nikki."[46]

Mangum's allegation was her ticket out of the center. Rather than spending the night or longer locked up, Mangum was on her way to the Duke University Medical Center's emergency room. For the first time, Mangum told police officers about the assault. She told Durham officer Gwendolyn Sutton that she "ended up in the bathroom with five guys who forced her to have intercourse and perform sexual acts." She alleged that "she was penetrated by all five." It would be the first of many different accounts. When later questioned by Shelton, Mangum stated that "some of the guys in the party pulled her from the vehicle and groped her," but no one had "force her to have sex." Shortly thereafter, while Shelton was reporting to his superiors that Mangum had recanted, she told a doctor that she had been dragged into a bathroom and raped.[47]

---

44. *Id.* at 30–31; Luck & Seigel, *supra* note 22, at 7–8.
45. Taylor & Johnson, *supra* note 5, at 31; Luck & Seigel, *supra* note 22, at 7–8.
46. Taylor & Johnson, *supra* note 5, at 31; Probable Cause Affidavit, *supra* note 34.
47. Taylor & Johnson, *supra* note 5, at 31–32.

Other officers reported similarly. A Duke police officer, Christopher Day, wrote in his report that Mangum "was claiming that she was raped by approximately twenty white males at 610 N. Buchanan" but had changed her story multiple times. Mangum apparently told a different story to female Durham police officer B.S. Jones, stating "Brett knew the deal," but "the guys weren't with it."[48]

The chief reason for Mangum's transfer to Duke was for authorities to assemble a rape kit, which would bear crucial importance later on in the case. Dr. Julie Manly took samples of Mangum's clothing, collected cheek scrapings and oral, vaginal, and rectal swabs, and administered a pubic hair combing. She also conducted a physical exam in which she noted that three small non-bleeding cuts on Mangum's right knee and heel were the only evidence of trauma. Three other doctors and five nurses also conducted physical examinations. They were unanimous in finding no physical evidence of an assault—no bruises, no bleeding, and no vaginal or anal tearing. The only thing Dr. Manley did find was fluid that she believed to be semen. She would later state that upon this basis alone she believe Mangum had been raped.[49]

Tara Levicy, a sexual-assault-nurse trainee at Duke, was not so skeptical. In her report, she included Mangum's newest account of her assault. In a four-page narrative, Mangum now alleged that "Nikki" began pushing her into a sexual threesome shortly after the pair had begun dancing. Magnum's response was to storm out of the house. Nikki then helped a lacrosse player drag Mangum out of her car and back into the house where Adam, Brett, and Matt took off her clothes and assaulted her orally, vaginally, and anally. Curiously, Mangum specifically described how Matt had expressed his reluctance to take part because he was getting married the next day—she had originally been told she would be performing at a bachelor party. She also was emphatic in stating that none of her attackers had used condoms. She stated that when they were through, Nikki had helped them to clean her up and then drove her away in her car before robbing her of all her money. In regard to physical evidence, Levicy could only note that Dr. Manley had found "diffuse edema of the vaginal walls."[50] This would later become the prosecution's smoking gun, even though the condition can be caused by smoking, consensual sex, frequent sex, or a reaction to antidepressant medication. Mangum fit all four categories. No other physical evidence of trauma was found on Mangum's body.[51]

---

48. *Id.* at 32.
49. *Id.* at 32–33; Luck & Seigel, *supra* note 22, at 8.
50. Taylor & Johnson, *supra* note 5, at 33–34.
51. Luck & Seigel, *supra* note 22, at 9.

Nifong Swallows the Pill

Eleven days after the incident, and one day after Durham's *News & Observer* ran a picture of the team members covering their faces as they walked into the police station to give DNA swabs pursuant to a court order, Nifong officially took over the case.[52] Though he would not be fully briefed by police for three more days,[53] Nifong gave word that he would be supervising the investigation and handling the prosecution. At the time, everything Nifong knew about the case was based on a document he found lying on an office copier.[54] Nevertheless, he made it personal. Nifong was firmly behind "his victim," as he called Mangum, and he would not hesitate to make that blatantly apparent.

Appearing on Rita Cosby's *Live & Direct* show on MSNBC on March 28, the day after his briefing, Nifong explained why he personally took over the case. "Well, this is the type of case that because of the—on top of the rape, which is already an abhorrent crime enough, you have the additional racial animus and hostility that just seems totally out of place for this community in this day and age. And I felt that this was a case that we needed to make a statement, as a community, that we would not tolerate this kind of behavior here in Durham. And I felt that the best way to make that statement was to take this case myself."[55]

He was also not shy about divulging details of the investigation. "The rape and the other sexual assaults took place in the bathroom. My understanding is that the estimates of time range from about fifteen minutes to about thirty minutes. A lot of times, when things like that are going on, they seem to last longer than they actually do. And there were three men involved in the direct assault on her."

Nifong added that, in addition to expected DNA evidence, his investigation had other evidence that a rape had occurred. "The victim's demeanor, the fact that when she was examined by a nurse who was trained in sexual assault, there was swelling and pain in the areas that would have been affected by the rape. The victim gave signs of having been through a traumatic situation. She seemed to be absolutely honest about what had occurred to her."[56]

---

52. *Id.* at 11.

53. Amended Complaint at 17, North Carolina State Bar v. Nifong (January 24, 2007).

54. Joseph Neff, *Quest to Convict Hid a Lack of Evidence*, NEWS & OBSERVER (Raleigh, N.C.), April 14, 2007.

55. *Rita Cosby Live & Direct* (MSNBC television broadcast March 28, 2006).

56. *Id.*

Nifong had already asserted his personal belief earlier in the evening on *The Abrams Report* that members of lacrosse team had raped Mangum.[57] Despite these public statements, Nifong could not have been so personally convinced. For one thing, he had yet to interview Magnum personally; for another, Sgt. Mark Gottlieb of the Durham Police Department had—and the results were anything but reassuring.

Gottlieb, who had a reputation for coming down hard on Duke students, had taken control of the case immediately after Mangum made her allegations. On March 16, he met with her to see if she could identify her assailants. It was a far from fruitful endeavor. Mangum's description of her attackers seemed hopelessly off the mark. "Adam" was "short" with "red cheeks," a "chubby face," and brown "fluffy hair." "Matt" had a "short haircut" and weighed around 260 pounds. She could only describe Brett as "chubby."[58] Besides being vague, Mangum's recollection seemed to exonerate the Duke lacrosse players, who were world-class athletes—not chubby teens. She could not pick any of the three out of a photo line-up.

Gottlieb tried again five days later. To ensure that there would be no confusion this time around, he showed Mangum pictures of lacrosse team members taken from Duke's website. Mangum still could not pick out her attackers, but she did identify four members of the team as being at the party. Trouble was, she was wrong even on this account. Brad Ross, one of the players Magnum identified with "100 percent certainty," had not even been in Durham on the night of the party, and he could prove it.[59]

Nevertheless, Nifong pressed on. He had every reason to believe that he would soon have his incriminating physical evidence. His victim had told police that her attackers had not used condoms. In conducting the rape kit, Dr. Manley had found what she believed to be semen. The police had obtained a court-order compelling all forty-six white lacrosse players to give DNA swabs by asserting that the results would clearly separate the guilty from the innocent.[60] Simply put, it would just be a matter of time before cold, impartial science would distinguish the innocent from the guilty, an assumption Nifong readily shared with anyone who would listen.

On March 28, the DNA results came in. North Carolina's State Bureau of Investigation (SBI) found no matches. Worse (for Nifong), it determined that

---

57. The Abrams Report (MSNBC television broadcast March 28, 2006).
58. Luck & Seigel, *supra* note 22, at 9.
59. TAYLOR & JOHNSON, *supra* note 5, at 39.
60. *Id.* at 153.

"there had been no semen, blood, or saliva anywhere on or in Mangum."[61] Nifong personally confirmed these results with an agent in the lab two days later.[62] Nifong knew he was in trouble. Though the results had not yet been made public, it would only be a matter of time before the lab released its official report. Without DNA evidence to support his victim's evolving tale, the case appeared doomed. He knew that if the case floundered, so would his hopes for re-election. He needed a credible witness, he needed DNA evidence, and he needed to be able to keep himself in the limelight. He set about getting all three.

On April 4, Nifong had Gottlieb conduct a third photo identification session with Mangum. On April 5, he had the rape kit transferred to DNA Security, Inc. (DSI), a private forensic laboratory in Burlington, North Carolina,[63] for more sensitive tests that might be able to isolate male DNA.[64] Through it all, Nifong never stopped talking to the media.

Third Time's the Charm: The Problem of Lineups and Mustaches

In 2006, the Durham Police Department had revamped its photo-identification procedures in response to a North Carolina initiative to minimize false identifications. General Order 4077 left no room for interpretation. It required police lineups to be conducted by an officer uninvolved in the investigation. That officer was required to instruct the witness that the lineup may or may not contain suspects. Furthermore, five filler photos were required to be used for every suspect in the lineup.[65]

Nifong needed a positive identification, and he was going to ensure that he got one. Though Mangum's previous two lineups had not been perfect, some attempt had been made to comply with the general order. By direction of Nifong, the April 4 lineup would completely ignore it. First, he put Gottlieb, who had been investigating the case since day one, in charge of "the show." The district attorney instructed Gottlieb to show Mangum photographs of each of the forty-six white Duke lacrosse team members. Furthermore, Gottlieb was not to use any fillers, let alone the 230 that were required

61. *Id.* at 96.
62. Amended Complaint, *supra* note 53, at 17.
63. *Id.*
64. Luck & Seigel, *supra* note 22, at 11.
65. TAYLOR & JOHNSON, *supra* note 5, at 154–57.

by the rules. Lastly, Nifong wanted Mangum to be told explicitly that she was only being shown photographs of people the police believed to have attended the party. Gottlieb obliged Nifong's every request.[66] Nifong had set up a test that Mangum could not fail.

Even so, Mangum's responses were troubling. Once again, she mistakenly identified Brad Ross as being present that night. On the other hand, she failed to identify the other three individuals whom she had previously claimed were there.[67] For the first time, she pointed to three attackers: Collin Finnerty, David Evans, and Reade Seligman. None of them matched her original descriptions. Moreover, her identification of Evans posed special problems for the prosecution. Mangum told Gottlieb that he "look[ed] like one of the guys that assaulted me, sort of." Asked why she was uncertain, Mangum replied, "He looks like him without the mustache." Evans had not had a mustache at the time of the party. In fact, he had never had one.[68] Regardless, the die had been cast. The three "Duke Defendants" had been chosen, and eventually they were indicted for rape, sexual assault, and kidnapping.[69]

DNA Round Two: False Positives

On April 10, Nifong got the news for which he had been hoping. DSI had "found DNA characteristics from up to four different males on epithelial and sperm fractions from several pieces of evidence from the rape kit." Having finally gotten a break, the district attorney rushed to meet Dr. Brian Meehan, president and director of DSI. On the way to the lab, Nifong called his campaign manager to alert him that he was expecting important information. He wanted the campaign team primed to capitalize on it. Unfortunately, Meehan was soon to drop a bomb on Nifong's parade. According to preliminary testing, none of the DNA found in the rape kit matched any of the lacrosse players. On the contrary, each and every lacrosse player was excluded as a potential contributor. Nifong would now have to explain the presence of DNA from four unidentified males.[70]

With the election less than a month away, Nifong's solution was simple: if no one knew the results, no one could ask any questions.[71] But things

---

66. *Id.* at 156.
67. *Id.* at 157.
68. *Id.* at 157–58.
69. Amended Complaint, *supra* note 53, at 18.
70. *Id.*
71. *Id.*

quickly got more complicted. The official DNA report compiled by SBI had just gone public—thirteen days after Nifong had been privately apprised of the results. The apparent lack of DNA evidence was no longer a secret. The question on everyone's mind now was whether Nifong would continue with the case.

Addressing a crowd of over 700 students, community members, supporters, and media news crews at the historically black North Carolina Central University the next day, Nifong answered this question. "A lot has been said in the press, particularly by some attorneys ... that this case should go away. I hope you understand that my presence here means that this case is not going away."[72] Specifically addressing the lack of DNA evidence, he said, "It doesn't mean nothing happened. It just means nothing was left behind."[73] He would later add that he "would not be surprised if condoms were used. Probably an exotic dancer would not be your first choice for unprotected sex."[74] The statement was not only in direct contrast to Nifong's previous public statements, but it also contradicted his victim's account of what happened.

None of that mattered to the crowd at NCCU; it drowned Nifong in thunderous applause. The underclass had found its champion and Nifong ate it up. Commenting on the pressure he was under to drop the case, he said, "Well, ladies and gentlemen, that's not doing your job. If I did that, then you should vote against me. Because that's not what this job is about. The reason I took this case is because this case says something about Durham that I'm not going to let be said. I am not going to allow Durham in the mind of the world to be a bunch of lacrosse players from Duke raping a black girl in Durham!"[75]

Not everyone was completely convinced of the district attorney's motives, though. One student asked Nifong if his efforts were motivated by the upcoming election. Nifong's response was curt. "As the district attorney, you do not get to choose what crimes occur and when they occur," he said flatly. "This is not about an election. This is about justice."[76]

---

72. Kelly Whiteside, *Prosecutor to Crowd: Duke Case Will Proceed*, USA TODAY, April 12, 2006, at C1.

73. Tim Whitmire, *DA Says Rape Case 'Not Going Away,'* HOUSTON CHRON., April 12, 2006, at A4.

74. Amended Complaint, *supra* note 53, at 11.

75. S.L. Price et al., *The Damage Done*, SPORTS ILLUSTRATED, June 26, 2006, at 75.

76. Whitmire, *supra* note 73.

Nifong's Brief But Torrid Affair with the Media

Since taking over the case, the district attorney had been a busy man. He made that point clear to defense attorneys, refusing to meet with them or consider evidence they said exonerated their clients. Still, Nifong always made time for some people—those with press badges. To say he was a media darling would be an understatement. Between the time he took over the case and his comments at NCCU on April 11, Nifong gave over seventy interviews. He made so many extrajudicial statements that the North Carolina State Bar would eventually divide them into nine distinct categories of "improper pretrial public statements and misrepresentations."

He attacked the lacrosse team's integrity. "There are three people who went into the bathroom with the young lady, and whether the other people there knew what was going on at the time, they do now and have not come forward," he told ABC TV News. "I'm disappointed that no one has been enough of a man to come forward. And if they would have spoken up at the time, this may never happen."[77] He told the Raleigh *News & Observer* newspaper, "I would like to think that somebody [not involved in the attack] has the human decency to call up and say, 'what am I doing covering up for a bunch of hooligans?' "[78]

When shame tactics did not work, Nifong resorted to threats, musing to the *New York Times*, "My guess is that some of the stone wall of silence that we have seen may tend to crumble once charges start to come out."[79] He also publicly questioned why the players needed attorneys, telling ESPN, "one would wonder why one needs an attorney if one was not charged and had not done anything wrong."[80]

The district attorney also liberally described his evidence. Interviewed on MSNBC, he described how a nurse had found evidence of trauma to the victim's genitals and that Mangum's "general demeanor was ... suggestive of the fact that she had been through a dramatic situation."[81] He proceeded to demonstrate how Mangum had been attacked, and stated, "Somebody had an arm around her like this, which she then had to struggle with in order to breathe ... she was struggling just to be able to breathe."[82]

---

77. Amended Complaint, *supra* note 53, at 3.
78. *Id.* at 12.
79. *Id.* at 3.
80. *Id.* at 5.
81. *Id.* at 6.
82. *Id.* at 7.

Perhaps worst of all, the district attorney seemed to be blatantly catering to voters on the basis of race. "In this case, we have the act of rape—essentially a gang rape—is bad enough in and of itself, but when it's made with racial epithets against the victim, I mean, it's just absolutely unconscionable," he told ABC TV News. "The contempt that was shown for the victim, based on her race, was totally abhorrent. It adds another layer of reprehensibleness to a crime that is already reprehensible."[83]

While most first-year law students would recognize the danger such comments placed on both the state's ability to guarantee the accused a fair trial and on Nifong's career, the district attorney seemed oblivious. When questioned by a reporter about defense attorneys' concerns that the accused would be unable to get a fair trial, Nifong glibly responded that "if the defense attorneys [are] angling for a change of venue they [won't] have much luck. 'After all the media that have been here this week,' he said, 'we'd have to move it to China.'"[84] Not uncharacteristically, he would later turn that argument on its head and accuse defense attorneys of prejudicing the case. "It's not me who is trying his case in the media," he said. "The defense is trying this case in the media. Maybe they want us to move it to Aruba or someplace like that."[85]

Nifong's seemingly willful blindness to his blatant violations of state rules barring extrajudicial comments was not shared by many. Black, his chief opponent, publicly stated that Nifong had irreparably harmed the case and biased potential jurors. "Any case should be tried in a court of law and not a court of public opinion," she said at an election forum. "Frankly, in my opinion it would be impossible to find unbiased jurors in the whole United States of America. I would've handled it differently."[86]

Bishop was less polite. "All you need to do is open your rule book and not open your mouth to the press," he said. He also criticized Nifong for exploiting Mangum's situation. "You just can't treat people that way," he said. "It absolutely does no justice for the victim. I have compassion for the victim. I would exercise better judgment.... I would've kept my mouth shut, analyzed the data."[87]

Nifong's opponents weren't the only ones alarmed by his media blitzkrieg. "You've got a prosecutor playing to race," said James Coleman, a professor at Duke Law School. "It's disgusting. If he's willing to [make race an

---

83. *Id.* at 13.
84. Sal Ruibal, *Attorneys for Players Go on the Offensive*, USA Today, March 31, 2006, at C9.
85. Stevenson, *supra* note 14.
86. *Id.*
87. *Id.*

issue] to go after what he thinks are three white kids with influence, what will he do against some poor black kid in a case where people are saying, 'You've got to convict somebody?' To me, a prosecutor who's willing to cut corners in any case is a prosecutor who's subverting justice."[88]

Even fellow district attorneys seemed to agree. "It would probably be fair to share that Mike should've been a little more circumspect with some of the comments he made early on," said Tom Locke, the district attorney for three North Carolina counties. According to Locke, during an early April meeting of the North Carolina Conference of District Attorneys, Nifong's fellow prosecutors made their opinions known to Nifong, telling him that his actions "have the potential to tar every one of us."[89] Whether that pressure finally got through to Nifong, or whether it was the mounting evidence against his case, Nifong's love affair with the media ended April 11. He stopped giving interviews cold turkey.[90] Of course, the damage had already been done.

What I Don't Tell Them Cannot Be Used Against Me

After Finnerty and Seligman's indictment on April 17, the latter's counsel wasted no time. Within two days, he served Nifong with a request for discovery material, including witness statements, the results of any tests, all DNA analysis, and any exculpatory information.[91] This put Nifong in a pickle. DSI had completed its testing on April 20. The lab had definitively determined that all the lacrosse players, including the two players that Nifong had already sought and obtained indictments against, were excluded as possible contributors of the DNA found in the rape kit.[92] Nifong had also uncovered potentially exculpatory evidence explaining the source of this DNA. In an interview with police, Mangum's "driver" had testified that he had taken her to one-on-one dates with three different men at local hotels in the days leading up to the lacrosse party. He also testified that he had had sex with her that Saturday night.[93] This would certainly explain the diffuse edema found by Dr. Manley at Duke.[94]

---

88. Price et al., *supra* note 75, at 75.
89. *Id.*
90. Luck & Seigel, *supra* note 22, at 14.
91. Amended Complaint, *supra* note 53, at 18.
92. *Id.* at 18–19.
93. Taylor & Johnson, *supra* note 5, at 159.
94. Luck & Seigel, *supra* note 22, at 9.

Even the lone bright spot among DSI's findings appeared worthless when considered under the totality of the circumstances. DSI had found traces of DNA on Magnum's discarded acrylic fingernail taken from the trash in the co-captains' bathroom that was consistent with that of Evans. On the face of it, this was a positive development. But DSI had also made a 100-percent DNA match to Meehan himself.[95] If the lab's tests were sensitive enough to pick up Meehan's transferred DNA, Evans's DNA on the fingernail, which had been found amid tissues and other garbage in Evans's own trashcan, was meaningless.[96] Revelation of all this was likely to bring the case to a close, which could not happen. So Nifong came up with a fix. His solution was as simple as it was illegal. He would suppress the counter-indicative evidence.

On April 21, Nifong met with Meehan and told him that he only wanted so-called "positive results" to be included in DSI's forthcoming report. There was to be no mention of the lab's findings that the four unidentified DNA specimens from the rape kit excluded lacrosse players as contributors. In fact, there was to be no mention that such specimens even existed. There would also be no mention of Meehan's DNA being found on Mangum's fingernail. The report was only to disclose those findings that would help Nifong's case. Meehan agreed.[97]

On May 12, Nifong met with Meehan and personally obtained the resulting ten-page report. The censored report was provided that same day to attorneys for both the indicted players and Evans, whom Nifong indicted three days later on the strength of the report.[98]

Discovery Proceeds—and Questions Get Raised

A month after obtaining the first round of indictments, the district attorney began complying with his obligations under North Carolina's open discovery law by turning over 1,278 pages of documents, two videotapes, and a compact disc containing photos.[99] Along with these materials, Nifong included the following certification: "The State is not aware of any additional material or information which may be exculpatory in nature with respect to

---

95. Taylor & Johnson, *supra* note 5, at 221–22.

96. *Id.* at 221.

97. Amended Complaint, *supra* note 53, at 17–20.

98. *Id.*

99. Taylor & Johnson, *supra* note 5, at 230.

the Defendant."[100] But the defense team for the indicted players was not convinced. It specifically requested that all expert witnesses "prepare, and furnish to the defendant, a report of the results of any (not only the ones about which the expert expects to testify) examinations or tests conducted by the expert."[101] They also wanted a report or written statement of the meetings between Nifong and Meehan. Nifong's response was to lie and deny. "I turned over everything I have," he told Judge W. Osmond Smith, who was presiding over the case.[102]

But of course he had not. Nifong did not provide in the discovery materials any written or recorded memorializations of the substance of his meetings with Meehan. He certainly did not disclose the evidence of additional male DNA specimens that DSI had discovered.[103] For the next five months, Nifong kept up this game of hide and seek. He ducked every defense motion to compel discovery—each more specific and detailed than the last—concerning the results of all DNA tests that DSI had performed. Finally, on October 27, even the court had had enough. Judge Smith ordered Nifong to turn over the complete file and underlying data from both SBI and DSI. At this point, the district attorney had no choice. He turned over 1,844 pages of requested documents.[104]

These documents were the mother lode. After nearly a month of digging, one member of the defense team, attorney Brad Bannon, stumbled upon what would become the defense's smoking gun. Buried within these documents was highly technical data detailing DSI's discovery of other male DNA in Mangum's rape kit, including Meehan's.[105] Nifong's worst nightmare was about to become reality.

On December 13, the defense filed a motion entitled "Motion to Compel Discovery: Expert DNA Analysis," which alleged that the previously hidden DSI documents showed conclusively that DSI had discovered the presence of four other male DNA specimens as early as April 10 and had confirmed those results shortly thereafter. It further alleged that Nifong had met with Meehan on several occasions to discuss the evidence found. Stopping short of stating that Nifong was therefore aware of the suppressed evidence, the defense pointed out that DSI had failed to turn over its communication logs. As a re-

---

100. Amended Complaint, *supra* note 53, at 21.
101. *Id.*
102. *Id.* at 22.
103. *Id.* at 21.
104. *Id.* at 24.
105. Taylor & Johnson, *supra* note 5, at 303.

sult of these findings, the defense's requests were explicit. They wanted a re-port of all DNA analysis conducted by the lab related to the case, and they wanted to know exactly what had been said between Nifong and Meehan.[106]

They weren't the only ones. Judge Smith also wanted answers. In chambers on December 15, Nifong claimed ignorance. "I just, in terms of the discovery issues, frankly, you know, I got the report and I was, like, whoa," he said. "So I immediately faxed a copy to Dr. Meehan and said, 'Read this, and I'll call you in the morning and get your opinion about this.' And we discussed it and I said, 'This is a major issue for the defense. They are entitled to hear about it, and I think it needs to be addressed right away. And so that's what w[er're] going to try to do, okay.'"[107] In open court, Nifong reiterated his ignorance. "The first I heard of this particular situation was when I was served with these reports—this motion on Wednesday this week," he said.[108]

Nifong's next move surprised everyone. Possibly hoping to catch the defense off guard, he announced that Meehan was in the courtroom and prepared to testify. The defense team jumped on the opportunity. Over the course of the next several hours, it elicited from Meehan confirmation that the lab had indeed found specimens from four unidentified males and that its analysis had excluded each and every lacrosse players as a contributor. If that weren't enough, Meehan confirmed many people's worst fear: Nifong had been made aware of the exculpatory evidence and specifically requested that the lab not disclosed it.[109]

"Our client, Mr. Nifong, specifically wanted ... to know ... do any of the referenced specimens [of lacrosse players] match any of the evidence," Meehan explained. "And that's the report that we gave him."[110] Meehan described how he had discussed with Nifong at the April 10, April 21, and May 12 meetings the details of the results of DSI's tests, including the potentially ex-culpatory DNA findings, and admitted that the resultant report was the result of "an intentional limitation" arrived at between the two "not to report on the results of all examinations and tests" that DSI performed.[111]

Meehan stopped short of confessing an illegal motive for the limitation. He explained that his and Nifong's deliberate limitation had been motivated

---

106. Motion to Compel Discovery: Expert DNA Analysis, North Carolina v. Evans (Dec. 13, 2006), available at http://www.newsobserver.com/content/news/crime_safety/duke_lacrosse/20061213_dukelacrosse.pdf.

107. TAYLOR & JOHNSON, *supra* note 5, at 307.

108. Amended Complaint, *supra* note 53, at 25.

109. TAYLOR & JOHNSON, *supra* note 5, at 309–11.

110. *Id.* at 310.

111. Amended Complaint, *supra* note 53, at 25–26.

by privacy concerns for the unidentified sources of the discovered semen. Bannon, the defense attorney conducting Meehan's cross examination, was not about to let that slide. "Let me ask you," he said, "who's privacy would have violated if you had simply reported the male DNA characteristics found on multiple rape kit items from multiple different males who didn't have reference labs for? Who's privacy would [be] violate[d]?" Meehan finally waved the white flag. "That wouldn't have violated anybody's privacy," he conceded. Nifong, however, still denied any wrongdoing. "We were trying to, just as Dr. Meehan said, trying to avoid dragging any names through the mud at the same time his report made it clear that all the information was available if they wanted and they have every word of it," he said immediately after the hearing.[112]

The Truth Hurts (and So Does Hiding It): The Aftermath for Mike Nifong

Though he always denied that it was his motivation, Nifong's handling of the Mangum's rape allegations had made him a household name and a hero to some Durham residents. It also won him the position of district attorney. Polling two-to-one among African-American voters, he won the May 2 primary by a victory margin of 883 votes[113]—squeaking past Black by a mere three percent of the total. "I felt I was the best candidate all along, and I'm glad that the people of Durham agree with me," he commented afterward.[114] He was able to ride that same support to victory in November, sweeping the black vote to overcome two challengers by winning 49.1 percent of the vote.[115]

Nifong's victory would prove short-lived, however. Five days after the disastrous evidentiary hearing, the North Carolina State Bar contacted the district attorney with a chilling message: it had been working on a complaint against him for his violations of pretrial publicity rules, and it was now broadening its investigation to consider more violations based on his with-

---

112. *Id.* at 26.

113. Price et al., *supra* note 75, at 75.

114. Oren Dorell, *Nifong Wins Election to Remain As D.A. in Durham, N.C.*, USA TODAY, May 3, 2006

115. John Stevenson & Tara McLaughlin, *Lawyers: Nifong Right Pick for DA*, HERALD-SUN (Durham, NC), Nov. 9, 2006, at A1.

holding of the exculpatory DNA evidence.[116] Nifong now seemed to panic. Hoping to downplay the significance of the DNA evidence, he sent a lackey to re-interview Mangum. Not surprisingly, the iteration of her testimony represented a marked departure from previous versions.

Now, Mangum couldn't recall whether her attackers actually raped her. She now thought it was possible that they had used an object to penetrate her vagina. She also claimed that Evans had cleaned her and the crime scene with a white towel after the attack. Curiously, Mangum no longer believed that Evans had a mustache when he attacked her—it had become a mere five o'-clock shadow.[117] Her new story greatly diminished the value of the evidence Nifong had failed to disclose.

Mangum was not the only one singing a new tune. On December 22, Nifong faxed a simple one-page form to the defense team. The message was simple: he was dropping the rape charges. "The victim in this case indicated that, while she initially believed she had been vaginally penetrated by a male sex organ, she cannot at this time testify with certainty [to that]," the message said. "Therefore, the state is unable to meet its burden of proof with respect to this offense." Nifong wasn't ready to completely drop the matter, however. He was pressing on with the sexual assault and kidnapping charges.[118]

The North Carolina State Bar was not impressed. On December 28, it released a seventeen-page ethics complaint charging Nifong with making extra-judicial statements "prejudicial to the administration of justice." The complaint specifically focused on statements it found to be "fraudulent, dishonest, deceitful."[119] The same day, Nifong issued what can best be described as a rambling, often inconsistent eight-page response. In it, the district attorney first asserted that he had not perceived the DNA evidence to be "specifically exculpatory." Instead, he simply considered the evidence "non-inculpatory." Next, Nifong described how he had never agreed with or asked Meehan to "exclude data from evidence specimens explicitly." Rather, Nifong stated that he told Meehan to compile a standard report in light of Meehan's concern for the Duke players' privacy. Finally, Nifong asserted that any "inadvertent failure to provide the evidence in question" was a result of his inability "to give the case [his] full attention" because of the election, mistakes by his

---

116. TAYLOR & JOHNSON, *supra* note 5, at 313.
117. *Id.* at 313–16.
118. *Id.* at 316.
119. *Id.* at 321; Luck & Seigel, *supra* note 22, at 25.

staff, and his focus on ensuring that the defense got documents obtained by the district attorney's office after May 18.[120]

The Bar had heard enough excuses, and it was not buying any of them. On January 24, 2007, it amended its complaint against the district attorney. Now, in addition to the charges stemming from Nifong's media blitzkrieg, Nifong was charged with "withholding or failing to provide potentially exculpatory evidence to the defense," as well as making "misrepresentations and false statements to [both] the court and opposing counsel." Worse, it seemed that Nifong's response to the grievance committee had not just fallen on deaf ears, but had actually aggravated his troubles. The Bar's final charge accused Nifong of making misrepresentations and false statements to the bar's grievance committee in his December 28 response.[121] It would not be the last time that Nifong would end up digging himself a deeper hole while scrambling to explain away his discovered misconduct.[122]

With his case floundering and his career in even more jeopardy, many critics considered Nifong's demise a certainty. The only lingering question was when it would become official. They did not have to wait long. After being sworn in as Durham's district attorney on January 2, Nifong recused himself from the Duke lacrosse players' prosecution on January 12 and asked North Carolina Attorney General Roy Cooper to take over. Cooper wasted no time. He appointed two of his senior prosecutors to start the investigation from scratch. By April 11, a conclusion had been reached. In a public statement, Cooper dismissed all charges against Reid Seligman, Colin Finnerty, and David Evans. The Attorney General did not merely find that there was "insufficient evidence"; instead he declared that "the three players were innocent, that no rape had taken place, that a 'rogue prosecutor' had overreached, and that, in the rush to condemn, a community and a state lost the ability to see clearly."[123]

Cooper summed up the case as "the result of a tragic rush to accuse and a failure to verify serious allegations."[124] The same would not be said

---

120. Letter from Mike Nifong, Durham District Attorney, to Katherine Jean, North Carolina State Bar Grievance Committee, Point-by-Point Response to the Three Allegations Contained in the Substance of the Grievance 3–4 (December 28, 2006), *available at* http://www.newsobserver.com/content/news/crime_safety/duke_lacrosse/20070301_nifongletter.pdf.

121. Amended Complaint, *supra* note 53, at 27–29.

122. William West, *Nifong Guilty, Gets Day In Jail*, HERALD-SUN (Durham, NC), Sept. 1, 2007, at A1.

123. Meadows et al., *supra* note 42, at 40–51.

124. Goldstein, *supra* note 12, at 59.

for Nifong's disciplinary case. On June 16, 2007, after a meticulous five-day hearing, the North Carolina State Bar disciplinary committee unanimously determined "that there is no discipline short of disbarment that would be appropriate"[125] for what it described as a prosecutorial "fiasco."[126] "Sometimes character is called upon ... and it is found wanting," said the panel's chair, F. Lane Williamson. "That is what happened to Mr. Nifong." He concluded publicly that Nifong had been driven to prosecute the Duke lacrosse case out of nothing more than "self-interest and self-deception."[127] On July 10, the order became official. Nifong could no longer practice law.[128]

Nifong's punishments would not stop there, however. After resigning from his position as the district attorney shortly after the board's decision, he appeared once more before Judge Smith. This time he was the defendant, accused of lying to the judge—a charge that carried a potential penalty of thirty days in jail. After presiding over two days of testimony, Judge Smith found Nifong guilty and sentenced him to twenty-four hours behind bars. "It's about the candor, accuracy and truthfulness in representations to the court, particularly in important matters where the liberties and rights to a fair trial of those accused of crimes may be jeopardized by the absence of such honesty by counsel," Judge Smith said.[129]

Finally, on January 15, 2008, Nifong filed for Chapter 7 bankruptcy protection. The move came on the very day Nifong's response to a civil lawsuit brought by Evans, Finnerty, and Seligman was due. In his petition, the disgraced prosecutor listed over $180 million in potential debts, including $30 million apiece to the three indicted lacrosse players, as well as three unindicted players. His assets included his home, $10,000 in vintage guitars, and his nearly $5,000 monthly pension.[130] The move came after the state denied Nifong's request that North Carolina pick up the cost for his legal bills. He had argued that because the complaint against him had arisen out of the exercise of his official duties, it was the state's responsibility "to secure his representation in this matter." The response he received was curt: "The state

125. Lara Setrakian & Chris Francescani, *Former Duke Prosecutor Nifong Disbarred*, ABC News, June 16, 2007, *at* http://abcnews.go.com/thelaw/Story?id=3285862&page=1.

126. William West, *Nifong Disbarred*, Herald-Sun (Durham, NC), June 17, 2007, at A1.

127. Setrakian & Francescani, *supra* note 125.

128. Luck & Seigel, *supra* note 5, at 26.

129. West, *supra* note 122.

130. Anne Blythe, *Nifong Bankruptcy Hearing Reveals More Assets*, News & Observer (Raleigh, N.C.), Feb. 8, 2008.

must refuse to pick up the legal tab if the state employee acted fraudulently, with malice or outside the scope of his official duties," wrote Grayson Kelley, chief deputy attorney general. Nifong's response was ironic. "I don't know why I continue to expect people to do the right thing," he said.[131]

A Closer Look at Nifong's Transgressions

Given the breadth and depth of Nifong's ethical breaches, the North Carolina State Bar did not have to delve deeply into North Carolina's Rules of Professional Conduct—which largely mirror the 2008 ABA Model Rules of Professional Conduct—to find sufficient cause to disbar the district attorney. Even considered individually, Nifong's extrajudicial statements, his failure to turn over exculpatory evidence, and the misrepresentations he made to the court, disciplinary committee, and opposing counsel would have been sufficiently damning to make the disciplinary committee's decision an easy one. Considered cumulatively, the grossness of Nifong's violations made the committee's decision a foregone conclusion. No lawyer could, or should, ever be trusted to practice law after such actions.

Of course, Nifong wasn't merely an ordinary attorney. He was the district attorney—charged with a sacred duty "to represent the State with integrity and professionalism, while protecting victims and their rights, in the pursuit of justice."[132] As explained in 1940 by United States Attorney General Robert H. Jackson, who would later become an Associate Justice of the Supreme Court, few individuals wield as much power over the lives of their fellow citizens as prosecutors. As a result, much is expected—and required —of such individuals.

> The prosecutor has more control over life, liberty and reputation than any other person in America. His discretion is tremendous. He can have citizens investigated, and, if he is that kind of person, he can have this done to the tune of public statements and veiled or unveiled intimations...."[133] [T]he citizen's safety lies in the prosecutor ... who seeks

---

131. Anne Blythe, *State Won't Assist Nifong in Defense of Lawsuit*, NEWS & OBSERVER (Raleigh, N.C.), Oct.19, 2007.

132. Durham County District Attorney's Office, http://www.ncdistrictattorney.org/14/ home.html (last visited April 30, 2009).

133. Editorial, *Prosecutorial Indiscretion; It's Past Time to Drop All Charges in the Duke Lacrosse Case*, WASH. POST, Dec. 31, 2006, at B6.

truth and not victims, who serves the law and not factional purposes.... [134]

Cognizant of this extraordinary power and the damage a "rogue prosecutor" can inflict, the Model Rules not only require that such individuals follow
the strict ethical guidelines required of all attorneys, but also special ethical
duties owed by virtue of the office they hold. Rule 3.8(f) "prohibits a prosecutor for making extrajudicial comments that have a substantial likelihood of
heightening public condemnation of the accused,"[135] unless they're necessary
to inform the public of the nature and extent of the prosecutor's action or
serve a legitimate law enforcement purpose. The Rule explicitly incorporates
the duty placed on all lawyers by Rule 3.6, which prohibits "extrajudicial
statements that the lawyer knows or reasonably should know will be dissemi-
nated by means of public communication and will have a substantial likelihood of materially prejudicing an adjudicative proceeding."[136]

Although the drafters intended to "strike a balance between protecting
the right to a fair trial and safeguarding the right of free expression"[137] by
having the prejudicial effect of any statements determined on a case-by-case
basis, the Comment to the Rule does describe types of statements that are
"more likely than not to have a material prejudicial effect." These include
statements relating to:

(1) the character, credibility, reputation or criminal record of a party,
suspect in a criminal investigation or witness, or the identity of a witness, or the expected testimony of a party or witness;

(2) in a criminal case or proceeding that could result in incarceration,
the possibility of a plea of guilty to the offense or the existence or
contents of any confession, admission, or statement given by a defendant or suspect or that person's refusal or failure to make a statement;

(3) the performance or results of any examination or test or the refusal or failure of a person to submit to an examination or test, or
the identity or nature of physical evidence expected to be presented;

(4) any opinion as to the guilt or innocence of a defendant or suspect
in a criminal case or proceeding that could result in incarceration;

---

134. TAYLOR & JOHNSON, *supra* note 5, at 77.
135. MODEL RULES OF PROF'L CONDUCT R. 3.8(f) (2008).
136. *Id.* R. 3.6.
137. *Id.* R. 3.6 cmt. [1].

(5) information that the lawyer knows or reasonably should know is likely to be inadmissible as evidence in a trial and that would, if disclosed, create a substantial risk of prejudicing an impartial trial; or

(6) the fact that a defendant has been charged with a crime, unless there is included therein a statement explaining that the charge is merely an accusation and that the defendant is presumed innocent until and unless proven guilty.[138]

In Nifong's case, it might be easier to count the statements he made that did not violate these cautionary guidelines than those that did. He referred to the lacrosse players as "hooligans" who "gang-raped" the victim because of their "general racial hostility." The day he took over the case, he stated on national television that the evidence—which he described in great detail—clearly demonstrated that members of lacrosse team had committed the assault. Finally, he commented on many different occasions about the players' refusal to make a statement.[139] The one thing he did not say was what he was required to say—that the charges against Seligman, Finnerty, and Evans were merely accusations and that each should be presumed innocent until and unless proven guilty. Given all this, it certainly should not come as a surprise that the Bar found that Nifong had clearly violated Rules 3.6 and 3.8(f).[140]

Rule 3.8 does not simply stop at extrajudicial statements, however. Rule 3.8(d) requires prosecutors to "make timely disclosure to the defense of all evidence or information known to him that tends to negate guilt of the accused."[141] Of course, discovery-related obligations are not unique to prosecutors. Rule 3.8(d) simply places a proactive enhancement on the obligations imposed on every lawyer by Rule 3.4, which prohibits an attorney from knowingly disobeying discovery obligations[142] and requires attorneys to make reasonably diligent efforts to comply with proper discovery requests.[143] Nifong's action in regard to just the DNA evidence discovered by Meehan's DSI lab place him in clear violation of his proactive duties. Rather than disclosing the evidence, he took steps to

---

138. *Id.* R. 3.6 cmt. [5].

139. Amended Complaint, *supra* note 53, at 4.

140. Amended Findings of Fact, Conclusions of Law and Order of Discipline at 20–22, North Carolina State Bar v. Nifong (July 31, 2007) [hereinafter Amended Findings of Fact].

141. MODEL RULES OF PROF'L CONDUCT R. 3.8(d) (2008).

142. *Id.* R. 3.4(c).

143. *Id.* R. 3.4(d).

hide it.[144] Furthermore, even when the defense filed proper discovery requests for such information, Nifong did not disclose it but played a five-month long game of evidentiary hide-and-seek.[145] Such actions clearly support the Bar's determination that Nifong violated both Rule 3.4 and Rule 3.8(d).[146]

Nifong's misstatements, perhaps better considered outright lies, supplied the final nails for his coffin. Rule 3.3(a)(1) prohibits a lawyer from knowingly making "false statement of fact or law to a tribunal" in the representation of a client. Rule 4.1 extends that requirement to statements made to third persons. Essentially, the rules require lawyers to be truthful when dealing with others on a client's behalf.[147] Rule 3.3(a)(1) contemplates both actual statements, either verbal or written, as well as the veracity of evidence offered to the court. Lawyers are not permitted to offer evidence that they know to be false, a duty "premised on the lawyer's obligation as an officer of the court to prevent the trier of fact from being misled by false evidence."[148]

As the reader may recall, not only did Nifong offer the "limited" lab report, but he certified that he had disclosed all requested discovery evidence verbally to Judge Smith in open court.[149] The Bar determined this to be a blatant violation of Rule 3.3(a)(1). Considering the number of false statements he made to third parties, including defense attorneys and the media, in his attempts to prosecute the Duke defendants, it should not be surprising that the Bar also found that Nifong had violated Rule 4.1.[150]

Ironically, the final charges against Nifong were based on the misrepresentations he made to the Bar once it filed its complaint against him. Rule 8.1(a) prohibits an attorney from knowingly making a false statement of material fact in connection with a disciplinary matter. In his mad scramble to dig himself out of trouble, Nifong just dug himself a deeper hole. The disciplinary committee found that such conduct additionally contravened the catchall prohibition against making misrepresentations and prejudicing the administration of justice found in Rule 8.4.[151] Of course, given the general language of Rule 8.4, it would be hard to identify any of Nifong's misconduct that did not also violate that Rule.

---

144. *See supra* notes 95–102 and accompanying text.
145. *See supra* notes 103–108 and accompanying text.
146. Amended Findings of Fact, *supra* note 140, at 20–22.
147. MODEL RULES OF PROF'L CONDUCT R. 4.1 cmt. [1] (2008).
148. *Id.* R. 3.3 cmt. [5].
149. Amended Complaint, *supra* note 53, at 22.
150. Amended Findings of Fact, *supra* note 140, at 20–22.
151. Amended Findings of Fact, *supra* note 140, at 20–22

Clearly, Justice Jackson's cautionary reminder bears careful consideration still today. Had the district attorney "sought truth and not victims" and served "the law and not factional purposes,"[152] his life and reputation, as well as those of everyone involved, would certainly be different today. Instead, Nifong chose to serve his own selfish interests. He chose to sacrifice his responsibilities and the lives and anonymity of Reade Seligman, Collin Finnerty, and David Evans—and even the misguided Crystal Mangum—in an attempt to win a local election and perpetuate himself in office. The mere fact that the "Duke Defendants" were eventually declared innocent does not negate the harm caused to them by the "exceptionally intense national and local media coverage" and "heightened public scorn and loss of privacy" they endured.

Nifong's actions harmed the profession itself, creating "a perception among the public within and outside North Carolina that lawyers in general and prosecutors in particular cannot be trusted and can be expected to lie to the court and to opposing counsel" and that "there is a systemic problem in the North Carolina justice system in that a criminal defendant can only get justice if he or she can afford to hire an expensive lawyer with unlimited resources to figure out what is being withheld by the prosecutor."[153] In light of his violations, and the harm he caused, Nifong's disbarment might be considered the only just outcome in the entire affair.

Comments and Questions

1. Much was made of Nifong's extrajudicial statements. However, as Nifong pointed out, he was not the only one talking to the media. Some members of the defense team were making equal use of their moment in the spotlight to the extent that Nifong accused them of deliberately trying to prejudice the jury in order to obtain a change of venue. Rule 3.6 makes no distinction between prosecutors and defense attorneys. Nevertheless, in contrast to Nifong, no charges were ever brought against any member of the defense team by the North Carolina State Bar. Do you think this was right? Is there any basis for giving more leeway to criminal defense attorneys in interpreting Rule 3.6?

2. The Comment to Rule 3.6 specifically deals with what might be considered "counter" statements. It provides that statements that might other-

---

152. TAYLOR & JOHNSON, *supra* note 5, at 77.
153. Amended Findings of Fact, *supra* note 140, at 23.

wise constitute a violation are excused when necessary to counteract prejudicial statements made publicly by another person. Clearly, Nifong was the first to strike. He was on national news shows the day he took over the case. As a result, the defense team was presumably within its rights to speak publicly to mitigate the undue prejudice created by Nifong statements. Does this make sense? Do two wrongs make a right in this context?

3. When considered at its most basic level, the Duke lacrosse "fiasco" was precipitated by one man's desire to remain in public office. Though Nifong had been appointed to the position on the basis of merit—his experience, the quality of his work, and his outstanding ethical reputation—he needed a community scandal in order to obtain the necessary name recognition to remain district attorney. Arguably, the election transformed him from a white knight to a rouge prosecutor. Given this example of what can go wrong, do you think that requiring district attorneys to campaign for office is a good idea? What are the costs and benefits of electing prosecutors? In the federal system, United States Attorneys are appointed by the President on a supposedly merit-selection basis. Do you think states should adopt this model?

4. On December 9, 2008, U.S. Attorney Patrick Fitzgerald held a press conference. He announced that federal investigators had recently placed a listening device in Illinois Gov. Rod Blagojevich's campaign office, as well as a wiretap on his home phone. The reason: according to Fitzgerald, Blagojevich had been on "a political corruption crime spree" that needed to be stopped. Fitzgerald told the media that secret tape recordings showed that Blagojevich was attempting to sell to the highest bidder the U.S. Senate seat that Barack Obama had left vacant after being elected to the presidency. Under Illinois' Constitution, the governor is solely responsible for filling Senate seat vacancies. "The conduct would make Lincoln roll over in his grave," Fitzgerald said, quoting Blagojevich as saying the Senate seat is "a bleeping valuable thing. You just don't give it away.... I've got this thing and it's bleeping golden."

Do you see any violations here? If Nifong's comments did not qualify as a type "necessary to inform the public of the nature and extent of the prosecutors action or server legitimate law enforcement purpose," how can Fitzgerald's? Don't these statements violate the same principles of Rule 3.6 that Nifong's did? Don't they potentially prejudice expected proceedings? Can you think of any reason that Fitzgerald should not be reprimanded for violating his ethical obligations?

5. In the eyes of most people, Nifong's greatest transgression was his attempt to "hide" exculpatory evidence from the defense. Arguably, the only reason he was caught was because of the quality and quantity of attorneys working for the Duke defendants. This type of legal defense obviously comes

at great expense. Most defendants cannot afford to hire one private defense attorney, let alone an entire team. Without those resources, what guarantee does a defendant have that the prosecutor is complying with all of his or her discovery obligations? Many people have alleged that Nifong-type discovery abuses occur on a daily basis. Do you think that this is true? Can you think of any procedures that could be enacted to ensure that all exculpatory evidence is disclosed to the defendants? Many states have enacted open discovery policies, which require prosecutors to turn over all their evidence. Does this take things too far?

6. According to Rule 3.8(a), criminal prosecutors have a duty to "refrain from prosecuting a charge that the prosecutor knows is not supported by probable cause." Seemingly, Nifong violated this rule as well. He sought and obtained an indictment after discovering that he had no real physical evidence. He had yet to interview Mangum personally, but he knew that she was providing multiple, conflicting accounts of what happened that night. He also knew that she had been incapable of identifying any of the Duke lacrosse players as her attackers until he had effectively "fixed" the identification process. Yet, the North Carolina State Bar did not accuse him of violating this principle. Why not? Do you think that the Bar had so much ammunition to use against Nifong that it only needed to consider the most obvious violations? Some Nifong supporters have alleged that even though there were flaws in the case, the charges against the Duke defendants should not have been dismissed. They believe that the case should have proceeded and been decided on its merits at trial. What is your opinion on this? Attorney General Cooper did not just simply dismiss the charges, he declared the defendants innocent. While dismissals are not uncommon, declarations of innocence are extraordinarily rare. Do you think that this signified that there was no probable cause in the first place?

Chapter 3

The Ironic Road to Club Fed[1]

"For decades, few things have inspired as much fear and loathing in the executive suites of corporate America as the law firm of Milberg Weiss and the two outsized personalities who ruled the place, Mel Weiss and Bill Lerach. Through creativity and ruthlessness, they transformed the humble securities class-action lawsuit into a deadly weapon.... But somewhere along the way, the work made its ruling partners a little like the CEOs they sued."

—Peter Elkind, FORTUNE 500 MAGAZINE[2]

Introduction: An Unusual Chain of Events

What police expected to be just another domestic disturbance turned out to be a lead that would culminate in the collapse of America's meanest law firm. On August 22, 1996, police responded to a call from a woman named Pamela Davis in Rocky River, Ohio, an affluent Cleveland suburb. Davis claimed that her boyfriend, James "J.J." Little, had assaulted her with a blow to the face that left her mouth bloody. Police quickly learned that Davis was known as a socialite in Rocky River, and was on felony probation for feeding her shopping habit with stolen credit cards, while Little was a prominent attorney with the Cleveland firm of Arter & Hadden—with a substantial crack habit.

In the course of the investigation that day, Davis made several claims to the police regarding Little, including that he was in possession of stolen paintings worth millions of dollars. A few months later, the FBI connected Davis's story to an unsolved art theft that had taken place in Los Angeles several years earlier. After additional investigation, the FBI confronted Little

---

1. Based on the original research and writing of **Susan Malove**.

2. Peter Elkind, *The Fall of America's Meanest Law Firm*, FORTUNE 500 MAGAZINE, November 13, 2006, *available at* http://money.cnn.com/magazines/fortune/fortune_archive/2006/11/13/8393127/index.htm.

about the stolen art. Once an immunity deal was struck, Little led them to the paintings and explained how they had come into his possession years earlier.

Little had recently moved to Ohio from California, where he had worked for a well known entertainment lawyer, James Tierney. Tierney, who represented clients including Gloria Estefan and Timothy Hutton, had given the paintings to Little while the latter was still in California and had asked him to take possession of them for safekeeping. Tierney had obtained the paintings from a friend, who—in seeking to defraud his insurance company—had claimed the paintings were stolen.

The owner of the paintings was a retired California eye surgeon named Steven Cooperman. He had insured the paintings, Picasso's 1932 "Nude Before a Mirror" and Monet's 1882 "The Customs Officer's Cabin in Pourville," for $12.5 million. In 1992, Cooperman reported the paintings stolen but the insurance company smelled a rat and refused to pay for the alleged loss. Not deterred, Cooperman sued for bad faith and demanded the full-insured amount plus punitive damages; eventually he received $17.5 million.

Once the paintings were discovered and the plot unraveled, Cooperman found himself at trial for insurance fraud. The 1999 trial ended in a conviction, and Cooperman was facing up to ten years in prison for his crime. After being released on $10 million bail, he hired a new lawyer from New York, Russell Gioiella, who began brainstorming ways to cut a deal with prosecutors to reduce Cooperman's sentence. Of course, the best way to negotiate a deal would be to find something of interest to the federal government, the bigger the better. Luckily for Cooperman, he knew something huge: the secrets of the law firm Milberg Weiss.[3] As a result of the deal to reveal Milberg's fraud, Cooperman ended up serving a 21 month sentence. Thus began the investigation of Milberg Weiss in 2001.

A Brief History of Milberg Weiss

Milberg Weiss, a New York based firm founded in 1965 by Larry Milberg and Melvyn Weiss, was once regarded as the top firm for shareholder class action lawsuits in the country. Since its founding, the firm, with offices in New York and California, has been credited with recovering over $45 billion dol-

---

3. *Id.*

lars for investors who claimed they were wronged by corporate fraud. This type of shareholder class-action litigation involves claims of investors who allege they suffered losses based on misleading statements, actions, and omissions on the part of corporate executives regarding a company's financial well-being. In such cases, a lead plaintiff comes forward with the suit to represent the class of all shareholders or investors in a corporation who have potentially suffered a similar loss as a result of the same corporate misconduct. Over the years, Milberg attorneys were involved in mammoth securities class-action suits against corporations such as AT&T, Lucent, Enron, Sears, Microsoft, Prudential Insurance, and Lincoln Savings & Loan.[4]

Within the firm, Melvyn Weiss and Bill Lerach were the big fish. Weiss headed the firm's New York operations, while Lerach was the head of the California office in San Diego, which he opened for the firm in 1976. (Larry Milberg passed away in 1989.) Weiss, born in the Bronx, started small and over the years built the firm's practice while expanding the frontiers of securities class actions nationwide. When Lerach joined Milberg, he focused his efforts on the volatile stocks of many Silicon Valley corporations.[5] He built "Milberg West" quickly, and was soon competing with the New York office for power and control within the firm. To many, Weiss was regarded as the noble hero, fighting for the little guy, the poor investor who was defrauded by corporate America; Lerach had a reputation for being relentless, outlandish, and the top plaintiff's class action attorney in America. He held the record for the largest recovery in a securities class action, $7.3 billion against Enron Corporation,[6] was known to scream at CEOs, and was generally disliked by opposing counsel.

Also at the top of the firm were attorneys David Bershad and Steven Schulman.[7] Bershad lived in New Jersey and was a named partner in the New York office. Bershad also served as Chief Operating Officer, led the accounting department, and was responsible for the financial affairs of the firm. He was reported to have earned $160.9 million during his 22 years at Milberg. Schulman was also a top partner in the New York office who specialized in Delaware-corporation shareholder derivative suits. He earned a reported $67.1 million in his 14 years as an equity partner at Milberg and became a

---

4. *Id.*

5. *Id.*

6. Carrie Johnson, *SEC to Side with Enron Plaintiffs*, Wash. Post, June 2, 2007, *available at* http://www.washingtonpost.com/wpdyn/content/article/2007/06/01/AR2007060102359.html.

7. *Id.*; *see also* Julie Creswell, *Milberg Weiss Is Charged with Bribery and Fraud*, N.Y. Times, May 18, 2006, *available at* http://www.nytimes.com/2006/05/18/us/18cndlegal.html?ex=1305604800&en=b01b688a560ca3d5&ei=5088&partner=rssnyt&emc=rss.

named partner in 2004. Both men served on the firm's executive committee. As such, both had the authority to oversee decision-making and the financial affairs of the firm.[8]

How It All Unraveled

As the investigation began, Dr. Cooperman revealed how his involvement with Milberg Weiss developed. According to Cooperman, in 1989 he contacted the firm about a potential shareholder lawsuit, which came to be known as the Newhall Land case. After discussing it over the phone with attorneys in the California office, Cooperman and a friend, Dr. Ronald Fischman, met with Lerach for the first time in San Diego to discuss the case. As Cooperman explained it to investigators, Lerach told them upfront that it was very hard to get people to serve as plaintiffs, and because of that, the firm compensated plaintiffs by paying them amounts equal to 5%–10% of the attorney's fees in a case.[9] At the meeting, Lerach urged Cooperman and Fischman to make investments to position themselves as plaintiffs for future lawsuits. The scheme picked up for these two right away, and dozens of cases and payments ensued.

What was Milberg's incentive for paying plaintiffs? In most class action cases, more than one plaintiff and attorney seek to represent absent class members against the defendant. When that is the case, each plaintiff and attorney competes to team up as "lead plaintiff" and "lead counsel." To obtain the lead position, a firm and its client must be approved by the court. At the time Milberg's scheme began, the lead counsel role was virtually guaranteed to the firm that filed the case first. Milberg found that by paying plaintiffs, the firm was able to maintain a ready group of individuals with investments in a wide variety of corporations, so that when the circumstances giving rise to a class action case sprung up, Milberg could be ready with a plaintiff on hand to file the suit within hours, ensuring the role of lead counsel.[10]

The benefits of securing the lead counsel role are many. Typically, lead counsel in a case controls the overall litigation strategy, has the

---

8. First Superseding Indictment at 2, United States v. Milberg Weiss Bershad & Schulman, LLP, Bershad, Schulman, Lazar and Selzer, CR 05-587 (A)-DDP (C.D. Cal. Oct. 2004) *available at* http://74.125.47.132/search?q=cache:UzpuaEvWVp0J:fl1.findlaw.com/news.findlaw.com/ wp/docs/clssactns/usmlbrg51806ind.pdf+milberg+weiss+bershad+%26+schulman+indictmen t&hl=en&ct=clnk&cd=1&gl=us&client=safari [hereinafter First Superseding Indictment].

9. *Id.* at 64.

10. *Id.* at 6–7.

power to assign work among other attorneys, and—most importantly—receives the most substantial fees in the case. Oftentimes, lead counsel also has the responsibility of determining how fees will be divided among the many law firms and attorneys working on the case, which is a very powerful position.[11]

Lerach explained to Cooperman and Fischman that, to facilitate the scheme, they needed to enlist intermediary attorneys to pass the money from Milberg to its final resting place in their hands. By using intermediaries, Milberg was able to use the pretext that the money was being paid to other attorneys as a referral fee or for the intermediary attorney's participation or assistance in the case. For example, Milberg would send a check, usually signed by Bershad, to an intermediary attorney with an attached cover letter stating that the enclosed payment was "in consideration of your consultation and referral of Dr. Cooperman to our firm." After the check was received by the intermediary attorney, Cooperman would usually direct that the proceeds of the check be used to satisfy legal fees owed to the intermediary attorney for work done for Cooperman in other matters.[12] If Cooperman had no outstanding legal bills with the intermediary, he would direct the money be forwarded to him or his family members in cash, or be used for his benefit through payment of third party debts.

Who were these intermediary attorneys? In Cooperman's case they were Richard Purtich and James Tierney. Purtich was a Los Angeles insurance lawyer who had represented Cooperman in other matters. He ultimately received about 35 checks from the Milberg firm on Cooperman's behalf totaling $3.5 million. James Tierney was the entertainment lawyer in Los Angeles who had helped Cooperman stage the theft of his own paintings. He received about $2 million from Milberg that he passed along to Cooperman. Cooperman also brought his brother-in-law, Bruce Bjork, a non-attorney, into the scheme. Milberg paid Bjork $245,000 for fictional "consulting work" in a case. Bjork eventually passed at least $203,000 of this money back to Cooperman.[13] All told, Cooperman received about $6.5 million in "first plaintiff" payments though his conduits.[14]

Cooperman also involved other family and friends in the Milberg fraud. His wife Nancy Cooperman, a second unnamed brother-in-law, Dr. Fischman, and a Beverly Hills pop psychologist named Mel Kinder all served as

---

11. *Id.* at 7.
12. *Id.* at 65.
13. *Id.* at 23.
14. Elkind, *supra* note 2.

plaintiffs for Milberg. Each of these named plaintiffs received payment for their involvement, either directly from Milberg or through Cooperman and his intermediaries.

In addition to requiring intermediaries, Milberg and its plaintiffs were required to make false representations to various courts for the scheme to succeed. In each case, the plaintiff gave some sort of perjured testimony or submitted false affidavits attesting to the fact that his or her interests "do not in any manner conflict with, nor are they antagonistic to, those of the class."[15] Lead plaintiffs were also typically questioned about financial compensation in their case, specifically, if any arrangements or incentives existed that would cause them to receive any payment or consideration for participation that would be different from the payment or consideration received by other members of the class. To this question, Cooperman was quoted as responding in one case, "I will not be treated differently than any other class member regarding any recovery."[16]

Cooperman also explained the role of David Bershad to the authorities. As COO, Bershad signed the majority of checks to intermediary lawyers and doled out cash from a safe in his office.[17] He sent the checks with cover letters thanking attorneys for the phantom client referral, or crediting the payment to nonexistent work performed "in this matter." Sometimes Weiss, Lerach, Bershad and other partners paid plaintiffs with personal checks or out-of-pocket cash, which required Bershad to create a phony bonus scheme within the firm to facilitate their reimbursement.[18]

In 2002, after Cooperman led investigators through his involvement in the fraud, federal prosecutors informed the firm and its top partners that they were potential targets of the investigation. Then they began looking for other members of the scheme unknown to Cooperman, and started by subpoenaing Milberg's records for as far back as 1972. A review of these records soon revealed the other repeat plaintiffs.

Seymour Lazar — The Plaintiff Who Started It All

The next serial plaintiff to be discovered was Seymour Lazar. Lazar's reputation preceded him. He was a wealthy Palm Springs retiree with careers in

---

15. First Superseding Indictment, *supra* note 8, at 69.
16. *Id.*
17. *Id.* at 1.
18. Elkind, *supra* note 2.

entertainment law, finance, and real estate. He dated Maya Angelou in the 1950s, managed comedian Lenny Bruce in the 1960s, apparently got into the LSD scene, went abroad for years, and then came back and settled in California where he made millions in desert real estate. Lazar was fairly litigious, and before he was involved with Milberg, he had already sued his father's estate, Donald Trump, and Carl Icahn.

In 1973, Lazar met Weiss when Lazar was a defendant in one of Milberg's cases. In that case, Lazar was accused of failing to disclose stock holdings before a takeover. Just three years later, Lazar became a paid plaintiff for Milberg, and he blazed a trail for the many that would follow him. Milberg paid not only Lazar to be a plaintiff, but his wife, son, and daughter as well.

Lazar's go-to intermediary was Paul Selzer, a well respected real estate attorney from the Palm Springs firm Best Best & Krieger (BB&K). Selzer received the first checks for Lazar beginning in 1984 in the Arcata case, totaling $94,000. Selzer received the money under the guise of a referral fee, and used it on Lazar's behalf. For example, in 1984 alone, he paid $6,000 to a law firm in Downey, California, that had done outside work for Lazar, placed $27,000 in Lazar's wife's trust, paid $742 to a surveying company working for Lazar, and used at least $15,000 to satisfy Lazar's bills at BB&K. In the following years, Selzer regularly received checks for Lazar in amounts anywhere between $50,000 and $200,000.[19] After paying off whatever Lazar owed BB&K for legal work (hundreds of thousands over about 20 years), Selzer used remaining payments from Milberg to pay off Lazar's other outstanding debts, including paying his accountant and a group of engineers and surveyors who worked on Lazar's real estate projects, and even forwarded thousands of dollars in cash directly to Lazar's son.[20]

At one point, Daniel Olivier, a partner at BB&K, grew skeptical of the arrangement between Selzer and Lazar. In 1994, he wrote a memo noting his discomfort in Lazar wanting it both ways: he wanted the Milberg lawyers to label the payments as referral fees to BB&K, but he also wanted BB&K to apply the money to Lazar's bills and other debts. The money was either BB&K's or it was Lazar's; it could not be both. Additionally, Olivier noted that Lazar did not want the relationship documented, and Olivier knew that Lazar's cover story that the payments to outside debtors were "business favors for a profitable client" wouldn't stand up to scrutiny.[21]

---

19. First Superseding Indictment, *supra* note 8, at 17.
20. *Id.* at 42.
21. Elkind, *supra* note 2.

Despite the circulation of Olivier's internal memo, the relationship be-tween Selzer and Lazar continued. Indeed, a few years later when Selzer left BB&K to start his own practice, Olivier personally took over Selzer's previous role with Lazar and Milberg, somehow overcoming his original objections to it. Olivier remained at BB&K until 2004, at which time he began cooperating with the government investigation.[22]

Besides BB&K, Lazar also used his son Job Lazar, an attorney, as an inter-mediary. In one instance, Job received a $250,000 check from Milberg for his "work in the United Airlines case," which of course he took no part in. Sey-mour Lazar reportedly used six total intermediary attorneys in three states, specifically Oregon, Kansas, and California.[23] Because Lazar was the first serial plaintiff, Milberg was still working out the kinks in its scheme. On two occa-sions, it accidentally paid two law firms for "referring" Lazar in the same case. Lazar received an estimated $2.4 million in kickbacks and served as lead plain-tiff in about 70 Milberg cases until he received his federal subpoena in 2002.[24]

The Break Up—Weiss and Lerach Part Ways

After the federal investigation was announced in 2002, rising tensions caused latent conflicts between the New York and San Diego offices of Mil-berg Weiss to come to a head. The opposite styles of their lead partners had always been a source of trouble. Lerach took pride in being loathed by oppo-nents. He considered being labeled "lower than pond scum" by a fellow Cali-fornia attorney a compliment. Weiss, on the other hand, craved respect, viewing himself as "dean" of the plaintiff's bar. Over time, disputes had arisen between the two over power, money, and credit, but the final straw came when Lerach sent a demand letter against the advice of Weiss to a firm that was serving as co-lead counsel in one of Milberg's cases. Weiss wrote a letter of apology to the recipient firm, and the split was set in stone. The firm was dissolved in 2004, with Lerach getting the San Diego office and all of its clients. He renamed his group Lerach Coughlin Stoia Geller Rudman & Rob-bins. Weiss got everything else, including the original firm name.[25]

Despite the fallout between Lerach and Weiss, both parties continued on with business, and the investigators continued searching for evidence.

---

22. *Id.*

23. First Superseding Indictment, *supra* note 8, at 13.

24. *Id.* at 98; *see also* Elkind, *supra* note 2.

25. Elkind, *supra* note 2.

The First Indictment and the Final Paid Plaintiff

Soon after the firm split, in June 2005, federal prosecutors handed down the first indictment in the case, naming Lazar and Selzer as defendants. Then, Bob Sugarman, an attorney in Milberg's New York office, made a deal for immunity and led prosecutors to the third serial plaintiff in the case: Howard Vogel.[26] Vogel sealed the deal for prosecutors. He quickly cooperated and had a clean background compared to Cooperman, who had been convicted of insurance fraud, and Lazar, who was known for his involvement in the 1960s LSD scene.

Vogel was also the freshest repeat plaintiff of the bunch, having been involved only since 1991. At that time he lived with his wife in New Jersey and legitimately contacted Milberg when his investment in Valero, a Texas energy company, plunged. Vogel initially spoke to Sugarman about his case. Unsolicited, Sugarman assured Vogel that he would receive a percentage of the attorney's fees for being lead plaintiff. Ultimately, after Vogel negotiated with Bershad and Schulman in New York, Milberg agreed to give him 14% of the attorney's fees and $10,000 to cover his lost investment.[27]

Milberg filed the Valero class action naming Vogel as lead plaintiff on August 21, 1991. As in all such filings, Milberg attorneys made representations to the court that Vogel had the same interests in the outcome of the case as the other members of the class. However, unlike the other class members, Vogel received $637,223 from the attorney's fees awarded in the case at the time of settlement.[28]

After his involvement in Valero, Schulman worked with Vogel to position him as plaintiff for a number of shareholder derivative suits against Delaware corporations, Schulman's specialty. Schulman advised Vogel of several corporations that were potential buyout targets, and drafted the documents for the suits ahead of time so they would be ready when the time was right. When a takeover bid was announced, Schulman could file his suit that day seeking a higher buyout price.[29] Altogether, Vogel served in about 40 Milberg cases as lead plaintiff, and also enlisted his wife and son to do the same. Over the course of the years that Vogel participated in Milberg cases, it is estimated that he received about $2.49 million in illegal kickback payments.[30] Milberg

---

26. *Id.*

27. First Superseding Indictment, *supra* note 8, at 51.

28. *Id.* at 18.

29. Elkind, *supra* note 2.

30. *Id.*

continued filing cases with Vogel well into 2005, years after the firm had been informed that it was a target of the federal investigation.

Normally, payments to Vogel went through Gary Lozow, a friend and fraternity brother of Vogel's who was a criminal attorney in Denver, Colorado. Lozow's claim to fame was that he had represented the family of Dylan Klebold, the Columbine High shooter. He knew nothing about securities litigation and certainly hadn't referred Vogel to Milberg, since he only became involved well after the relationship was under way. Vogel also admitted to using an unnamed New York real estate attorney as an intermediary, and reported that he was given envelopes stuffed with cash directly from Milberg partners.

Vogel's biggest payment from Milberg came in the Oxford Health Plans case in 2003. After the case had settled, Milberg received $30 million in attorney's fees and needed to negotiate a percentage to pay Vogel. Schulman informed Vogel to contact Weiss for a deal, and when he did contact Weiss, he was told to come into the New York office because Weiss didn't want to risk any phone conversations being recorded due to the pending criminal investigation.

The two men met and made an arrangement that resulted in a $1.1 million check being sent to Lozow in Denver for his "joint representation" of Vogel in the Oxford case. Another check was sent to Lozow on the same day as payment in a case in which Vogel's step-son had participated. After receiving both checks, Lozow wired over $1.2 million into a bank account set up by Vogel.[31]

Indictments Pile Up

After discovering Vogel's involvement, prosecutors were ready to start painting with a broader brush. In May 2006, the Department of Justice amended the original indictment to include Cooperman, Bershad, Schulman, Vogel and Milberg Weiss itself.[32] At that point, only the two big fish— Weiss and Lerach—had escaped charges. Moreover, the momentum had shifted. Defendants began cooperating left and right and investigators were learning more and more. Lerach finally resigned from his firm after Bershad

---

31. *Id.*

32. Press Release, Debra Wong Yang, U.S. Attorney for the Cent. Dist. of Cal., Milberg Weiss Law Firm, Two Senior Partners Indicted In Secret Kickback Scheme Involving Named Plaintiffs In Class-Action Lawsuits (May 18, 2006), *available at* http://www.usdoj.gov/usao/cac/press room/pr2006/061.html.

pled guilty and began cooperating with the government in July 2007.[33] He cited the need to protect his new firm of about 180 attorneys from being implicated in the case and wanted to ensure it would continue to zealously represent shareholders and consumers.[34]

Prior to formal indictments, Weiss and Lerach both turned down deals with the government through which each would have served three-year prison terms. Eventually Lerach was indicted and, in September 2007, pleaded guilty to conspiring to obstruct justice and making false statements under oath. Just days later, Weiss was indicted for a multitude of conspiracy and false statements charges.[35] With everyone turned against him, Weiss finally threw in the towel and pleaded guilty as well.

Sentencing and Attorney Discipline

Guilty of multiple white collar offenses, Lerach and Weiss were both facing up to 40 years in federal prison. By pleading guilty they were able to secure sentences of only 24 months and 30 months respectively. Lerach was also ordered to forfeit $7.75 million and pay a $250,000 fine. Weiss was ordered to pay $9.75 million and also a $250,000 fine.

These sentences were not easy to negotiate. Weiss's plea deal allowed prosecutors to ask for a maximum of 33 months in prison, and in response to prosecutors seeking the full sentence, Weiss submitted his own sentencing memorandum.[36] Along with the memo, Weiss attached 275 letters from colleagues, friends, and family attesting to his generosity, kind nature, and remorse for his acts.[37] In the memo filed June 2, 2008, Weiss asked the

---

33. Carrie Johnson, *Lerach to Leave Law Firm As He Tries to End Probe*, WASH. POST, Aug. 29, 2007, *available at* http://www.washingtonpost.com/wpdyn/content/article/2007/08/28/AR2007082801636.html.

34. Carrie Johnson, *Plaintiff Lawyer To Quit His Firm*, WASH. POST, May 31, 2007, *available at* http://www.washingtonpost.com/wpdyn/content/article/2007/05/31/AR2007053100004.html.

35. Carrie Johnson, *Class-Action Lawyer Weiss Indicted*, WASH. POST, Sept. 21, 2007, *available at* http://www.washingtonpost.com/wpdyn/content/article/2007/09/20/AR2007092002397.html.

36. Ashby Jones, *Examining Mel Weiss's Life in Letters*, WALL STREET J. L. BLOG, May 27, 2008, *available at* http://blogs.wsj.com/law/2008/05/27/examining-mel-weisss-life-in-letters/.

37. Nathan Koppel, *Feds Want Mel Weiss to Serve 33 Months, Weiss Asks for 18*, WALL STREET J. LAW BLOG, May 23, 2008, *available at* http://blogs.wsj.com/law/2008/05/23/feds-want-mel-weiss-to-serve-33-months-weiss-asks-for-18/.

judge to sentence him to the shortest prison term allowable under the deal, 18 months.

Weiss' attorney argued for leniency on the basis that Weiss's career included an extraordinary amount of good work, and improved the quality of life for millions. Also of significance in the memo was a focus on Weiss' humanitarian contributions throughout his career involving pro bono work benefiting Holocaust survivors and other efforts aimed at peace in the Middle East, Parkinson's disease research, and the Alzheimer's Association.[38] Among the letter writers were Arthur Miller, Kenneth Feinberg, David Boies, Burt Neuborne, and Stephen Sussman.[39]

Ultimately, U.S. District Judge John Walter of the Central District of California was not swayed. He explained that in reaching the sentence of 30 months he considered Weiss's numerous charitable contributions, but they were "difficult to reconcile" with his criminal conduct. The judge also stated that Weiss's actions went directly to "the core and heart of the judicial system."[40] Weiss reported to prison August 28, 2008, for his 30-month term.[41]

Lerach, who was sentenced first, also submitted numerous letters to Judge Walter seeking leniency in his sentencing, but was largely unsuccessful. He received the longest sentence allowable under his plea deal, 24 months. Lerach reported to prison in May 2008 and after release will be required to complete 1,000 hours of community service.

Judge Walter explained the disparity in sentences between the two as a result of Weiss's obstruction of the investigation and continuing involvement in the scheme after the investigation was underway.

The other parties to the conspiracy were sentenced as follows. David Bershad received six months in prison and was ordered to forfeit $7.75 million and pay a fine of $250,000. Steven Schulman was also sentenced to six months, but was ordered to forfeit $1.85 million in addition to the $250,000 fine. Cooperman received four months in prison, Vogel received three months, and Lazar—the first paid plaintiff—received six months home detention and two years of probation.

---

38. Defendant Melvyn I. Weiss's Sentencing Memorandum, United States v. Melvyn I. Weiss, CR 05-587(E)-JFW (C.D. Cal. 2008), *available at* http://online.wsj.com/public/resources/documents/weisssentencing.pdf.

39. Koppel, *supra* note 37.

40. Amanda Bronstad, *Mel Weiss Sentenced to 30 Months for Kickback Scheme*, NAT. L.J., June 3, 2008, *available at* http://www.law.com/jsp/article.jsp?id=1202421890210.

41. *Id.*

Richard Purtich, the Cooperman intermediary who funneled about $3.5 million from Milberg to Cooperman and various third parties, pled guilty to a felony tax charge in the case, but no information is available as to his sentence.[42] Selzer, Lazar's main intermediary, was sentenced to six months of home detention and two years of probation. Milberg Weiss itself was fined $75 million in the case, less than the $251 million prosecutors originally sought.

On August 11, 2008, the New York Departmental Disciplinary Committee filed a petition against Melvyn Weiss seeking an order that his name be stricken from the roll of New York attorneys on the ground that Weiss was automatically disbarred as a result of his federal felony conviction. The petition noted that Weiss's federal conviction also constituted a felony under New York law. Weiss did not respond to the petition and was duly disbarred.[43]

Lerach forfeited his license to practice in California as part of his federal plea deal; no formal disciplinary actions were conducted.

Like Weiss, Schulman faced automatic disbarment as a result of his conviction of a federal felony that also constituted a felony under New York law. Schulman, however, chose to fight. The disciplinary petition in his case was filed on February 19, 2008. He responded to it by arguing that, in fact, his federal felony conviction had no specific equivalent under New York law, and that—contrary to the Bar's contention—the verbal and written admissions he made while disposing of his federal case did not amount to a concession of conduct that would bring him within the purview of New York's penal law on enterprise corruption. The Bar Committee was not impressed; it responded that Schulman's arguments placed form over substance and reiterated that the automatic suspension rule applied to him. Not surprisingly, despite his protests, Schulman was disbarred.[44] In March 2009, Schulman consented to his disbarment in the state of Delaware.[45]

No disciplinary records could be located for David Bershad.

Paul Selzer, the intermediary attorney, was placed on interim suspension by the California Bar after his conviction.[46] Additionally, Selzer was suspended in-

---

42. Elkind, *supra* note 2.

43. *In re* Melvyn I.Weiss, An Attorney, Departmental Disciplinary Comm. for the First Jud. Dep't v. Weiss, M-3362 (N.Y. App. Div. 2008), *available at* http://www.criminallawlibrary blog.com/NY_AppDiv1_Weiss_12-18-08.pdf.

44. *In re* Steven G. Schulman, An Attorney, Departmental Disciplinary Comm. for the First Jud. Dep't v. Schulman, M-6355 (N.Y. App. Div. 2008), *available at* http://www.criminallaw libraryblog.com/NY_AppDiv1_Shulman_03-20-08.pdf.

45. Order, *In re* Steven G. Schulman, 2008-0427-B, (Del. 2009), *available at* http:// courts.delaware.gov/opinions/(mkauhfzupwl31j452pqgaqio)/download.aspx?ID=119670.

46. Avvo.com, Lawyer Paul Selzer Palm Springs Attorney, *at* http://www.avvo.com/attorneys/ 92264-ca-paul-selzer-339667.html (last visited Apr. 29, 2009).

definitely from representing taxpayers in front of the IRS because his federal conviction involved violations of Internal Revenue Code.[47] With disciplinary charges pending, Selzer resigned from the practice of law in California in 2008.[48]

Which ABA Model Rules Were Implicated?

In class actions lawsuits, the whole class is the client, not just the lead plaintiff. By putting the lead plaintiff's interest ahead of the class, Milberg Weiss breached its fiduciary duty to the latter. Milberg's scheme created a direct conflict of interest between lead plaintiff and lead counsel on the one hand, and the absent class members, on the other. A lead plaintiff sharing in a percentage of the attorneys' fees has an interest in moving the case to settlement quickly and ensuring a high fee award. The absent class members' interest is in maximizing the recovery of damages and minimizing the percentage of that recovery that will be siphoned off for the attorneys.

As a result of their actions, the Milberg attorneys violated ABA Model Rule 1.7, which addresses conflicts of interest between current clients. The representation of the paid plaintiffs was without a doubt "directly adverse" to the representation of the class. Obviously, the scheme was secret, so there was no opportunity for the class members to waive the conflict; moreover, if they knew about it, they would not have agreed to a waiver.

Also violated by the attorneys involved in Milberg's scheme, partners and intermediaries alike, was Model Rule 1.5 regarding attorneys' fees. This rule states in subsection (e) that a division of a fee between lawyers who are not in the same firm may be made only if: (1) the division is in proportion to the services performed by each lawyer or each lawyer assumes joint responsibility for the representation; (2) the client agrees to the arrangement, including the share each lawyer will receive, and the agreement is confirmed in writing; and (3) the total fee is reasonable. Here, the intermediary attorneys performed no work, agreements between the parties were not in writing, and the

---

47. Announcement of Disciplinary Sanctions, Office of Prof'l Responsibility, Internal Rev. Serv., Dep't of the Treas., 2009-8 I.R.B. (Feb. 23, 2009), *available at* http://www.irs.gov/irb/2009-08_IRB/ar17.html.

48. *Palm Springs Lawyer Resigns After Guilty Plea in IRS Case,* 2008 CAL. ST. B. J. *available at* http://calbar.ca.gov/state/calbar/calbar_cbj.jsp?sCategoryPath=/Home/Attorney%20Resources/California%20Bar%20Journal/December2008&MONTH=December&YEAR=2008&sCatHtmlTitle=Discipline&sJournalCategory=YES&sCatHtmlPath=cbj/2008-12_Discipline_Feature.html&sSubCatHtmlTitle=Feature.

purpose of the fee sharing arrangement was ultimately to share fees with non-lawyers, which is specifically prohibited by Model Rule 5.4. Though there are exceptions to the prohibition found in Rule 5.4, participation in a racketeering conspiracy is not one of them.

Also implicated in the case, mostly by Bershad's conduct, but also by all of the attorneys involved at Milberg, is Rule 1.15 on safekeeping property. Although this case didn't directly implicate the commingling of client trust funds, the spirit of the rule was certainly violated by Milberg's failure to keep legitimate books and records. Certainly, one purpose of safekeeping is to legitimize all financial dealings and ensure that the lawyers with access to funds are not dipping into accounts for illegal purposes.

The most flagrant of Milberg lawyers' violations involved Model Rules 3.3, Candor Toward the Tribunal, and 3.4, Fairness to Opposing Party and Counsel. Rule 3.3 states, in pertinent part, that a "lawyer shall not knowingly ... make a false statement of fact or law to a tribunal ... or ... offer evidence that the lawyer knows to be false." It goes even further, stating that a

> lawyer who represents a client in an adjudicative proceeding and who knows that a person intends to engage, is engaging or has engaged in criminal or fraudulent conduct related to the proceeding shall take reasonable remedial measures, including, if necessary, disclosure to the tribunal.

Rule 3.3 strikes at the heart of Milberg's fraudulent conduct.

Rule 3.4 (b) states in pertinent part that a lawyer shall not falsify evidence, counsel or assist a witness to testify falsely, or offer an inducement to a witness that is prohibited by law. By encouraging plaintiffs to participate in cases, Milberg attorneys counseled and assisted clients in testifying falsely, falsifying evidence regarding their position in relation to absent class members, and offered inducements to the plaintiffs in return for making these false statements in court.

One of the shocking things about this case is that over the decades that Milberg's scheme was ongoing, not one attorney reported the misconduct. Under Rule 8.3, Reporting Professional Misconduct, a lawyer who knows that another lawyer has committed a violation of the ABA Model Rules that "raises a substantial question as to that lawyer's honesty, trustworthiness or fitness as a lawyer ... *shall inform* the appropriate professional authority (emphasis added)." No one with knowledge of the scheme reported anyone else for acting dishonestly or violating the Model Rules. That likely includes all of the Milberg attorneys employed on the East and West coasts, which amounted to about 250 individuals at one point, as well as all of the intermediary attorneys.

On the same note, the general ABA rule against attorney misconduct applies across the board in this case. Rule 8.4 states that it is professional misconduct for a lawyer to: "(a) violate or attempt to violate the Rules of Professional Conduct, knowingly assist or induce another to do so, or do so through the acts of another; (b) commit a criminal act that reflects adversely on the lawyer's honesty, trustworthiness or fitness as a lawyer in other respects; (c) engage in conduct involving dishonesty, fraud, deceit or misrepresentation; (d) engage in conduct that is prejudicial to the administration of justice."

Finally, Rule 5.1, Responsibilities of Partners, Managers and Supervisory Lawyers, is implicated by the special duties it puts on attorneys at the top of a firm. In this respect, Milberg's partners were a complete failure. The rule requires that partners in a law firm make reasonable efforts to ensure that the firm has measures in effect that give reasonable assurance that all lawyers in the firm will conform to the rules of professional conduct. It also requires that a lawyer having direct supervisory authority over another lawyer make reasonable efforts to ensure that the other lawyer conforms to the rules. Senior Milberg lawyers not only flunked these standards, but they created a firm that was an incubator for unethical conduct. While the firm purported to represent shareholders against corporate fraud, it was actually defrauding those very same shareholders. They believed that the purpose of their suit was to recover for the class, when it was mostly a vehicle to maximize illicit profits for the paid plaintiffs and the attorneys themselves.

Where Are They Now?

One would think that, at this point, with Milberg LLP forging ahead with new leading attorneys, Weiss and Lerach would be laying low in prison and staying out of the news. What a naïve thought.

Less than one month after reporting to prison, Lerach got himself into even hotter water. Soon after arriving at the minimum-security federal penitentiary in Lompac, California, Lerach was conversing with a guard when the conversation turned to sports. The guard reported that after mentioning that he was a San Diego Chargers fan, Lerach offered him the use of his season tickets.[49] There was no report of whether Lerach was trying to strike a deal with the guard, or was just being generous, but the guard reported the statement to authorities and a disciplinary investigation began.

---

49. Dan Levine, *Going Gets Rough for Lerach*, RECORDER (California), Sept. 9, 2008, *available at* http://www.law.com/jsp/ca/PubArticleCA.jsp?id=1202424375556.

According to Bureau of Prisons guidelines, offering anything of value is considered a "high category" offense, only one level below the most egregious kinds of violent behavior on the four-tier scale. Other "high category" offenses include escape, wearing a disguise, and making sexual advances to other inmates.

During the investigation, Lerach was placed in 23-hour per day administrative segregation, which is customarily the case until an administrative hearing is held. Possible disciplinary measures include transfer from the minimum-security camp facility to a low-security prison, or loss of personal property or recreational privileges.

And Weiss? Also in prison, but continuing to make headlines, and it seems there is just no end to the irony.

On February 4, 2009, Weiss was listed in a U.S. Bankruptcy Court filing among the investors who fell victim to Bernie Madoff's $50 billion Ponzi scheme.[50] Weiss had four separate accounts with the Madoff funds, but it is unclear exactly how much money he invested. On the upside, Weiss wasn't alone in his decision to invest in Madoff's funds. The February 2009 filings also named David Bershad and Howard Vogel as investors.

Despite Weiss's investment losses, the Madoff scheme actually benefited Milberg LLP. The attorneys leading Milberg after Weiss's incarceration took advantage of the fraud in an effort to rebuild their reputation. In 2009, the firm signed up more than 100 Madoff victims for a suit, the largest group amassed by any law firm in the case. No information could be obtained regarding whether Weiss was personally involved as a plaintiff. Regardless, Milberg's clients as a whole sustained an estimated loss of $1.5 to $2 billion. To share the load in this monumental case, Milberg LLP teamed up with Seeger Weiss, a law firm in which Weiss's son is a name partner. If the team is successful, it will probably mean a windfall in attorneys' fees and a step towards Milberg regaining its credibility.

Comments and Questions

1. Milberg Weiss was at one time a firm of around 200 attorneys, and the newly renamed Milberg LLP, with about 100 attorneys, is made up of many attorneys who were present during the conspiracy but somehow managed to

---

50. *Convicted Felon Mel Weiss Was A Madoff Investor*, Feb. 5, 2009, *at* http://bitterqueen.typepad.com/friends_of_ours/2009/02/convicted-felon-mel-weiss-a-madoff-investor.html (last visited Apr. 29, 2009).

escape charges. Now leading the firm, those attorneys have the opportunity to seek contributions toward the $75 million the firm was ordered to pay in the case from the specific partners convicted of engaging in conspiracy and fraud. At this point, there is no evidence that any such contributions have been sought. Although $75 million might not be enough to really damage the firm, one might wonder if the real reason no contributions have been sought is to avoid further controversy that might implicate Milberg's remaining attorneys in the conspiracy.

How likely is it that these attorneys knew of the twenty-some-year conspiracy to pay plaintiffs? Considering the evidence that it was common practice and that clients were told upfront about the payments, can these attorneys make a credible argument they were unaware? If they knew of the conspiracy but did not participate, what were their obligations under the Model Rules?

2. As the story goes, Lazar was the plaintiff who started it all. He first served as a plaintiff in 1976, with Cooperman joining him in 1989, and Vogel in 1991. According to the investigation, Cooperman was paid approximately $6.5 million from 1989–1999, but Lazar was only alleged to have received $2.4 million, an amount similar to the one imputed to Vogel, who was involved for a much shorter time. If Lazar was involved the longest, how likely is it that he received millions of dollars less than Cooperman? Is this disparity in numbers due to the fact that Cooperman's cooperation led the investigation and Lazar was relatively uncooperative? Is it unethical to hide ill-gotten gains?

3. During the course of litigation, the government's focus was more on misrepresentations and fraud, and less on harm to Milberg's clients. However, the assumption by the government and others condemning Milberg's practice was that the requirement to pay plaintiffs led Milberg to inflate its legal fees, shrinking the recovery for the class in each case. In regards to an attorney's ethical requirements, would it help if Milberg could make a showing that the fees charged in cases where plaintiffs were being paid were the same as those where they were not? If there was no reduction in size of the award to the class, what other fiduciary duties owed to the class were breached?

Chapter 4

The Legal Doctor Kevorkian[1]

Q: Mr. Glazer, what consultations and/or conferences if any, did you conduct with more experienced professional colleagues in the capital field concerning the litigation of a capital case?

A: Well it was like, you know, a round table on a Friday afternoon. I mean, all the lawyers go to a bar in Gainesville and sit around. I don't know if it came up or not but in general the answer is, I would say no one.[2]

—Attorney Steven Glazer, quoted in a 1999 deposition in *Wuornos v. State*, SC00-1748 (Fla. Feb. 1, 2001)

Introduction

Between 1989 and 1992, eight men were murdered on the highways of the State of Florida. The police began looking for two women, the "Angels of Death," who were thought to be responsible for these murders. One of these women, Aileen Wuornos, was eventually apprehended and charged with the first degree murder of Walter Antonio, Troy Burress, Charles Carskaddon, Charles Humphreys, Richard Mallory, and David Spears. The news media immediately took up the story and it became a national spectacle. America had its first female serial killer.[3]

Defendant Aileen Wuornos

No one can argue that Aileen Wuornos had an easy life. Her parents were already divorced when she was born in 1956. Her father eventually killed himself in prison, where he was serving time for the rape and kidnapping of a

---

1. Based on the original research and writing of **Elizabeth Manno**.
2. Initial Brief of Appellant at 36, Wuornos v. State, SC00-1748 (Fla. Feb. 1, 2001), *available at* http://www.floridasupremecourt.org/clerk/briefs/2000/1601-1800/00-1748_ini.pdf.
3. AILEEN WUORNOS: THE SELLING OF A SERIAL KILLER (Lafayette Films 1992).

seven year old boy. Wuornos's mother abandoned her, forcing her to be adopted by her grandparents. She never had contact with her mother again. Wuornos's grandfather was an alcoholic and eventually committed suicide. Her grandmother also drank excessively and died of a liver disorder. Wuornos's brother died of cancer at the age of twenty-one.[4] Quite clearly, there was a profound history of depression and substance abuse in her family.

While in school, Wuornos's IQ was established at 81, which is in the low range of "dullness." At age thirteen, she was raped by a family friend. She waited six months before revealing her resulting pregnancy to her grandparents. They blamed her for the pregnancy, and she was forced to give the child up for adoption. There is also evidence that Wuornos was physically and verbally abused while living with her grandparents. However, when called by the State to testify at one of her murder trials, Wuornos's uncle claimed that his family had a "normal lifestyle" and was a "straight and narrow family."[5]

Wuornos ultimately left her grandparents' home at age sixteen for a life on the streets dominated by prostitution and drug and alcohol abuse. For a while she lived in an abandoned car in the woods in Michigan, enduring the snow and freezing winter temperatures common there. Eventually, she moved to Florida, continuing her life of prostitution and drug use. In the late 1980s, Wuornos met Tyria Moore, and the two became lovers. Their relationship was serious: Wuornos considered Moore her wife. Wuornos wanted to do whatever she could to support and protect Moore, and make her happy. Wuornos stated that part of the reason she began engaging in prostitution with unknown men on Florida highways, rather than just with her "regulars," was Moore's encouragement and Wuornos's desire to bring home money to her lover.[6]

Moore was once a prime suspect in the investigation of the murders with which Aileen Wuornos was eventually charged. However, Moore would ultimately cooperate with law enforcement and aid them in obtaining a confession from Wuornos. Specifically, Moore allowed the police to secretly record conversations between herself and Wuornos. The police set Moore up in a hotel room and recorded phone calls Wuornos made to her from prison. Moore cried on the phone and told Wuornos that she was worried she would be implicated in the crimes, and insisted that Wuornos confess to the police. It was not

---

4. Wuornos v. State, 644 So. 2d 1000, 1005 (Fla. 1994).

5. *Id.*

6. AILEEN WUORNOS: THE SELLING OF A SERIAL KILLER (Lafayette Films 1992), AILEEN: LIFE AND DEATH OF A SERIAL KILLER (Lafayette Films 2003).

long before Moore had convinced Wuornos to do just that. Moore then became the State's star witness at trial and was never charged with any crime.[7]

The original investigating officer assigned to the murders, Sergeant Bryan Jarvis of the Marion County police, stated in a 1992 interview that there was initially a lot of evidence that two people were involved in the crimes.[8] It was Moore who showed law enforcement officers where to find the murder weapon as well as the location of some of the victims' property.[9] In fact, Moore was personally in possession of some of this property, including one of the victim's cars. Moore was even identified as being with Wuornos at a gas station at the same time that one of the victims was believed to have met Wuornos.[10] Still, she was never charged, as the State and police focused their efforts on Aileen Wuornos alone.

After raising questions about the investigation of the case and the lack of prosecution of Moore, Jarvis and his family received death threats. His house was broken into and the Wuornos investigation files were stolen. Jarvis has voiced his belief that the police refused to properly investigate the source of these threats, and that he was being targeted for his questioning of the investigation.[11]

Wuornos's story was immediately national news, and it was not long before it began to be exploited for financial gain by others connected to the case. Sadly, even as the police were conducting the investigation, they were simultaneously involved in discussions with movie producers, as was Wuornos's lover, Tyria Moore. In fact, the same attorney represented the police officers and Moore in the movie discussions.[12] The Florida Film Bureau was taking steps to ensure that any movies about Wuornos would be shot on location in the state.[13] The movie deal discussions would eventually lead to resignations and public apologies by police officials. It was rumored at the time that this might lead to the overturning of Wuornos's convictions, but that never occurred.[14]

---

7. AILEEN WUORNOS: THE SELLING OF A SERIAL KILLER (Lafayette Films 1992).

8. *Id.*

9. Wuornos v. State, 644 So. 2d 1000, 1004 (Fla. 1994); Wuornos v. State, 676 So. 2d 972, 973 (Fla. 1996).

10. AILEEN WUORNOS: THE SELLING OF A SERIAL KILLER (Lafayette Films 1992).

11. *Id.*

12. *Id.*

13. Chris Lavin & Jim Ross, *Murders, Movies, and a Plea to Die,* ST. PETERSBURG TIMES, Apr. 20, 1992, at 1B.

14. AILEEN WUORNOS: THE SELLING OF A SERIAL KILLER (Lafayette Films 1992).

While she was in prison awaiting trial, Wuornos began to communicate with Arlene Pralle, an Ocala horse and wolf breeder. Pralle later testified that her relationship with Wuornos began when Wuornos prayed for God to send her a "good Christian woman," and Jesus personally told Pralle to write to Wuornos in prison.[15] As odd as it sounds, Pralle and her husband, Robert, legally adopted the adult Wuornos in November 1991. Steven Glazer was the Pralles's attorney for the adoption.[16] He would continue to represent the Pralles as an attorney and an agent, even after he eventually assumed representation of Aileen Wuornos in her criminal cases.[17]

Attorney Steven Glazer

Steven Glazer was a high school drop-out from New York, who then spent several years playing in a 60s rock band, and later worked as a truck driver. Eventually, Glazer moved to his brother's hometown of Gainesville, Florida, and enrolled in Santa Fe Community College. He ignored Santa Fe's continued requests for a high school transcript, and went on to attend the University of Florida, where he obtained his undergraduate and law degrees.[18]

Glazer assumed legal representation of Wuornos in 1992, just three years after being admitted to the Florida Bar. At the time, his phone number spelled out "Dr. Legal," which Glazer used in TV commercials. At one point, Glazer's answering machine greeted callers with the Beatles' song "Help," and informed the caller that if help was needed, the caller had come to the right place. Later, the message was changed to the Bob Marley song "Get Up Stand Up," and the caller was told that Steve Glazer would stand up for the caller's rights.[19] Even today, Glazer carries a laminated card with one word written on it: Liberal. He gives this card as one of his credentials—he is a "card-carrying liberal."[20] This inexperienced and flippant lawyer became a self-proclaimed "Legal Doctor Kevorkian" for Aileen Wuornos, speeding her on her way to her death through his actions as her attorney.

---

15. Wuornos v. State, 644 So. 2d 1012, 1015 (Fla. 1994).

16. Associated Press, *Couple Adopts Woman Charged in Serial Killings*, St. Petersburg Times, Nov. 7, 1991, at 6B.

17. Aileen Wuornos: The Selling of a Serial Killer (Lafayette Films 1992).

18. Lavin & Ross, *supra* note 13.

19. *Id.*; Aileen Wuornos: The Selling of a Serial Killer (Lafayette Films 1992).

20. Interview with Steven Glazer, Attorney, in Gainesville, Fla. (Mar. 29, 2009); Lavin & Ross, *supra* note 13.

Events

After seeing her own and Wuornos's police sketches on television, Moore became worried. She left Wuornos and went up North to her family. Wuornos was quickly arrested on an outstanding warrant for a charge unrelated to the murders. After police discovered Moore in Pennsylvania, they did not arrest her, but instead placed her in some type of "custodial arrangement." Later they transferred custody to Florida law enforcement, which arranged for Moore to call Wuornos and get her to confess.[21]

After prompting by Moore, Wuornos agreed to confess and indicated her desire to speak to the police and also an attorney.[22] A lawyer from the Public Defender's Office was summoned and advised Wuornos not to confess, but Wuornos ignored this advice.[23]

All of the victims had picked up Wuornos as a prostitute in their vehicles. Wuornos's story of the murders would ultimately vary somewhat in her different statements. But, in general, she asserted that, although she did kill the men, she did so in self-defense after they had tried to rape, abuse, or rob her. For example, she claimed that Richard Mallory (her first victim) picked her up while she was hitchhiking and took her to a secluded area to engage in an act of prostitution. In her first statement, Wuornos stated that she became afraid he would rape her and take her money, so she shot him. At the trial for this murder, the only guilt-phase trial Wuornos ever had, she told the jury in graphic detail that she had been violently raped by Mallory and killed him after she believed that he intended to kill her.[24] Mallory's alleged actions toward Wuornos were important, because it became a theory of the defense that they had ignited her psyche and caused her to commit the other murders. It was eventually discovered that Mallory had a history of violence and sexual abuse, but this was not brought to light until after the trial had ended.[25] This information possibly could have been introduced at trial because Wuornos was claiming self-defense, making a victim's past crimes potentially relevant.

---

21. State v. Wuornos, No. 91-0257CFAES, 1991 WL 352757, at *1 (Fla. Cir. Ct. Dec. 13, 1991) (order denying Defendant's Motion to Suppress).

22. AILEEN WUORNOS: THE SELLING OF A SERIAL KILLER (Lafayette Films 1992).

23. Wuornos v. State, 644 So. 2d 1000, 1003 (Fla. 1994).

24. AILEEN WUORNOS: THE SELLING OF A SERIAL KILLER (Lafayette Films 1992); Wuornos v. State, 644 So. 2d 1000, 1003–04 (Fla. 1994).

25. Associated Press, *Information on Wuornos Victim Makes Case for New trial*, Oct. 13, 1992.

In a rare move, and despite vigorous objection by her public defender, the judge permitted the State to introduce evidence of the six other murders that Wuornos was accused, but not convicted, of committing.[26] The judge determined that this evidence was admissible under Florida's "Williams rule" to show the intent of the defendant, and to rebut claims of self-defense.[27] In light of this evidence, the jury not only found Wuornos guilty, but it recommended death, 12 to 0. The judge chose to follow the jury's recommendation and sentenced Wuornos to death.[28]

After this trial was over, Wuornos surprised everyone by firing her top-notch capital public defenders and hiring newly graduated Gainesville attorney Steven Glazer to represent her.[29] Glazer was not paid by Wuornos; he donated his time as an attorney.[30] During an interview, Glazer later explained that he took the case without being paid because he wanted to help Wuornos achieve what her public defenders would not help her with: getting herself executed. "If you saw someone drowning, wouldn't you throw them a life preserver?" Glazer asked.[31] Glazer claimed that he did receive a nominal payment of $7,500 from Wuornos—not much for several years of representation for a capital crime defendant. He was adamant that this money came from Wuornos's personal funds from being a prostitute, and not from numerous media deals.[32]

After hiring Glazer, Wuornos quickly entered pleas in her remaining five cases. Specifically, on March 31, 1992, mere moments after a judge approved Wuornos's request to appoint Glazer to her case, Wuornos pleaded no contest to three first degree murder charges for the deaths of Charles Humphreys, Troy Burress, and David Spears.[33] Later, she pleaded guilty to first degree murder in the Walter Antonio and Charles Carskaddon cases. Glazer, on Wuornos's behalf, requested to waive the penalty phases for these cases. Penalty phases are held in capital cases so that a jury can consider the possible existence of aggravating and mitigating factors surrounding the killing and make a recommendation to the judge about whether the defendant should be sentenced to death. Because of the seriousness of the death penalty, the presiding judge in each of Wuornos's cases would not let her waive the penalty

---

26. AILEEN WUORNOS: THE SELLING OF A SERIAL KILLER (Lafayette Films 1992).

27. *Wuornos*, 644 So. 2d at 1006–07.

28. *Id.* at 1005–06.

29. Lavin & Ross, *supra* note 13.

30. Bryanna LaToof, *Wuornos to Undergo More Tests*, ST. PETERSBURG TIMES, July 15, 1992, Pasco Times at 1.

31. Interview with Steven Glazer, Attorney, in Gainesville, Fla. (Mar. 29, 2009).

32. *Id.*

33. Lavin & Ross, *supra* note 13

phase.[34] Ultimately, Glazer agreed to minimally participate in these proceedings, so as to prevent the case from coming back on appeal as a result of procedural deficiencies.[35]

So, despite Wuornos's protestations, penalty phases were held for the Antonio, Carskaddon, Humphreys, Burress, and Spears murders, but Wuornos chose to waive her right to be present at these proceedings. Thus, she was never seen in person by the juries that evaluated whether or not she should be put to death. In the Humphreys, Burress, and Spears cases, the jury recommended death by a vote of 10 to 2, which Judge Sawaya followed.[36] After the Antonio penalty phase was delayed to allow Glazer to get heart bypass surgery, the jury ultimately returned a death recommendation of 7 to 5, which the judge implemented. Wuornos also received death in the Carskaddon case. All told, while being represented by Glazer, Wuornos received six death sentences in a little over a year's time.

The Legal Kevorkian

The outcome in Wuornos's cases is hardly surprising given that Glazer's publicly stated goal was to see that she be put to death, claiming that this is what she wanted. However, Glazer's unflinching march toward this goal ignored Wuornos's probable mental incompetence and likely amounted to conflict-ridden and ultimately ineffective assistance of counsel. These issues are examined, in turn.

Conflicts of Interest

Throughout his representation of Wuornos, Glazer was also simultaneously acting as both an agent and attorney to Arlene Pralle. In this capacity, he negotiated cash payments for media interviews with both Pralle and Wuornos, and was even personally paid for his role in the interviews as well.[37] For example, Glazer accepted $300 from the Geraldo Rivera talk show, and a $2,500 cut of the $10,000 total paid by a British documentary crew for the right to film. Glazer denied taking money from the Montel Williams talk

---

34. Bryanna LaToof, *Wuornos' Lawyer Stands by her Wish for No Trial*, St. Petersburg Times, Apr. 24, 1992, Hernando Times at 10.

35. Interview with Steven Glazer, Attorney, in Gainesville, Fla. (Mar. 29, 2009).

36. Wuornos v. State, 644 So. 2d 1012, 1016 (Fla. 1994).

37. Aileen Wuornos: The Selling of a Serial Killer (Lafayette Films 1992).

show, but Pralle testified in a deposition that he received $3,300 from it. Regardless of the exact amounts, Glazer admitted in a 1999 deposition that he had a financial interest in the outcome of Wuornos's case.[38]

Pralle was also receiving thousands of dollars for interviews, and was set to receive 33% of the proceeds of a book written about Wuornos, although the publisher went out of business before she was paid.[39] At one point prior to her execution, Wuornos expressed concerns in interviews that Glazer and Pralle were "just out for the money," and claimed that she didn't trust them.[40]

These business and legal arrangement led Glazer to become embroiled in multiple conflicts. ABA Model Rule of Professional Conduct 1.7(a)(2) prohibits the representation of a client if "there is a significant risk that the representation of one or more clients will be materially limited by the lawyer's responsibilities to another client, a former client or a third person or by a personal interest of the lawyer." In representing both Pralle in her media negotiations and Wuornos as her criminal attorney, Glazer was representing two people with directly conflicting interests. Pralle had an interest in earning as much money as possible for media interviews, and the more sensational Wuornos's story became, the more money she would make. On the other hand, Wuornos had an interest in seeing her case resolved in the most favorable way for her personally, which may not have been the biggest headline grabber. In fact, Wuornos expressed anger at the media's involvement in her case a number of times; she disliked the hype. The media attention was, of course, being fed by the actions of Glazer and his client Pralle.

Pralle and Wuornos's interests in the outcome of Wuornos's case were clearly not aligned, and Glazer certainly could not represent them both without a significant risk that the representation of one of these clients would be materially limited by his representation of the other. The conflict was present before Glazer assumed representation of Wuornos (because he already represented Pralle), so he should have declined to take her on as a client. The rules do provide that this type of conflict may be waived, but *only* if the lawyer believes that he will be able to provide "competent and diligent representation to each client" *and* each client gives informed consent. The first condition could not have been met in this case, and the second condition wasn't.

Glazer also had a personal conflict in the matter, in violation of Model Rule 1.7 and the corresponding Florida Rule 4-1.7. By receiving money from

---

38. Chase Squires, *Inmate's Ex-Lawyer Says He Guaranteed an Appeal*, St. Petersburg Times, Apr. 15, 2000, Pasco Times at 2.

39. *Id.*

40. Aileen Wuornos: The Selling of a Serial Killer (Lafayette Films 1992).

the media for interviews, as well as a percentage of the money Pralle received, Glazer acquired a monetary interest in the outcome of Wuornos's cases. Again, the more sensational and newsworthy the case became, the more money he and Pralle would receive. As a result, the risk that Glazer's personal interests would negatively impact his representation of Wuornos was too great for him to be her lawyer.

Glazer's personal interests also conflicted with those of his client when it came to Wuornos entering pleas. Glazer openly admitted that he did not have the experience or resources to proceed with a full guilt-phase trial in a capital murder case.[41] Given this, Wuornos would have been at a severe disadvantage had she chosen to go forward with a trial rather than enter a guilty or no contest plea. This situation arguably left her with little meaningful choice in her course of action as long as Glazer was her attorney. Moreover, Glazer had a strong personal interest in coaxing Wuornos to enter pleas so that he could continue to represent her and reap the concomitant financial remuneration and national attention. If Wuornos exercised her right to a jury trial, Glazer would either expose himself to widespread ridicule by trying a case over his head, or lose the limelight by giving the case up.

Indeed, this exact scenario is what apparently came to pass. Wuornos alleged in an interview that Glazer and Pralle had pressured her into entering pleas.[42] Glazer, of course, maintains that it was always Wuornos's decision to plead guilty, but her statement to the contrary is troubling. Model Rule 1.2 provides that a lawyer shall abide by the client's decision as to what plea should be entered. If Glazer pressured Wuornos, it would have been a blatant violation of this ethical constraint.

In a 2009 interview conducted for this book, Glazer denied that his representation of Wuornos was compromised by conflicts. He admitted that if he had represented Pralle, it would have been a conflict of interest. However, Glazer claimed that he was never an attorney or agent for Arlene Pralle. He maintained that he was Wuornos's, not Pralle's, attorney for the adoption and claimed that any interactions he had with Arlene Pralle were as an attorney for Wuornos.[43] But video footage shot for a documentary contemporaneous with Glazer's representation of Wuornos shows otherwise; it reveals that Glazer was personally involved with Pralle and her negotiations with the media. In the documentary, Pralle refers to Glazer as her attorney and agent

---

41. *Id.*; Initial Brief of Appellant at 24, Wuornos v. State, SC00-1748 (Fla. Feb. 1, 2001), *available at* http://www.floridasupremecourt.org/clerk/briefs/2000/1601-1800/00-1748_ini.pdf.

42. Aileen Wuornos: The Selling of a Serial Killer (Lafayette Films 1992).

43. Interview with Steven Glazer, Attorney, in Gainesville, Fla. (Mar. 29, 2009).

numerous times, and states that he receives a "cut" of any money she makes.[44] In addition, it is clear that it was Pralle who retained Glazer for the adoption of Wuornos.[45] All of these facts contradict Glazer's later assertions, and demonstrate that an attorney-client relationship was present between Pralle and Glazer.

Glazer's Competency as an Attorney

In addition to the conflicts of interest that arose in Glazer's representation of Wuornos, his actions seriously call into question his effectiveness as an attorney, which became one of the primary issues on appeal. The first issue is Glazer's competency as a capital attorney in general. He had only been in practice for three years when Wuornos hired him. Prior to Wuornos's case, Glazer had represented only twelve felony defendants, none in a capital case.[46]

Model Rule 1.1 provides that an attorney must ensure that he has the "legal knowledge, skill, thoroughness, and preparation reasonably necessary for the representation." The Rule's comments make clear that an attorney can be competent with little experience in an area, but only if the attorney undertakes the necessary study or associates with a lawyer with established competence in the field. Glazer did not do any additional study of death penalty cases to become competent to represent Wuornos, nor did he consult with a single experienced capital attorney for advice or guidance. According to Glazer's own admission, the only advice he received from other attorneys came during happy hour discussions in a Gainesville bar. When asked in a 1999 deposition why he didn't seek help from a more experienced attorney, Glazer replied "I just didn't. I was probably ineffective."[47]

Along with his lack of competency in capital cases, Glazer's preparation and resources devoted to his representation of Wuornos were shockingly deficient. He did not request any discovery in any of Wuornos's cases, and he admitted that he never reviewed or even sought to obtain the previous discovery in the possession of the Public Defender's Office.[48] In the later interview for this book, Glazer maintained that he did not need to review the discovery

---

44. AILEEN WUORNOS: THE SELLING OF A SERIAL KILLER (Lafayette Films 1992).

45. Initial Brief of Appellant at 17, *Wuornos*, (SC00-1748).

46. Chase Squires, *Lawyer Did Bad Job in Serial Killer Case*, ST. PETERSBURG TIMES, Apr. 18, 2000, Pasco Times at 1.

47. Squires, *supra* note 46.

48. Initial Brief of Appellant at 23, 35, *Wuornos*, (SC00-1748).

because he was present in the courtroom for most of Wuornos's first trial. He did not, however, elaborate on how seeing a portion of the discovery admitted at trial in her first case negated the need for viewing or requesting discovery in her five remaining cases.[49]

Glazer's "office" was his living room, a far cry from the resources and workspace necessary for most capital attorneys to do even a mediocre job of representing their client.[50] Glazer had no staff: no paralegals, no investigators, no junior attorneys, no law clerks. Glazer admitted that he did not have the resources to mount a full-fledged defense of his client.

Glazer's lack of competency as an attorney led to numerous mistakes that would affect Aileen Wuornos and render Glazer's legal assistance woefully ineffective. Perhaps the most egregious example of Glazer's shortcomings is evident with respect to the issue of Wuornos's mental status. At the time in question, Wuornos was obviously unstable to anyone who met or saw her. Her profane outbursts in the courtroom and rambling statements in prison are well documented and were well known to the public. She made wild claims of having sex with as many as 250,000 men as a prostitute. During court proceedings, she hurled profanities at the judge, the assistant state attorney, and their families. She was unable to sit through court proceedings and maintain appropriate decorum.[51] She was even declared incompetent to stand trial at one point.[52] Any normal person who saw Wuornos's actions would have, at a minimum, questioned her sanity. Her cognitive and behavioral abilities were obviously less than that of an average person.

But more than just appearing to have mental issues, Wuornos's instability was well documented by medical professionals. For example, in the Mallory case, every psychologist who examined Wuornos, for the defense and prosecution alike, found that she had a personality disorder. Specifically, three defense psychologists testified that Wuornos suffered borderline personality disorder at the time of her crime, resulting in an extreme mental or emotional disturbance; that her ability to conform her conduct to the requirements of the law was substantially impaired; and that Wuornos exhibited evidence of brain damage. The State's sole expert witness agreed that

---

49. Interview with Steven Glazer, Attorney, in Gainesville, Fla. (Mar. 29, 2009).

50. AILEEN WUORNOS: THE SELLING OF A SERIAL KILLER (Lafayette Films 1992).

51. AILEEN WUORNOS: THE SELLING OF A SERIAL KILLER (Lafayette Films 1992).; AILEEN: LIFE AND DEATH OF A SERIAL KILLER (Lafayette Films 2003); Associated Press, *supra* note 240.; Bryanna LaToof, *Convicted Killer's First Plea is Denied in Pasco Court*, ST. PETERSBURG TIMES, June 24, 1992, Hernando Times at 3.

52. *Female Serial Killer Pleads Guilty Again*, LEGAL INTELLIGENCER, October 29, 1992, at 5.

Wuornos had an impaired capacity and mental disturbance at the time of the crime, but believed the impairment was not substantial and the disturbance was not extreme.[53]

Despite all this, when Glazer took over as Wuornos's lawyer, he consistently maintained and represented to the court that Wuornos was completely competent. Not only did these assertions convince the trial judges not to pursue the issue, but they also gave the appellate courts reviewing Wuornos's cases reasons to deny her a new trial on these grounds.

In the Humphreys, Burress, and Spears cases, for example, Glazer stipulated to Wuornos's competency, based on his "study" of her psychological evaluations, and thus it was impossible for Wuornos to appeal on competency grounds.[54] In the Carskaddon sentencing, Wuornos "vehemently and profanely" complained of mistreatment and was unable to control her outbursts to the point that the trial court threatened to bind and gag her. The State itself agreed that her disruptive behavior was consistent with the existence of a personality order. Glazer, on the other hand, stated that "she understands exactly what's happening here and she is competent to make these decisions." Glazer continued on, saying, "I can represent to this court this woman is not insane. She understands what's going on and she is in full control of her mental facilities."[55]

Glazer did not request any further psychological evaluation of his client until July 1992, after she had already entered guilty pleas. He then backtracked on his previous statements from merely a month before, and now said that "I see the change over the past year, and it led me to think I could be wrong about her ability to perceive what's happening to her."[56] At this point, however, it was too late. The Florida Supreme Court ultimately used Glazer's in-court assurances of Wuornos's competency as part of the basis for its denial of relief for her on appeal.[57]

Wuornos's bizarre behavior should have alerted Glazer to consider the instability of her mental status. He should not have made representations to the court that so deeply affected his client without first having her evaluated by professionals. Glazer also failed to present any evidence of her lack of competency during the many penalty phases, which at least could have pro-

---

53. Wuornos v. State, 644 So. 2d 1000, 1005 (Fla. 1994).

54. Wuornos v. State, 644 So. 2d 1012, 1017 (Fla. 1994).

55. Wuornos v. State, 676 So. 2d 966, 968–70 (Fla. 1995).

56. Bryanna LaToof, *Wuornos to Undergo More Tests*, St. Petersburg Times, July 15, 1992, Pasco Times at 1.

57. *Wuornos*, 676 So. 2d at 969.

vided some mitigation for Wuornos. Glazer did not call any expert witnesses to testify about Wuornos's mental condition, nor did he call any friends of Wuornos whose testimony might have revealed her incompetence, or at least that she legitimately thought she was acting in self defense.[58] Of course, Glazer presently maintains that he did not put on any substantive mitigation because that was Wuornos's desire. But, considering Wuornos's questionable competency, it is unclear if this is truly what she wanted, or if she even had the capacity to make such an important decision.

Although his actions in promoting Wuornos's competency despite signals to the contrary may seem unethical, Model Rule 1.14 requires no affirmative action on the part of an attorney who is representing a client with a suspected diminished capacity. It provides only that the attorney *may* take protective action or seek to appoint a representative for the client. Thus, under Rule 1.14, Glazer had no affirmative duty to take protective action for his client, such as seeking the appointment of a guardian ad litem. However, an attorney still has a duty under Model Rule 1.3 to diligently represent his or her client, and act with dedication to the interests of the client. Presumably, most criminal defense attorneys would agree that representing to the court that your client is completely competent, when there is at least some question whether or not this is true, would be acting against a client's best interests. Furthermore, general moral values would suggest that a person with potentially diminished capacity should not be permitted to make self-destructive decisions.

Glazer's Ineffective Assistance

Steven Glazer's representation of Aileen Wuornos was deficient in many other ways as well. For instance, Wuornos raised on appeal in connection with the Humphrey, Burress, Spears, and Antonio penalty phases the inadequacy of the trial court's "cold, calculated premeditation" jury instruction. The instruction used by the courts in these cases had been specifically condemned by the Florida Supreme Court. The Supreme Court agreed that the giving of this instruction was obviously improper, but it did not grant any relief due to Glazer's failure to object.[59]

Also in her appeal from the Humphrey, Burress, and Spears cases, Wuornos was deemed to have waived her right to appeal the impropriety of

---

58. Bill Thompson, *New Trial Sought for Aileen Wuornos*, Tampa Tribune, Apr. 18, 2000, at 3.

59. Wuornos v. State, 676 So.2d 972, 974 (Fla. 1995); *Wuornos*, 644 So. 2d at 1020.

statements made during the State's closing argument about her other conviction, both because Glazer failed to object, and because he had opened the
door when he spontaneously told jurors during voir dire that Wuornos had
been convicted and sentenced to death in an earlier case. Another issue on
appeal involved hearsay that had been admitted against Wuornos during the
penalty trial, but the Court held once again that defense counsel had opened
the door, this time with his own cross-examination, and thus that this issue
had been waived as well.[60]

The Florida Supreme Court almost agreed to remand the Carskaddon case
for a new trial due to the many insufficiencies of the plea colloquy. First, the colloquy did not meet the standard set forth in Florida Rule of Criminal Procedure
3.172 because the trial judge failed to inform Wuornos of the mandatory minimum and maximum penalties for her crime. Furthermore, Wuornos made
continued and contradictory assertions that she was (1) guilty and wanted to
abandon her right to trial, and (2) that she acted in self-defense. Her statements
were so problematic that the judge noted at one point that Wuornos was "making it very difficult, if not impossible" for the court to accept her plea. The
Supreme Court specifically stated that it would have likely granted a remand in
the case but for the following comments directed by Glazer to the trial judge:

> Ms. Wuornos understands specifically that she's giving up the right to
> claim self-defense. She understands she's giving up the right to claim invol-
> untary intoxication as a defense, and she understands that she's giving
> up the right to insanity at the time, the offense as a reason. She under-
> stands those things. If you care to question her on it, you will find that she
> understands exactly what is happening here and she is competent to make
> these decisions.

This detailed statement convinced the Court that Wuornos must have understood her plea, and on this basis it denied her appeal.[61]

Model Rule 1.3 requires a lawyer to act with diligence in representing a
client. Naturally, any attorney will make mistakes. But the aggregation of
Glazer's errors throughout his representation of Wuornos appear to rise to the
level of ineffective assistance of counsel, especially when considering that Glazer
had conflicting personal interests and a desire to help Wuornos receive the death
penalty.

What makes Glazer's ineffective assistance particularly disturbing is
that, to some degree, it was calculated. According to his own statements,

60. *Wuornos*, 644 So. 2d at 1018.
61. Wuornos v. State, 676 So. 2d 966, 968–70 (Fla. 1995).

Glazer put up just enough of a defense, a "token effort," to make it difficult for Wuornos's appellate lawyers to make a case to overturn her death sentence later on.[62] This is why he chose to "put on a show" for the penalty phase, despite Wuornos requesting to waive that phase and present no witnesses on her behalf. Because Glazer found the law to be unclear on whether a penalty phase could be waived in a capital case, and he did not want the case to be remanded later, he decided to put on just enough evidence so that a penalty phase could be said to have occurred, the verdict would be death, and the death sentence would be insulated from successful challenge.[63]

Glazer's efforts, of course, succeeded. Wuornos's appeals were all denied and she was put to death. Glazer claims that this was Wuornos's desire, but her mental instability and attitudinal vacillations should have given anyone, lawyer or not, pause in accompanying her down this path. Instead, whether through ignorance, inexperience, or otherwise, Glazer blazed the trail for her.

Other Inappropriate Behavior

In addition to his poor performance as an attorney, Glazer also exhibited other behavior that was inappropriate, distasteful, and demonstrated that he did not take his representation of Wuornos seriously. These actions were no doubt detrimental to Wuornos's legal case as well.

Glazer openly smoked marijuana during his representation of Wuornos. He was willingly filmed in a documentary smoking marijuana while driving to visit Wuornos in prison. Glazer expressed no concern about his ability to represent his client while high; instead, he laughed and called the trip to the prison in South Florida from Gainesville a "six joint drive."[64]

In the same documentary, Glazer continued to joke about Wuornos and her case. He joked that his advice to Wuornos on the death penalty was a quote from Woody Allen: "Don't sit down." Glazer is also shown laughing and playing songs on his guitar that he composed for Wuornos. When he tells the documentary crew about being with Wuornos as she is executed, he smiles at an extremely inappropriate time.[65] Glazer later explained these actions as being part of his personality and a result of his years in show business. He cited his decades as a musician as making him a "ham" in front of the cam-

---

62. Squires, *supra* note 46.
63. Interview with Steven Glazer, Attorney, in Gainesville, Fla. (Mar. 29, 2009).
64. AILEEN WUORNOS: THE SELLING OF A SERIAL KILLER (Lafayette Films 1992).
65. *Id.*

eras, which in his opinion was not an indication of his lack of seriousness toward the case.[66]

The fact that Glazer allowed himself to be filmed in a documentary during his representation of Wuornos, let alone the attitude and behavior he evinced therein, raises serious ethical questions. (It should be noted that the State Attorney's Office, Public Defender's Office, and police all refused to participate in interviews with the documentary crew.) Model Rule 1.6 states that a lawyer shall not reveal information relating to the representation of a client without the client's informed consent. None of the exceptions provided for in the rule applies here. Glazer's willingness to openly share information about his representation of Wuornos to a documentary crew, as well as other media, without Wuornos's informed consent, was inappropriate and likely violated Rule 1.6. Wuornos believed that Glazer was lying to the media, confirming that she never gave consent for Glazer to reveal and discuss in detail his conversations with her and information he gleaned from the representation.[67] This, coupled with the fact that Glazer benefited financially from these interviews (in violation of Rule 1.7), makes his behavior in speaking with the media especially suspect.

Glazer presently says that he now regrets participating in the documentary. He chalks his behavior up to his inexperience as a lawyer and his experience in show business. He also claims that he was tricked by the documentary producer, Nick Broomfield, who led him to believe that they were just filming him to document their trip, not for use in the final documentary.[68] Still, at the time of the filming, Glazer was nearly forty and had been an attorney for three years. He should have had some sense of the seriousness of the case and the importance of client confidentiality.

Death Penalty Issues

Any case becomes more complicated when the death penalty is part of the mix. Glazer was an unusual defense attorney in that he took the case under the guise of helping Wuornos in her desire to expedite her execution, and used his role as her attorney to assist Wuornos in being sentenced to death. Despite being a self-proclaimed "anti-death penalty attorney," Glazer dubbed himself in Wuornos's case a "Legal Jack Kevorkian" who wanted to

---

66. Interview with Steven Glazer, Attorney, in Gainesville, Fla. (Mar. 29, 2009).
67. AILEEN WUORNOS: THE SELLING OF A SERIAL KILLER (Lafayette Films 1992).
68. Interview with Steven Glazer, Attorney, in Gainesville, Fla. (Mar. 29, 2009).

aid his client in the pursuit of a quick death.[69] His efforts were not limited to the courtroom; he also admitted to trying to manipulate press coverage to "guide" Wuornos to the outcome she wanted.[70]

The role of an attorney representing a client who definitively wishes to die is necessarily fraught with ethical issues, but when the client's intentions are uncertain or possibly the result of mental illness, the ethical stakes are raised even higher. Glazer, however, did not see any gray. When critics questioned his actions, Glazer steadily maintained that execution is what Wuornos wanted, and since it was his job to obey his client's wishes, he was doing the right thing.[71]

In a recent interview, Glazer continued to maintain that Wuornos, despite having a personality disorder, was competent, and thus he did nothing wrong in guiding her to her death. He also implied that Wuornos confessed her guilt to him, saying that "attorneys have confidential information from their clients" and based on what he "knows," her potential innocence was not an issue he had to consider.

Glazer's judgment is questionable on several fronts. First, Wuornos's decision was not necessarily well-grounded. She did not desire death out of remorse or guilt. To the contrary, in almost every plea colloquy she participated in, Wuornos emphatically asserted her innocence, based primarily on her claim that she had killed in self-defense.[72] (Despite later contradictory statements, Glazer himself acknowledged in court that Wuornos had a colorable claim of self-defense.[73]) Wuornos instead claimed that her religious beliefs required her to go to the electric chair. She wanted to be executed to "get off this crooked, evil planet" and "go to God, go live in heaven where there's peace and harmony."[74] Her desire for death, moreover, did not always remain strong. At one point, Pralle stated that, although Wuornos said she wanted to die, in her heart she really wanted to live.[75]

Second, Wuornos stated that both Pralle and Glazer encouraged and even pressured her to change her pleas to no contest or guilty. Indeed, when

---

69. Chase Squires, *CCR: Lawyer Did a Bad Job in Serial Killer Case*, St. Petersburg Times, Apr. 18, 2000, Pasco Times at 1.

70. Squires, *supra* note 46.

71. Lavin & Ross, *supra* note 13.

72. *See* Wuornos v. State, 644 So. 2d 1012, 1016 (Fla. 1994); Wuornos v. State, 676 So. 2d 966, 967 (Fla. 1995).

73. *Wuornos*, 676 So. 2d at 968.

74. Lavin & Ross, *supra* note 13.

75. Aileen Wuornos: The Selling of a Serial Killer (Lafayette Films 1992).

discussing Wuornos's desire for the death penalty in the documentary, both Pralle and Glazer emphatically support the decision and even appear to be strangely excited that she will be sentenced to death.[76] In addition, there remains the issue of whether Wuornos had a meaningful choice to go to trial to prove her innocence, when her defense counsel admittedly did not have the resources or experience to do so.

Finally, there is again the issue of whether or not Wuornos was truly competent to understand the consequences of seeking the death penalty and make a rational decision. Wuornos's competency was always an issue, and it remains questionable whether she was truly competent in a legal sense. But more than that, there is significant evidence that life on death row can lead defendants to become depressed and suffer from "Death Row Syndrome." Like many death row defendants, Wuornos was living in a six foot by eight foot cell essentially 24 hours a day, 7 days a week. She claimed on one occasion that she wanted to die because she was tired of the whole process.[77] Glazer himself admits that Wuornos was depressed and sick of life on death row.[78]

It is extremely common for convicts on death row to suffer from anxiety and depression from years of appeals and waiting for death. This depression can lead many to the point that they are driven to volunteer for execution to escape it. Death Row Syndrome is a legal, not medical, concept that has been embraced by the international community, though it is still very controversial in the United States.[79]

What an attorney is expected to do when his client is "volunteering" for death is not completely clear. Certainly, insisting upon a competency hearing is responsible lawyering. If the client is found to be acting with diminished capacity, Rule 1.14 permits the lawyer to pursue actions in the best interests of the client that go against the client's wishes. But the threshold for competence is low and in most cases the client is likely to pass muster. If this turns out to be the case, the Model Rules are silent on what to do.[80]

Though no specific rule is applicable, an attorney facing this situation must consider his duty to his client, his obligation to uphold the integrity of the criminal justice system, and his more global sense of morality. Regarding

---

76. *Id.*

77. AILEEN: LIFE AND DEATH OF A SERIAL KILLER (Lafayette Films 2003).

78. Interview with Steven Glazer, Attorney, in Gainesville, Fla. (Mar. 29, 2009).

79. J.C. Oleson, *Swilling Hemlock: The Legal Ethics of Defending a Client Who Wishes to Volunteer for Execution*, 63 WASH. & LEE L. REV. 147, 222 (2006).

80. *Id.*

the first two factors, lawyers are required to follow their client's wishes, but they also have a duty to ensure that our justice system is not perverted, that is, that it is not used merely as a suicide machine by those so inclined. Regarding the third factor, a lawyer must consider whether he is personally comfortable in using his professional expertise to assist another person in facilitating his or her own death.[81]

Along this latter line, many suggest that lawyers look to the medical profession for guidance. Doctors are faced with this issue every time a terminally ill patient wishes to end his or her life. For them the answer is clear: the Hippocratic Oath forbids doing a patient physical harm.[82] Should lawyers take this same approach? If so, what should be considered aiding a client in his or her death? Would simply not filing an appeal in a capital case be enough, or is more required? Because the decision to file an appeal is explicitly the client's, failing to file does not seem to rise to the level of "aiding" a client in his or her death. In Glazer's case, however, such careful line-drawing is unnecessary. He took an extremely proactive approach to getting Wuornos the death penalty, making it a personal goal in the representation. By the standards of the medical profession, this would be unethical conduct. Of course, there are many who question whether doctors are right on this exceedingly difficult moral issue.

Epilogue

In 2001, Wuornos chose to abandon her remaining collateral appeals. These are the appeals that would have dealt with the issue of whether or not Glazer provided her with effective assistance of counsel.[83] Wuornos's mental state continued to deteriorate, and during her last interview she spoke of the "sonic pressure" she was convinced the government was using on her through the television in her cell. She also spoke of being beamed up in a spaceship and police conspiracies, and exhibited paranoia that her food in the prison was being poisoned. Nick Broomfield, the British documentary producer chosen by Wuornos to be the only person present for her final press conference, stated that to him it was evident that she had completely lost her mind and touch with reality.

---

81. *Id.* at 154.

82. *Id.* at 201.

83. Gwyneth Shaw, *Wuornos Requests an Earlier Execution: The Serial Killer Asked the State Supreme Court to Let Her Waive Any Further Appeals*, ORLANDO SENTINEL, May 2, 2001, at D3.

Despite her evident insanity, Wuornos sailed through Florida Governor Jeb Bush's psychiatrists' tests and was certified as competent for execution. Her final words were further evidence of her insanity: "I'd just like to say I'm sailing with the rock, and I'll be back like Independence Day, with Jesus June 6. Like the movie, big mother ship and all, I'll be back."[84]

Wuornos was executed on October 9, 2002, by lethal injection.[85] She was the third woman executed in Florida history.[86] Neither Glazer nor Pralle visited Wuornos before she was executed. Glazer's thoughts on Wuornos's execution? "Ob-la-di, Ob-la-da, life goes on."[87]

Since her death, there have been multiple books, movies, and even an opera about Aileen Wuornos. The most well known of these is the 2003 movie *Monster*, for which Charlize Theron won the Oscar award for "Best Actress" for her portrayal of Aileen Wuornos.

Arlene Pralle and her husband sold their Ocala horse farm and moved to the Bahamas.[88] Steven Glazer is still a practicing criminal defense attorney near Tallahassee, Florida. Although widely criticized for his actions in the Wuornos case—local attorneys would turn their back on him when he entered the courthouse—he is currently in good standing with the Florida Bar, and has no public discipline record. Glazer says taking the Wuornos case was the worst decision he ever made; it ruined his reputation and his life.[89] It may have cost Aileen Wuornos hers.

Comments and Questions

1. As noted in the narrative, it is not unusual for death row inmates to come to a point when they want to hurry up the process toward execution. Currently there is no Model Rule of Professional Conduct that addresses the death penalty or a client who wishes to die. Should there be an ethical rule in this area to provide guidance? If so, what should the rule be?

2. Model Rule 8.4(d) creates a violation for lawyers who engage in conduct that is "prejudicial to the administration of justice." By assisting

---

84. AILEEN: LIFE AND DEATH OF A SERIAL KILLER (Lafayette Films 2003).

85. *Id.*

86. Chase Squires, *Victim's Kin Plan to Pass on Wuornos Execution*, ST. PETERSBURG TIMES, Oct. 9, 2002.

87. *Id.*

88. Squires, *supra* note 46.

89. Interview with Steven Glazer, Attorney, in Gainesville, Fla. (Mar. 29, 2009).

Wuornos in being put to death, did Glazer violate this rule? Does the integrity of the legal system suffer when a defense attorney assists his or her client in receiving the death penalty, or is this acceptable assistance of counsel for criminal defendants?

3. Glazer took pains to prevent Wuornos from being granted relief on appeal. He "put on a show" and made just a "token effort" to give the appearance of effective counsel so that it would be nearly impossible for her case to be overturned. Should an attorney be permitted to manipulate the court in this respect, particularly in a death penalty case? Is this type of action also prejudicial to the administration of justice under Model Rule 8.4(d)?

In the case of *State v. Smith*,[90] at the request of her client, an Arizona defense attorney argued for the death penalty, while the prosecutors implored the jury to spare the defendant's life. If the client desires death, should that permit the attorney to assist the client in achieving that goal? Is it enough in the *Smith* case to say that a jury will get to decide?

4. In 1999, just seven years after Steven Glazer represented Aileen Wuornos in her murder cases, the Florida legislature enacted Rule of Criminal Procedure 3.112(f), which requires that defense attorneys in capital cases meet certain requirements. These requirements include that the attorney have at least five years of litigation experience in the field of criminal law, as well as experience as lead counsel or co-counsel in a minimum of nine "serious and complex cases" tried to completion. Of those nine trials, three must have been murder trials, and the attorney must have been lead or co-counsel in at least two trials in which the death penalty was sought. The rule also requires that the attorney have demonstrated the necessary proficiency and commitment in the investigation and presentation of evidence in mitigation of the death penalty, and the attorney must have, in the past two years, attended at least twelve hours of continuing legal education courses devoted specifically to the defense of capital cases. Are these requirements sufficient protection for capital criminal defendants? Why or why not?

---

90. Oleson, *supra* note 79.

Chapter 5

The Case of Casanova and His Clients[1]

"You can be a lawyer or a lover, but you can't be both."

—Washington Supreme Court Justice Charles W. Johnson

Sex between attorneys and clients became a hot topic in Washington during the spring of 2000 when a case involving a sexual affair between one of Washington's most highly respected attorneys and his client became public. Although the Washington State Bar Association had yet to adopt a rule expressly prohibiting sexual relationships between attorney and client, this case forced it to grapple with the issue head on.[2]

Prior to this explosive case, the Bar Association received inquiries about attorney-client sexual relationships "with enough frequency that it raise[d] our concerns," said Barrie Althoff, former chief disciplinary counsel for the Bar.[3] Nevertheless, in 1994, the Washington Supreme Court rejected a proposed rule on the subject.[4] In light of the Court's action, the Bar Association turned to its members to dissuade fellow attorneys from engaging in this exceedingly questionable practice.

Enter Lowell K. Halverson. A graduate of Harvard College and the University of Washington Law School, Halverson married his wife, Diane, in 1964, and four years later was admitted to the Washington State Bar.[5] Throughout his years in private practice, Halverson proved a dedicated family law attorney. He served as an American Academy of Matrimonial Lawyers Fellow and, in 1990, he became president of the Washington State Bar Asso-

---

1. Based on the original research and writing of **Emily Banks Jahr.**

2. Scott Sunde, *Lawyer Suspended a Year for Misconduct*, SEATTLEPI.COM, April 28, 2000, http://seattlepi.nwsource.com/local/halv28.shtml.

3. *Id.*

4. *Id.*

5. LOWELL K. HALVERSON & JOHN W. KYDD, DIVORCE IN WASHINGTON: A HUMANE APPROACH, (2d ed., Eagle House Press 1990); *In re* Disciplinary Proceeding Against Halverson, an Attorney at Law, 140 Wash. 2d 475, 478 (2000).

ciation.[6] Diane worked as his office manager.[7] By all outward appearances, Halverson was a model attorney and husband.

As an extensive publisher and prominent lecturer in the area of family law and as past president of the Washington State Bar Association, other attorneys, as well as the public, looked to Halverson for guidance and advice.[8] He warned fellow practitioners of the distinct dangers of attorney-client sex, especially in the emotionally volatile area of family law. His book, *Divorce in Washington: A Humane Approach*, explicitly discouraged people in the process of divorce from getting involved in new sexual relationships.[9] Ironically, the disciplinary board would later admit Halverson's book as an exhibit against him.[10]

In fact, Halverson did not stop at one book. As editor-in-chief of the Bar Association's *Family Law Deskbook*, he examined "the potential adverse ramifications of an attorney-client sexual relationship."[11] Halverson even authored materials for a Continuing Legal Education course, at which he spoke, dissuading attorneys from sexual relationships with their clients.[12]

Then Lisa Wickersham walked into Halverson's law office. Guided by love, or perhaps only lust, Halverson failed to follow his own advice.

The Wickersham Affair

Lisa Wickersham first met Halverson in late 1989 when she accompanied a friend to Halverson's office.[13] In addition to his law practice, Halverson was an artist who created Native American artwork.[14] At the time of Wickersham's visit, Halverson and his wife were in the process of designing a new office building featuring a second floor designed to resemble a Native American longhouse.[15] The new office would showcase Halverson's own Native-

---

6. *Halverson*, 140 Wash. 2d at 478.

7. *Id.* at 480.

8. *Id.* at 498–99.

9. *Id.* at 485.

10. *See id.* at 484–85.

11. *Id.* at 485.

12. *Id.*

13. *Id.* at 478.

14. Educational Media Collection, University of Washington, Not Your Average Lawyer (Lowell Halverson) (1991), *at* http://www.css.washington.edu/emc/title/5995.

15. Elizabeth Celms, *Island Crest Law Office, Courtyard is Artistic Cache*, MERCER ISLAND CITY REPORTER (Washington), March 11, 2009, *available at* http://www.pnwlocalnews.com/east_king/mir/lifestyle/41047589.html.

American inspired sculptures.[16] Wickersham expressed her own deeply-held interest in art. Halverson wasted no time. He immediately offered Wickersham a job in his office involving a special artwork project.[17] Wickersham accepted, and she worked on the special project for the next few months.[18] During Wickersham's initial visit, Halverson administered a personality questionnaire—which he used as part of his law practice—to both Wickersham and her friend.[19]

In May 1991, Wickersham returned to Halverson's office and retained him as her divorce attorney.[20] At that time, Halverson administered a second personality questionnaire to her.[21] Wickersham sought either a trial separation from her husband or a dissolution of marriage. Halverson filed a petition for the latter in June, and Wickersham left her husband, attorney Neil Sarles, in early July.[22] Later that month, during a meeting at Halverson's office, Wickersham confided to Halverson that she was "attracted to [her] attorney."[23]

Not long after this provocative confession, Halverson invited Wickersham on "a tour of photographs displayed at the Ranier Club in Seattle" to celebrate a successful court appearance.[24] According to Halverson, during the tour, Wickersham suggested that "they get a room." Wickersham later denied making this invitation.[25] In any case, after the tour, Halverson took Wickersham to a "restaurant on the waterfront where they expressed a mutual attraction" for each other and considered the possibility of a relationship.[26] As the couple dined, Halverson laid out his "ground rules" for any affair: (1) Halverson's wife could not discover it, and (2) Halverson did not want to spend time, or "bond," with Wickersham's young daughter.[27] The latter rule was consistent with the advice Halverson proffered in his book about divorce, where he wrote that "children are often confused, frustrated, or intimidated by their parents' involvement in another love relationship."[28] Halverson also

---

16. *Id.*
17. *Halverson*, 140 Wash. 2d at 478 (2000).
18. *Id.*
19. *Id.*
20. *Id.*
21. *Id.* at 479.
22. *Id.*
23. *Id.*
24. *Id.*
25. *Id.*
26. *Id.*
27. *Id.*
28. HALVERSON & KYDD, *supra* note 4, at 14.

explained to Wickersham that the affair would not "be of any significance" to her pending divorce as long as she followed his "ground rules."[29] Still, Halverson advised Wickersham to tell the truth if she was ever questioned about their relationship.[30] Halverson even told Wickersham that "he should not begin a sexual relationship with her," and he discussed with Wickersham "the ethical part of getting involved with a client."[31] Wickersham recognized the "need to be discreet," especially due to Halverson's current position as president of the Washington State Bar Association, and she agreed to play by his rules.[32]

Coincidentally, a few weeks later, Halverson's wife, Diane, left for a trip to Australia. After Diane was out of the country, Wickersham called Halverson at his office to arrange a time to meet.[33] Halverson invited Wickersham to his home that night. During their evening together, Halverson and Wickersham had sexual intercourse while Wickersham's daughter slept in the next room. For the next six months, Halverson and Wickersham continued their affair, undetected, "seeing each other whenever they could."[34]

The couple's clandestine affair continued until one of Halverson's "ground rules" was unexpectedly broken. On January 1, 1992, Diane discovered the affair.[35] For Diane, this was just the beginning of the horror. Halverson later admitted to the Washington State Bar Association that he had engaged in consensual sexual relationships with six female clients beginning in the early 1970s, all while married to Diane.[36] He represented each of the six women in divorce or child custody cases. Five of them retained Halverson as their attorney prior to the beginning of sexual relations—their cases progressing side-by-side with the level of intimacy between attorney and client.

As if his role as lawyer and lover were not enough, Halverson also played psychologist. He regularly conducted personality testing with each client, further complicating the attorney-client relationship. According to Dr. Laura Brown, a psychologist and expert in the field who would later testify during Halverson's disciplinary hearing, Halverson's use of personality tests "added a more psychological aura" to the professional relationship.[37] In Dr. Brown's

---

29. *Halverson*, 140 Wash. 2d at 479 .
30. *Id.* at 512 (Sanders, J., concurring in part, dissenting in part).
31. *Id.*
32. *Id.* at 479 (majority opinion).
33. *Id.* at 480.
34. *Id.*
35. *Id.*
36. *Id.*
37. *Id.* at 484.

opinion, this created an increased risk of harm to Halverson's clients because it increased the power differential between practitioner and person in need.[38]

Nevertheless, the potential psychological damage to his clients did not deter Halverson from seeking sexual gratification from them—and neither did the threat of financial damages. When Halverson closed a case, it seems he closed a relationship. However, it was not always that easy. In one case, a client threatened to reveal their affair to Diane unless Halverson "wrote off" the client's bill.[39] Halverson cooperated. All of the affairs remained a secret— at least to the public—until Halverson dumped Lisa Wickersham.

Upon Diane's discovery of the affair, Halverson withdrew as Wickersham's attorney. He explained to Wickersham that he could not maintain his "objectivity," and he "could no longer keep his roles separate."[40] Of course, Halverson's representation of Wickersham was further complicated by his wife's role as office manager. Wickersham wanted Halverson to continue as her attorney, but Halverson refused.[41]

Halverson provided Wickersham with names of several local family law attorneys who could complete the remaining work on her case.[42] Left with no other choice, Wickersham hired attorney Eric Watness, and Halverson transferred the balance of Wickersham's account to him.[43] Halverson also wrote off the unpaid portion of Wickersham's bill.[44] Ultimately, Halverson provided Wickersham with more than $13,000 of free legal work.[45]

Halverson did not end all contact with Wickersham, however. Despite the termination of their professional relationship, the affair continued—if only briefly. At first, Halverson left his wife, moved out of their marital home, and maintained his sexual relationship with Wickersham. But only six weeks later, Halverson told Wickersham that he was going back to Diane and moving home.[46] Wickersham did not take the break-up well. She later reported that Halverson "used me" and "abandoned my divorce case."[47]

---

38. *Id.*
39. *Id.* at 485.
40. *Id.*
41. *Id.*
42. *Id.*
43. *Id.*
44. *Id.*
45. *Id.* at 507 (Sanders, J., concurring in part, dissenting in part).
46. *Id.*
47. Rick Anderson, *Love Gone Wrong*, SEATTLE WKLY., February 11, 1998, *available at* http://www.seattleweekly.com/1998-02-11/news/love-gone-wrong.php.

The affair with Halverson negatively impacted Wickersham's ability to prosecute her divorce case. According to Wickersham, after her relationship with Halverson ended, she was "unable to trust her new attorney."[48] Indeed, Wickersham failed to tell Watness about her relationship with Halverson until almost three months after he agreed to represent her. Watness described Wickersham as "at times anxious, particularly fixated on the relationship between herself and Mr. Halverson, at times unable to focus off of that and onto resolution of issues, development of facts, that sort of thing."[49] Nevertheless, Watness claimed that Wickersham had received a "fair outcome" in her dissolution of marriage and described Halverson's work as "excellent."[50] Watness also added that, ultimately, Wickersham collaborated with him on her case "in an intelligent and competent way."[51] In September 1992, Watness settled Wickersham's case, and a final judgment of dissolution of marriage was entered.[52]

The Washington State Bar Association Complaint

In October 1993, approximately one year after the close of her divorce case, Wickersham filed a complaint against Halverson with the Washington State Bar Association. Although the content of the grievance is not public, it reportedly complained about Halverson's conduct and his case management.[53] In 1994, while the Bar Association was investigating her complaint, Wickersham filed a separate civil suit against Halverson, which was settled one year later in a sealed agreement for a "substantial sum with no admission of liability."[54] Neil Sarles, Wickersham's former husband, later sued Wickersham and recovered one-half of the settlement.[55]

In February 1997, the Washington State Bar Association finally filed a formal complaint against Halverson.[56] In December 1997 and February 1998, the Bar Association held proceedings to determine whether Halverson's conduct violated Washington's Rules of Professional Conduct (RPC), which

---

48. *Halverson*, 140 Wash. 2d at 484.

49. *Id.* at 480.

50. *Id.* at 481; *see also id.* at 508 (Sanders, J., concurring in part, dissenting in part).

51. *Id.* at 480 (majority opinion).

52. *Id.*

53. *Id.* at 481.

54. *Id.*

55. *Id.*

56. *Id.*

would subject him to professional sanctions. The hearing officer concluded that Halverson had, in fact, breached the rules and recommended that he be suspended from the practice of law for six months and placed on probation for two years. The officer's recommendation also provided that Halverson disclose the reason for his discipline to future female clients and continue treatment with a mental health physician.[57]

Not surprisingly, Halverson appealed the hearing officer's decision to the Bar Association disciplinary board.[58] The 14-member board unanimously upheld the hearing officer's factual findings and his conclusion that Halverson had violated RPC 1.7(b)—Duty to Avoid Conflicts of Interests. By split decision, the disciplinary board held that Halverson had also violated RPC 1.4(b)'s duty to communicate and RPC 2.1's duty to exercise independent professional judgment.[59] Also by split decision, the disciplinary board upheld the hearing officer's recommended sanction.[60]

Halverson refused to throw in the towel. He appealed to the Washington Supreme Court, challenging four of the hearing officer's factual findings and each of the disciplinary board's adverse legal conclusions. He also argued that "the sanction was too harsh."[61] In response, the Bar Association assigned error to the disciplinary board's failure to grant Halverson a harsher sanction. The Bar Association also assigned error to the disciplinary board's decision that Halverson had not violated the following ethical rules: RPC 1.8(b)—Duty to Avoid Using Information Related to Representation of a Client to Client's Disadvantage; RPC 1.13—Duty to Maintain Normal Client-Lawyer Relationship Under an Impairment/Disability; and section 1.1 of the Washington Rules of Lawyer Discipline (RLD)—Commission of Act of Moral Turpitude.[62]

In Re Disciplinary Proceeding Against Halverson, an Attorney at Law

In his appearance before the Washington Supreme Court, Halverson steadfastly maintained that he had not crossed any ethical lines. His position was that, because Washington had never adopted a rule expressly forbidding attorney-client sex, his conduct fell short of being sanctionable. His attorney,

---

57. *Id.* at 481.
58. *Id.*
59. *Id.*
60. *Id.*
61. *Id.*
62. *Id.*

David Allen, asserted that "Lowell (Halverson) is the kind of guy who doesn't cross the street if there is a red light."[63] Allen noted that Halverson should not be punished for Washington's "inability to pass a rule."[64] He argued that if Washington had enacted an explicit prohibition, Halverson would not have engaged in a sexual relationship with Wickersham.

At the start of his case, Halverson challenged the hearing officer's Finding of Facts 28, 29, 32 and 33. This would be an uphill battle. The Court noted that factual findings established by a hearing officer and unanimously accepted by the disciplinary board are generally "accepted as verities."[65]

Finding of Fact 28 stated:

> Ms. Wickersham depended on Respondent [Halverson] while he was her attorney to help her obtain temporary living arrangements, custody of her child with sufficient child support and maintenance. She also depended upon Respondent for a favorable property settlement which was important for her economic well being. This dependence created a large power imbalance between Ms. Wickersham and Respondent.[66]

Halverson disputed the hearing officer's conclusions that Wickersham was dependent on him and that there existed "a large power imbalance" between them, arguing that these facts were not supported by "substantial evidence."[67]

In response, the Bar Association directed the Court to the testimony of both an experienced family law practitioner and Dr. Laura Brown, a psychologist who, as noted earlier, studies sexual relationships between professionals and clients. The family law practitioner testified "to the inherent power imbalance in a dissolution attorney-client relationship."[68] In general, attorney-client sex has been called the "legal profession's dirty little secret."[69] Lawyers hold "tremendous power" over their clients.[70] Divorce clients are especially vulnerable to their attorneys' sexual advances. The representation comes at an extremely emotional time in the client's life. The attorney is savior and superman, helping the client to hold on to or obtain some of the most impor-

---

63. Scott Sunde, *Lawyer Suspended a Year for Misconduct*, SEATTLEPI.COM, April 28, 2000, *at* http://seattlepi.nwsource.com/local/halv28.shtml.

64. *Id.*

65. *Halverson*, 140 Wash. 2d at 483.

66. *Id.* at 482.

67. *Id.*

68. *Id.* at 484.

69. John M. O'Connell, *Keeping Sex Out of the Attorney-Client Relationship: A Proposed Rule*, 92 COLUM. L. REV. 887, 887 (1992).

70. *Id.* at 887.

tant things in her life: a place to live, marital assets, child custody, and child support. The result is a relationship in which the omnipotent attorney can prey on the defenseless client.[71] Dr. Brown added that, in light of Halverson's role as Wickersham's former employer, the power imbalance between them was even greater than a typical attorney-client relationship.[72]

According to the Court, Halverson failed to offer an authority or citation to rebut the Bar Association's evidence or undermine the hearing officer's finding.[73] In fact, even Halverson had written in his book, *Divorce in Washington: A Humane Approach*, that "recently divorced people can be traumatized by the thought of dating. They feel they are old, unattractive, awkward...."[74] Clearly, Wickersham depended on Halverson. Consequently, the Court rejected Halverson's attack on finding 28.[75]

Next, Halverson claimed that Finding of Fact 29 was a "generality, observation, or policy statement," not a factual finding.[76] This finding stated:

> Unlike many legal areas, dissolution practice requires some degree of intimacy between lawyer and client. Attorneys practicing dissolution law are not only attorneys but to some extent are personal counselors or quasi therapists. Respondent enhanced this feeling on the part of dissolution clients, both through his administration of a personality sorter and through the personal advice in his book.[77]

Once again, Halverson had supplied some basis for this finding in his own work. In the first chapter of *Divorce in Washington*, Halverson wrote that "the psychological process of the divorce is critical, and we need lawyers who are trained to deal with the divorce process as a whole, and not just its legal aspects in isolation.... Many of my clients find struggling with their feelings far more difficult than struggling with the legal process."[78] Further, in Chapter 2, Halverson wrote that the attorney-divorce client relationship is "a highly personal ... partnership where mutual confidence is a key consideration."[79] The Supreme Court accepted Halverson's self-incriminating guid-

---

71. *Halverson*, 140 Wash. 2d at 484.
72. *Id.*
73. *Id.* at 483.
74. HALVERSON & KYDD, *supra* note 4, at 13.
75. *Halverson*, 140 Wash. 2d at 484.
76. *Id.* at 482.
77. *Id.* at 483.
78. HALVERSON & KYDD, *supra* note 4, at 13.
79. *Id.* at 19.

ance. The Court held that Halverson's own words, as well as the testimony of at least two experts, refuted his legal position.[80] It added that "even if the first part of the finding is a generalization, it is one supported by the clear preponderance of the evidence."[81]

Finally, the Court considered Halverson's opposition to Findings of Fact 32 and 33. These stated, respectively:

> Respondent [Halverson] knew or should have known from his sexual relationships with other clients [that] those clients were being exposed to greater risks of emotional harm. Further, Respondent should have known that his sexual relationships with clients created greater legal risks for his clients in their pending dissolution proceeding(s).[82]

* * *

> In the instant case, Ms. Wickersham has suffered personal harm from Respondent's [Halverson] conduct. In addition, Ms. Wickersham was harmed by having to change attorneys during the dissolution proceeding. The change of attorneys required additional time on the part of Ms. Wickersham. It required her to establish a new relationship with another attorney.[83]

In opposition to these findings, Halverson argued that "Wickersham should have known what harm might result from the relationship because she was a willing participant."[84] He further claimed that no substantial evidence supported a conclusion that Wickersham was emotionally handicapped by the relationship or by changing attorneys during the dissolution proceedings. Regarding factual finding 33, Halverson's position relied on testimony from three witnesses that Wickersham obtained a "very good" outcome in her dissolution case.[85]

However, Halverson's admission to affairs with five previous clients supported finding 32 that he knew or should have known the potential harm his sexual relationship with Wickersham might cause her. The Court specifically pointed to Halverson's fee dispute with a former client and

---

80. *Halverson*, 140 Wash. 2d at 484.
81. *Id.*
82. *Id.* at 483.
83. *Id.* at 482.
84. *Id.* at 483.
85. *Id.* at 482.

lover, which forced Halverson to write off the client's bill.[86] In addition, Halverson's own writing once again hurt his cause. He stated in his book that "rebound relationships can be extremely exciting and dangerous, especially when relief is mistaken for love."[87] Regarding finding 33, mental health professionals had testified convincingly about the anxiety, stress, and inability to focus exhibited by Wickersham after Halverson withdrew from her representation.[88] In sum, all of this evidence was sufficient for the Supreme Court to reject Halverson's dispute of these factual contentions.

RPC 1.7(b) — Duty to Avoid Conflicts of Interest

After establishing the facts, the Court considered Halverson's challenges to the disciplinary board's findings that he violated various provisions of Washington's Rules of Professional Conduct. The burden of proof rested on the Bar Association to establish each "act of misconduct by clear preponderance of the evidence."[89]

First, Halverson contested the disciplinary board's finding that he violated RPC 1.7(b).

RPC 1.7(b) provided:

A lawyer shall not represent a client if the representation of that client may be materially limited by the lawyer's responsibilities to another client or to a third person, or by the lawyer's own interests, unless:

(1) The lawyer reasonably believes the representation will not be adversely affected; and
(2) The client consents in writing after consultation and a full disclosure of the material facts.... [90]

Halverson argued that he reasonably believed that his representation of Wickersham would not be adversely affected by his own interests. Further, he con-

---

86. *Id.* at 485.
87. HALVERSON & KYDD, *supra* note 4, at 5.
88. *Halverson*, 140 Wash. 2d at 485.
89. *Id.* at 486.
90. *Id.* The reader should note that the current Washington RPC 1.7 contains slightly modified wording. WASH. RULES OF PROF'L CONDUCT 1.7 (2009), *available at* http://www.courts.wa.gov/court_rules/?fa=court_rules.rulesPDF&groupName=ga&setName=RPC&pdf=1, at 20–21.

tended that, although he did not receive informed written consent from Wickersham, "this was merely a technical violation of the rule."[91]

The Court rejected Halverson's claims. It opined that Halverson's violation of RPC 1.7(b) was much more than a mere technical violation. To start, the Court noted that Halverson's belief that the representation would not be adversely affected by the sexual relationship was clearly unreasonable. An objective lawyer would have foreseen the potential material risks to Wickersham and discussed those risks with her.[92]

In his dissenting opinion, Justice Richard Sanders sharply disagreed with the majority's analysis on this point. He argued that a sexual relationship between attorney and client "does not inherently create a contrary interest."[93] He emphasized that "the personal relationship may strengthen the representation, increasing the zeal with which the attorney approaches the case."[94] Sanders also contended that, if Halverson truly believed that a sexual relationship would not affect the representation, the issue of informed consent was moot—even if this belief were unreasonable. To stress his argument, Sanders cited disciplinary board member and former appellate judge Charles Wiggins: "It makes little sense to analyze the ways in which Halverson failed to disclose [a] conflict he failed to recognize."[95]

Unfortunately for Halverson, Sanders was the sole justice who adhered to this line of reasoning. The majority concluded that Halverson's "ground rules" fell far short of the disclosure needed to advise Wickersham of the many serious risks of pursuing a relationship. First, as an experienced family law attorney, Halverson should have known that discovery of his affair with Wickersham could create animosity between Wickersham and her husband, complicating the dissolution proceedings.[96] Indeed, this turned out to be the case. After her husband discovered the affair, the interaction between them deteriorated sharply. It became "brutally adversarial; abusive and emotionally and financially difficult."[97]

The Court additionally noted that Halverson should have realized that the affair could adversely impact the custody determination of Wickersham's daughter. Given his experience, he should have predicted that Wickersham

---

91. *Halverson*, 140 Wash. 2d at 486.
92. *Id.*
93. *Id.* at 509 (Sanders, J., concurring in part, dissenting in part).
94. *Id.*
95. *Id.* at 510.
96. *Id.* at 487 (majority opinion).
97. *Id.* at 484.

might suffer anxiety and depression as a result of having an affair in the midst of a pending divorce, which her husband could then use to raise questions about her fitness to serve as primary caretaker. Despite this possibility, the only conversation that Halverson had with Wickersham regarding her daughter involved his "ground rule" of not bonding with the child.

Finally, the Court determined that Halverson should have known that if his wife discovered the affair, he would necessarily have to withdraw from Wickersham's representation.[98] This was especially true given that Diane worked as his office manager. Withdrawal in the middle of a case is almost by definition harmful to the client. Halverson failed to disclose this very real possibility to Wickersham.

Thus, the Court held that Halverson's "subjective belief that his relationship with Wickersham would not adversely affect the representation was not objectively reasonable."[99] It further held that, even assuming that Halverson's belief was reasonable, he still failed to communicate the relevant risks to his client. Instead, Halverson's conversations with Wickersham were designed to protect his own interests—to minimize the risk that he would get caught by his wife and to avoid having to deal with Wickersham's child. Accordingly, the Court rejected Halverson's arguments and affirmed the hearing officer's conclusion that he had violated RPC 1.7(b).[100]

RPC 1.4(b)—Duty to Communicate

Halverson contended that because Wickersham should have known that revelation of their affair could damage her relationship with her husband and further complicate the dissolution proceedings he had no duty to communicate this information to her. Alternatively, he claimed that he adequately discussed the risks of the affair with Wickersham prior to its start. Washington RPC 1.4(b) provides that "a lawyer shall explain a matter to the extent reasonably necessary to permit the client to make informed decisions regarding the representation."[101] For the same reasons that it concluded that Halverson had violated RPC 1.7(b), the Court upheld the disciplinary board's determination that he had also violated RPC 1.4(b).[102]

---

98. *Id.* at 486.
99. *Id.* at 487.
100. *Id.*
101. *Id.*
102. *Id.* at 487.

Once again, Justice Sanders disagreed, noting that Halverson discussed the "ethical part of getting involved with a client" with Wickersham.[103] Sanders also pointed out that Halverson had advised Wickersham "against rushing into any new relationships and … [that] doing so could jeopardize her position in the dissolution."[104] According to Sanders, this evidence was sufficient to conclude that Halverson lived up to his ethical duty under RPC 1.4(b).[105]

RPC 2.1 — Duty to Exercise Independent Professional Judgment

RPC 2.1 provides:

In representing a client, a lawyer shall exercise independent professional judgment and render candid advice. In rendering advice, a lawyer may refer not only to law but to other considerations such as moral, economic, social and political factors that may be relevant to the client's situation.[106]

Although pressed by the Bar Association, the Supreme Court rejected a per se rule that any lawyer who enters a sexual relationship with a client necessarily fails to exercise independent professional judgment.[107] However, the Court held that, on the facts of this case, Halverson fell below the threshold of independent professional judgment when he neglected to advise Wickersham of the possible adverse effects that their affair could have on her dissolution proceedings. Additionally, Halverson exercised unprofessional judgment by failing to advise Wickersham of his "published, professional opinion" that individuals in the process of a dissolution of marriage should not begin new sexual relationships.[108] Perhaps even worse, according to the Court, Halverson took no precautions to avoid pregnancy, and he never discussed the consequences of pregnancy with Wickersham.[109] For these reasons, the Court upheld the disciplinary board's decision that Halverson clearly violated RPC 2.1.[110] Without doubt, Halverson was guided by something other

---

103. *Id.* at 512 (Sanders, J., concurring in part, dissenting in part).
104. *Id.*
105. *Id.*
106. *Id.* at 488 (majority opinion).
107. *Id.* at 488.
108. *Id.*
109. *Id.*
110. *Id.*

than "independent professional judgment" when he decided to have sex with his client.

RLD 1.1 — Commission of Act of Moral Turpitude

On one ground, at least, Halverson won. The Bar Association urged the Court to find that Halverson had violated section 1.1 of the Rules of Lawyer Discipline by committing an "act of moral turpitude" when he had sex with Wickersham. The Court declined; it pointed out that Wickersham was the initiator of the relationship.[111] It also distinguished Halverson's case from *In re Disciplinary Proceeding Against Heard*, in which the attorney, Heard, had engaged in sexual intercourse with a mentally disabled 23-year-old client who suffered from drug and alcohol abuse.[112] Though in that case the Court had found Heard's conduct to be moral turpitude, it had been careful to make clear that the facts of the case were quite unique.[113]

The Court also distinguished Halverson's case from *In re Haley*[114] and *In re Heinmiller*.[115] In *Haley*, the Court held that a 66-year-old surgeon who provided his 16-year-old patient with alcohol and maintained a sexual relationship with her for more than two years was guilty of "moral turpitude."[116] In *Heinmiller*, it held that a social worker who initiated a sexual relationship with a former client only one day after the conclusion of counseling also committed such an act. In the latter case, the Court was guided by a bright line professional rule forbidding counselor-patient sexual relations for a period of time even after the conclusion of therapy.[117] As Halverson repeatedly pointed out, no such bright line rule existed for attorneys and clients.

The Washington Supreme Court's Bottom Line

The Washington Supreme Court upheld each of the disciplinary board's findings of fact, conclusions of law, and the conditions of the two-year pro-

---

111. *Id.* at 492.
112. *In re* Disciplinary Proceeding Against Heard, an Attorney at Law, 136 Wash. 2d 419 (1998).
113. *Id.*
114. Haley v. Med. Disciplinary Bd., 117 Wash. 2d 720, 722–25 (1991).
115. Heinmiller v. Dep't of Health, 127 Wash. 2d 595 (1995).
116. *Haley*, 117 Wash. 2d at 722–25.
117. *Heinmiller*, 127 Wash. 2d at 604–06.

bationary period.[118] Moreover, the Court held that the disciplinary board's recommended six-month suspension was too lenient and increased it to one year. The Court noted that the disciplinary board had overlooked Halverson's "pattern of misconduct."[119] Although the proceeding was limited to his sexual relationship with Wickersham, the Court emphasized that Halverson had openly admitted to sexual relationships with five additional clients.[120]

The Court found the contradiction between Halverson's professional advice and personal life extremely disturbing. Halverson advised clients and attorneys to avoid sexual relationships during dissolution proceedings. His book made clear that he understood the serious psychological and legal risks of such behavior. Nevertheless, he failed to warn Wickersham of any of these risks. As the majority noted, "Halverson violated the trust Wickersham placed in him by taking advantage of her status as his dissolution client for his own sexual gratification."[121]

Is Attorney-Client Sex Ever Okay?

Although the Supreme Court's decision in the *Halverson* case begged the question whether attorney-client sex is permissible under any circumstances, the Court soon provided the profession with a definitive answer. In June 2000, less than two months after it decided Halverson's fate, the Court adopted a version of Model Rule 1.8(j).[122] "It's really straightforward," said Washington Supreme Court Justice Charles W. Johnson, shortly after adopting the rule.[123] "You can be a lawyer or a lover, but you can't be both."[124]

The most recent version of the Washington rule (RPC 1.8(j)) states that a lawyer shall not:

> (1) have sexual relations with a current client of the lawyer unless a consensual sexual relationship existed between them at the time the client-lawyer relationship commenced; or

---

118. *Id.* at 500.

119. *Id.* at 499.

120. *Id.*

121. *In re* Disciplinary Proceeding Against Halverson, an Attorney at Law, 140 Wash. 2d 475, 499 (2000).

122. Alex Fryer, *High Court to Lawyers: No Sex with Clients*, SEATTLE TIMES, June 9, 2000, *available at* http://community.seattletimes.nwsource.com/archive/?date=20000609&slug=4025756.

123. *Id.*

124. *Id.*

(2) have sexual relations with a representative of a current client if the sexual relations would, or would likely, damage or prejudice the client in the representation.[125]

Rules barring sexual relationships between professionals and clients are slowly becoming the norm. For example, Washington's adoption of RPC 1.8(j) made it the twenty third state to adopt a bright line prohibition.[126] California, New York, and Florida are among the states that had already adopted such a rule. In addition, even before the Halverson case, Washington had enacted legislation barring doctors, dentists, nursing home administrators, psychologists, and nurses from having sex with their patients or clients.[127]

The Washington rule passed with an 8–1 vote. Justice Sanders was the lone dissenter. He contended that the rule is demeaning to women by implying that women are not emotionally capable of entering an adult relationship.

"While rules governing attorney-client sex appear to control male sexuality—by disciplining attorneys who engage in sexual relationships, the vast majority of whom are male—they indirectly control female sexuality by denying self-determination to female clients who desire a dual relationship with an attorney," Justice Sanders wrote in his opinion dissenting to the rule's adoption.[128] In an interview with the Seattle Times, Sanders added, "The court made itself into [a] bedroom policeman. It's a massive intrusion of the state into the private lives of lawyers. It presents an opportunity for blackmail."[129] Perhaps Lowell Halverson would agree.

As of January 13, 2009, Halverson remained listed as an active member of the Washington State Bar Association. However, Halverson's profile on the WSBA Web site indicated that he was no longer actively practicing law. It also included a "discipline notice" that thoroughly described the Halverson/Wickersham affair, as well as Halverson's sanction. The directory listed Halverson's practice area solely as "Indian."[130] Halverson's self-damning book, *Divorce in Washington: A Humane Approach*, is out-of-print. As of 2009, however, his sculptures could still be seen in the garden

125. WASH. RULE OF PROF'L CONDUCT 1.8(j), *available at* http://www.courts.wa.gov/court_rules/?fa=court_rules.display&group=ga&set=RPC&ruleid=garpc1.08.

126. *Id.*

127. Steve Miletich, *Lawyers' Bar Wants Rule Banning Sex with Clients*, SEATTLE POST-INTELLIGENCER REP., January 22, 1999, *available at* http://www.seattlepi.com/local/atty22.html.

128. Alex Fryer, *supra* note 121.

129. *Id.*

130. *Id.*

of his former office building. Ironically, Halverson's most prominent wooden sculpture is entitled "Broken Promises."[131]

Comments and Questions

1. Halverson routinely administered personality questionnaires to each of his clients. Although the Washington State Bar Association and Washington Supreme Court stopped short of deciding that Halverson should not have done so, the Bar Association offered expert testimony that Halverson's use of the questionnaires "added a more psychological aura" to his relationships with his clients. Dr. Brown testified that due to the personality questionnaires, "the risk of harm" was greater because "the power differential [between Halverson and his clients] was greater." Should lawyers be permitted to administer personality questionnaires to their clients? If so, should states regulate the types of questions that may be included on questionnaires? Finally, is the use of personality questionnaires with clients more appropriate in the area of family law than in other areas of legal practice?

2. The hearing officer for the Bar Association held in Finding of Fact 28 that a large "power imbalance" existed between Halverson and Wickersham. However, in his dissent, Justice Sanders argued that this "does not accurately portray the dynamics of an attorney-client relationship."[132] Who was right here? Should a client's emotional dependence on her attorney be a relevant factor in a disciplinary proceeding?

3. Finding of Fact 33 stated that Wickersham "suffered personal harm" due to Halverson's conduct. Justice Sanders wrote that "broken hearts and personal disappointments are not the proper subjects of an attorney discipline proceeding."[133] He added that "Halverson had no doubt sustained severe emotional distress which might have cost him his marriage but for the grace of his wife."[134] Was the majority's review of Wickersham's personal harm appropriate in its consideration of Halverson's violation of RPC 1.7(b)? Why or why not?

4. The dissent argued that the majority conducted a senseless analysis of Halverson's violation of RPC 1.7(b) and "the ways in which Halverson failed

---

131. Celms, *supra* note 14.

132. *In re* Disciplinary Proceeding Against Halverson, an Attorney at Law, 140 Wash. 2d 475, 507 (2000).

133. *Id.* at 508 (Sanders, J., concurring in part, dissenting in part).

134. *Id.* at 509.

to disclose the conflict that he failed to recognize."[135] Was the majority correct in its analysis of Halverson's violation of RPC 1.7(b)? Why or why not? Is it possible for an attorney who has an interest in starting or continuing a sexual relationship to provide conflict-free representation and candid advice to his paramour/client?

5. Justice Sanders wrote that "viewing female dissolution clients as 'victims' who need the support, assistance and guidance of their powerful male attorneys is degrading because it undermines women's right of independent self-determination."[136] Was Sanders correct that women are "victimized" and "degraded" by the majority's mind set? Are rules barring sex between professionals and their clients demeaning to women?

---

135. *Id.* at 510.
136. *Id.* at 507.

Chapter 6

Of Chinese Walls and Comfort Zones[*]

"If a client ever complained to you about your representation of a competitor, what would you do?

"In polite English, I would tell him to get lost."

> —Colloquy in *Maritrans G.P., Inc. v. Pepper, Hamilton & Scheetz* between counsel for Pepper and its expert witness

J. Anthony ("Jerry") Messina was a partner in the Philadelphia law firm of Pepper, Hamilton & Scheetz. Messina headed the firm's labor department and represented management in labor negotiations. Stephen Van Dyck was president of Maritrans G.P., Inc., a publicly-held company based in Philadelphia that transported petroleum products on the East and Gulf Coasts by tug and barge. Before a dispute arose between them in the fall of 1987, Messina and the Pepper firm had been representing Maritrans in labor negotiations for more than ten years. Messina and Van Dyck had developed a close, if sometimes difficult, relationship. John Harkins, another Pepper lawyer, thought the two "had a kind of love-hate relationship." Despite their difficulties, Van Dyck admired Jerry Messina's abilities, recalling how "he negotiates with the airline stewardesses when he gets on the plane."

During the spring of 1987, Messina began to represent four tug and barge companies based in New York harbor in joint negotiations with the longshoremen's union. Maritrans competed with the New York companies for business in New York harbor, but Messina did not tell Maritrans about his new clients. When Van Dyck learned about them from other sources in September 1987—months after Messina had become heavily involved in labor negotiations for the New York companies—he objected to Messina's repre-

---

[*] This chapter is based on the original research and writing of James L. Kelley. Because Judge Kelley used only original court records in composing his narrative, the chapter is without footnotes.

senting Maritrans's competitors. Messina and Alfred D'Angelo, another labor partner at the Pepper firm, met with Van Dyck and attempted, unsuccessfully, to allay his concerns. As D'Angelo recalled the meeting, Van Dyck "felt that Messina had been so close to them that somehow they had a right to Messina, exclusive of others." Messina took offense at Van Dyck's objections. "Steve, what you're saying is you don't trust me." Van Dyck responded: "Damn right I don't." Van Dyck demanded that Messina withdraw from representation of the New York companies.

Pepper, Hamilton & Scheetz, like most major law firms, maintains a professional responsibility committee to resolve conflict-of-interest and other ethics questions that arise from time to time. After Van Dyck objected to Messina's representing Maritrans's competitors, Messina asked D'Angelo "to run the issue past the committee." D'Angelo went to Jon Baughman, chairman of the professional responsibility committee, and described the situation. As Baughman understood Van Dyck's objections: "Jerry was using his considerable abilities the same way for other clients as he was for Mr. Van Dyck—that was the concern." Van Dyck had expressed that objection—perhaps his primary objection—succinctly: the Pepper lawyers were "his lawyers" and, having bought and paid for their loyalty, they shouldn't work for the opposition. The litigation to come would bring to the fore a different concern: that Messina might disclose to the competition confidential information he had acquired while representing Maritrans.

The Pepper firm's consideration of Van Dyck's objections was cursory at best. D'Angelo and Baughman met for about one half-hour. Neither put anything in writing. Baughman did not inquire further into the facts, did no research, and did not even refer the question to the full professional responsibility committee. As he saw it: "There was no need to." Baughman advised D'Angelo that there was "no general prohibition on representing the competitors of a client." The only question was whether Pepper, on a hard-headed business basis, was prepared to lose Maritrans to gain other, quite probably more profitable, clients.

Maritrans had been a valuable client, generating more than $2 million in fees over the years. Although its labor business had been declining, Pepper management decided to make a final effort to work things out with Van Dyck. Peter Hearn, a senior partner (and godfather of one of Van Dyck's children) was designated to attempt a compromise that would keep Maritrans in the fold. Hearn met with Van Dyck on November 3. The two reached a tentative compromise under which Messina would withdraw from representation of the New York companies after the current round of negotiations and would not undertake representation of other New York tug and barge companies.

Specifically, Messina and Pepper would not represent Bouchard Transportation, Maritrans's most formidable competitor. In the meantime, two other Pepper lawyers, D'Angelo and Anthony Haller, would represent Maritrans. In order to protect any confidential information D'Angelo or Haller might learn from Maritrans during that period, it was further agreed that a "Chinese wall" would separate them from Messina—in theory, preventing any exchange of information about their respective clients. Hearn and Van Dyck sealed the tentative compromise with a handshake.

The compromise of November 3 proved fragile. It hadn't been reduced to writing and resolution of several points had been deferred. Messina, a rainmaker and power in the firm, was opposed to giving up representation of other tug and barge companies. Hearn wrote a draft agreement which Van Dyck rejected. Van Dyck responded with a draft which Hearn rejected. Van Dyck's draft suggested a compromise that would have allowed Pepper lawyers, other than Messina, to represent the New York companies, indicating that Van Dyck was not seriously concerned about disclosure of confidential information. On December 1, Hearn abandoned the effort at compromise and wrote to Van Dyck, terminating Pepper's representation of Maritrans.

Maritrans G.P., Inc. v. Pepper, Hamilton & Scheetz

On February 1, 1988, Maritrans's new counsel filed suit against the Pepper firm and J. Anthony Messina, individually, in the Court of Common Pleas of Philadelphia County. Richard Sprague, a former Philadelphia District Attorney, represented Maritrans. Messina was represented by Arthur Raynes, another seasoned trial lawyer. Sprague and Raynes would spar throughout the trial—sometimes with barbed humor, sometimes with thinly veiled hostility. Counsel for the Pepper firm were joined by Stephen Gillers, a professor and prominent scholar of legal ethics. The case was heard by Judge Abraham Gafni.

Maritrans's complaint sought an injunction to bar Pepper and Messina from "continuing their conflicting legal representation of Maritrans's New York-based competitors." The crux of its claim was that Pepper, as a result of representing Maritrans for ten years, was privy to a broad range of information considered confidential throughout the industry. If Pepper continued to represent the New York competitors that information would inevitably be disclosed to them, whether intentionally or unintentionally, and Maritrans would suffer serious competitive injury.

Trial began on December 20, 1988, and continued over several months, generating a massive transcript with voluminous exhibits. As it developed, the case involved four basic issues:

> Did the Pepper firm have confidential information about its former client, Maritrans, which, if disclosed to its competitors, would harm Maritrans?

> Had Pepper lawyers disclosed confidential information to Maritrans's competitors, or was disclosure likely unless representation of the competitors were enjoined?

> Did Pepper's representation of Maritrans's competitors violate Pennsylvania's conflict-of-interest rules?

> Under the circumstances, was Maritrans entitled to an injunction barring Pepper from representing its competitors?

The first two issues were exclusively factual. The third issue presented legal questions which would produce a classic clash of experts. The last issue involved application of traditional tests for injunctive relief.

Did the Pepper Firm Have Confidential Information of Maritrans?

Maritrans called Heyward Coleman, its executive vice president of sales and marketing, as a witness on these issues. Coleman's educational background included an MA degree in nuclear physics from Duke and an MBA from Harvard. An articulate witness, Coleman testified concerning a 1987 public offering of Maritrans securities in which the Pepper firm had represented the company. In preparing disclosure documents for the Securities and Exchange Commission, representatives of Pepper became "intimately familiar with the cost structure of our company," including labor costs, the largest variable cost in the tug and barge industry and among the most sensitive information in labor negotiations. Pepper had also represented the company in securing loans through a private placement. That transaction included "a very detailed prospectus that went into a great deal of sensitive, confidential information concerning our market shares. It consisted of our revenues broken down by regions, statements of our long-term strategy, and a long-term financial forecast."

The parties disputed whether Maritrans's business strategies and forecasts would become stale in the near term and therefore useless to competitors. According to Coleman, that information is projected out as far as ten years, "particularly in regard to our strategy—how you are going to position yourself over the long term—is something that tends to change very, very little over time." Asked if strategy information could be used by Maritrans's New York competitors, Coleman replied: "Absolutely." As he explained: "I would love to have similar statements of strategy from our competitors. It would be of enormous use to me to know what markets they plan to concentrate on, how they plan to manage their cost structure, what types of competitive advantages they currently hold and expect to gain."

John Burns, manager of labor relations, had dealt extensively with Messina for a decade. The company had multiple labor agreements, union and nonunion, which Messina had for many years negotiated. Burns treated the agreements, which contained terms and conditions of employment and pay rates, as confidential. He gave an example of how knowledge of Maritrans's labor costs would be useful to a competitor: "If my total labor costs are $3,000 a day and my competitor wants to better me in the marketplace, he has to shoot for some figure under $3,000 a day. But if he knows I'm paying $3,300 a day to attract good employees, he may have to pay $3,400 a day to do the same. That's a decision he has to make, but he's got the information on which to base the decision."

Maritrans called Robert Bray—an attorney who, like Messina, had worked exclusively for management in labor negotiations since 1966—as an expert witness. Bray supported the testimony of Coleman and Burns from his perspective as lawyer-negotiator for scores of clients in hundreds of labor negotiations. On the need for information: "There is no labor counsel around who would not become intimately involved with all the information available to a client in terms of its economic future and its economic life blood. His whole job is to improve the competitive condition of his client." He described Maritrans as "the key player in the industry—the company competitors would be highly concerned with in their strategies for dealing with labor."

Ironically, some of the strongest evidence for Maritrans came from the mouths of its competitors. One towing company president confirmed the value of knowing a competitor's labor costs when he declined to reveal his company's estimates of Maritrans's recent labor costs. An official of Bouchard Transportation, Maritrans's most formidable competitor, provided (perhaps unintentionally) proof of the importance competitors attached to keeping business information confidential. The President of Maritrans was in the room during the official's deposition when Richard Sprague, counsel for Maritrans, asked: "Who is your largest customer?" The official replied: "I'm not going to tell you." Sprague asked why. The official responded: "Tell him to leave the room. He's my competitor."

Witnesses for the Pepper firm sought to rebut Maritrans's case, point by point. Pepper partner Alfred D'Angelo described the firm's contractual arrangements with Maritrans. Pepper did not have a retainer agreement with Maritrans. Nor had the firm ever agreed to represent it exclusively in the tug and barge industry. As with most of its clients, Pepper had done work for Maritrans when called upon, at their regular hourly rates. "We weren't prepared to allow Maritrans or anybody to foreclose us from representing other companies in the industry."

D'Angelo denied that Pepper lawyers had received a broad range of information about Maritrans during labor negotiations, including cost and price structures, financial forecasts, and overall corporate strategy. Asked if such information was "essential to function adequately as labor counsel," D'Angelo replied: "They are not essential to representing the client either adequately or superiorly or any other adverb you want to put in there." D'Angelo also denied it would be helpful in negotiations to know another company's competitive situation or its labor costs. While he occasionally found the labor agreements of other companies useful, D'Angelo had been able "to get collective bargaining agreements virtually any time I needed them or wanted them"— usually from a union representative.

The Pepper firm called H. Thomas Felix II as a labor law expert to rebut the testimony of Gray, the Maritrans expert. Asked what information he would request of a client when negotiating a labor contract, Felix listed personnel policies, fringe benefits, labor costs, and any specific goals in the negotiation. By contrast, in a renewal contract—such as the tug and barge company contracts involved here—less information would be needed. He would want to know how much the client is willing to spend on wages and benefits, and whether it is in a position to cope with a strike. Felix was asked whether or not he would ask the client for the other types of information that Maritrans had claimed were important in negotiations—such as cost and price structures, corporate strategy, revenues by customer and market segment and financial forecasts. Felix replied: "It's not only not necessary, but my client would never pay me to learn that information."

The evidence at that point was conflicting. It was fairly clear, however, as Judge Gafni would find, that over the years Maritrans had provided a range of information to Pepper lawyers which Maritrans expected to be kept confidential. Although some of that information, such as collective bargaining agreements, may have been available outside the company, other sensitive information was not. Moreover, there was evidence, supported by common sense, that some information—for example, labor costs—could be useful to a competitor and harmful to Maritrans.

Had the Pepper Firm Disclosed Confidential Information? Were They Likely to Disclose?

Disclosure of information in a situation like this can be difficult to prove. A customer list may be considered confidential, but a Maritrans tug pulling a Mobil petroleum barge through New York harbor becomes public information. The source of the leak may be unknown; it may have been an outside lawyer, or it may have been a company employee. Usually there will be no record of oral disclosures—only faded, and perhaps selective, recollections.

There was testimony indicating disclosures of information that might be termed "borderline confidential" because it was not closely held, or had somehow become general knowledge. A single, more serious, disclosure would weigh heavily in the court's decision. The "Chinese wall" erected to prevent D'Angelo and Haller from disclosing Maritrans information to Messina had been a key part of the November 3 compromise. Although that compromise had failed after a month, it was in place on November 5 when D'Angelo and Haller met with two Maritrans officers, Vice President Heyward Coleman and John Burns, manager of labor relations. The subject of the meeting was an impending strike by the longshoreman's union in New York harbor.

Those present at the meeting gave differing recollections of what had occurred. Judge Gafni summarized the testimony: "D'Angelo and Haller contend that the only thing discussed was a very general labor law question concerning the legal implications of attempting to obtain new work during a strike in New York harbor, since Maritrans was considering such action. Moreover, they insist that no strike plans, no operating plans, and no potential customers were discussed; rather the legal advice given was all generic." Contradicting the Pepper lawyers, Coleman testified that "Maritrans proposed options, strategy, and intentions in the event of a strike by [employees of the] New York-based competitors. [This information] was conveyed to D'Angelo and Haller for the purpose of securing both legal and practical advice. They also discussed how aggressive Maritrans intended to be in seeking new business."

Judge Gafni was satisfied that the meeting was "closer to Coleman's version" of what had taken place. "D'Angelo and Haller had conceded that the information conveyed at the meeting was considered by Maritrans to be confidential and was not to be conveyed to Messina, who was then representing the New York competitors. If only generic legal advice had been given, there would have been no reason for Maritrans to be so concerned that the information would be told to Messina." Despite that explicit understanding of confidentiality, in late December Peter Hearn, architect of the short-lived compromise agreement, convened a meeting of D'Angelo, Haller, and Messina in which the information provided to D'Angelo and Haller at the November 5 meeting was disclosed to Messina and Hearn, in violation of the compromise agreement.

That disclosure violated Pennsylvania Rule of Professional Conduct 1.6 which broadly prohibits a lawyer from revealing information about a present or former client's case, not only to competitors, but to anyone other than co-counsel. Beyond that, Judge Gafni found Hearn's trial testimony concerning the circumstances of the disclosure more disturbing than the disclosure itself. Hearn testified that in the late December meeting he had been acting as counsel to Maritrans, along with the company's designated lawyers, D'Angelo and Haller, and that, therefore, notes of the meeting were covered by the attorney-client privilege. (He claimed not to recall that Messina had been present.) Hearn was first allowed to testify with the notes before him without disclosing them to Maritrans counsel Sprague, who was cross-examining him. Sprague asked Hearn: "Is there anything [in those notes] indicating the assigned attorney?" Hearn replied in the negative. Following Sprague's cross-examination, Judge Gafni reviewed the notes and discovered that Hearn was not named among lawyers assigned to Maritrans labor matters. Reversing himself, the judge ruled that Hearn had not been acting as counsel for Maritrans as he had claimed; as a result, the attorney-client privilege was lost when D'Angelo and Haller told Hearn what had transpired in their November 5 meeting with the Maritrans officers.

Judge Gafni was sharply critical of Hearn's response to Sprague's question which, as he saw it, "could be interpreted as reflective either of an absence of candor or, at best, a disregard of fairness, when considering the disability under which Mr. Sprague was conducting his cross-examination." Stopping short of calling Hearn's response "a purposeful misstatement or a lie," it was, as the judge saw it, not something which "can inspire confidence in Maritrans as to Pepper's good faith or, at the very least, what careful attention and weight will be given to their assurances of what they will do with confidential information in the future." Hearn's disingenuous response to a single question showed how a lack of candor from a witness —particularly a lawyer from a blue-chip firm—can color a judge's view of an entire case.

Had the Pepper Firm Violated
Conflict-of-Interest Rules?

Courts commonly say that violating a rule of ethics is not, of itself, a basis for an enforceable claim in court. The stated purposes of the rules are to provide guidance and, where appropriate, to enforce discipline against lawyers. Nevertheless, as Judge Gafni recognized: "In determining the fiduciary duty an attorney owes his client, the courts will inevitably look to the ethical rules." Four leading experts on legal ethics became involved in the Maritrans litigation: Charles Wolfram and Geoffrey Hazard for Maritrans; Stephen Gillers and Marvin Frankel for the Pepper firm.

The expert witnesses focused on Rules 1.7(a) and 1.9(a) of the Pennsylvania Rules of Professional Conduct—identical in all relevant respect to the corresponding Model Rules—dealing, respectively, with concurrent and successive conflicts of interest. Rule 1.7(a) prohibits a lawyer from representing two present clients whose interests are "directly adverse." According to Maritrans, the Pepper firm violated that rule from the spring of 1987 until December 1, 1987—the period during which it represented Maritrans and its New York competitors concurrently.

Rule 1.9(a), the "former client" rule, addressed the situation after the Pepper firm terminated its relationship with Maritrans on December 1. The rule provides:

> A lawyer who has formerly represented a client in a matter shall not thereafter represent another person in the same or a substantially related matter in which that person's interests are materially adverse to the interests of the former client, unless the former client gives informed consent, confirmed in writing.

The rule implicates sometimes conflicting policy considerations. A former client should have confidence that its former lawyer will not disclose its secrets to competitors. This consideration relates not only to the former client's "comfort zone" (Judge Gafni's phrase) about future disclosures, but also to the willingness of clients generally to share fully with their lawyers information they need to provide effective representation.

On the other hand, law firms should not be completely foreclosed from taking on competing clients when they have information—in their files or in their memories—about former clients in the same field. This is a major concern for big law firms with specialized departments and for smaller (boutique) firms which specialize, for example, in representing television stations or airlines. A related concern, reflected in subpart (b) of the rule, is with the young lawyer who wants to move to another firm which happens to represent clients with interests adverse to clients of his present firm. If knowledge gained from his work at his present firm is to be attributed ("imputed") to the new firm, costing them clients, that firm will probably be unwilling to hire him. The drafters of Rule 1.9 attempted to balance these competing considerations.

Maritrans's Legal Position

Charles Wolfram was called as the ethics expert for Maritrans. Wolfram had practiced with Covington & Burling in Washington, D.C., joined the faculty at Cornell Law School, and serves as Reporter for the American Law Institute's *Restatement of the Law Governing Lawyers*. Wolfram, an industrious witness, had prepared thirty-nine pages of direct testimony. He was cross-examined by Stephen Gillers, also a professor and author of a widely-used textbook on professional responsibility.

Wolfram testified that the Pepper firm's representation of the New York competitors was not permissible under the "substantial relationship" standard of Rule 1.9(a). Under that standard, the issue is whether the former and present representations are factually related. Wolfram contended: "There is probably no information that a competitor might wish to know about Maritrans' labor policies, strategies, practices, or plans that Mr. Messina did not know or possess in documentary form." That same information is relevant to the labor negotiations work which Messina and other Pepper lawyers are performing for the New York operators.

Generally speaking, if a matter is "substantially related" under Rule 1.9(a), the interests of the former and potential new client are, in Wolfram's opinion, likely to be "materially adverse." Here, the evidence of adversity was strong. Maritrans and the New York competitors were both working the New York harbor—a shrinking market—and competing for some of the same customers. In these circumstances, competitors would want to know "as much as Messina knows about Maritrans in order to shape their labor relations." Wolfram did not, however, interpret the rule to impose a flat ban on working for a former client's economic competitor. As an example, he cited the lawyer who specializes in suing for delinquent accounts; that lawyer can work for Walmart and Sears, simultaneously or successively. The "matters"— different bills and different people—are not related, "substantially" or at all, and there is little danger that Walmart's commercial secrets will be passed on to Sears, or vice versa.

Wolfram rejected the Pepper lawyer's claims that they, "as honorable lawyers, would not use or disclose any information relating to their former representation of Maritrans." Without questioning the integrity of Pepper lawyers or lawyers generally, Wolfram nevertheless viewed those claims as "irrelevant" under the substantial relationship test—irrelevant because, in legal language, Rule 1.9(a) is a "prophylactic" or "per se" rule. Its application does not depend on a showing of abuse (disclosure of information) in a particular case. If a substantial relationship exists, looking only to the factual commonalities between the former case and the new case, the representation is barred, regardless of a lawyer's good conduct and honest intentions.

Nor does a prophylactic rule merely reflect a "Caesar's wife" approach. There are practical reasons supporting such as rule. As Wolfram saw it, "no lawyer in Mr. Messina's situation could have forgotten all of the mass of confidential Maritrans information known to him. At the very least, the subconscious impulse to employ that information, when relevant in the interests of the competitor clients, would be very difficult, if not impossible, to resist." In addition to psychological realities, serious practical problems arise when the former client seeks to prove that disclosures *have* been made. Here, for example, Pepper took the position—which the judge rejected—that Maritrans should be required to reveal in court the very information for which it was claiming confidentiality, effectively destroying that claim while trying to save it.

The Pepper Firm's Legal Position

Pepper called Marvin Frankel as its expert witness on the ethics rules. Frankel, a New York City practitioner, had behind him a distinguished career in the law. As a young lawyer he served under the Solicitor General of the United States, arguing cases before the Supreme Court. In private practice he specialized in labor litigation. For thirteen years, Frankel served as a United States District Judge. Most relevant here, Frankel was a member of the American Bar Association's "Kutak Commission" (after its chairman, Robert Kutak) which drafted the original 1983 version of the Model Rules of Professional Conduct.

Frankel's testimony also focused on Rule 1.9(a)—specifically, on whether the interests of the New York companies were "materially adverse to the interests of the former client." Drawing on his knowledge of the Kutak

Commission's deliberations, he advocated a narrow reading of "materially adverse" under which the rule would not be applicable to Pepper's representation of the New York companies. "We were aware that lawyers commonly represent competitors, concurrently and successively, especially if they are specialists, and we weren't about to include adversity between competitors, whether the clients were concurrent or successive." Frankel contended that lawyers should be free to work successively for economic competitors, for example, for Anheuser Busch, then Miller; for General Motors, then Ford.

Competition between big companies takes place in a national market among millions of potential customers. According to Frankel, the rule was intended to apply *only* in situations where client and former client were competing, head to head, for the same business—a situation he illustrated hypothetically: The City of Philadelphia is planning a bond issue and is looking for an investment banker to underwrite it. Goldman, Sachs and Morgan, Stanley compete on an ongoing basis for the city's bond business, and both bid for the upcoming bond offering. The Pepper firm represents Goldman, Sachs, which is initially selected as underwriter and later fired before the offering. Whereupon, Pepper terminates its relationship with Goldman, Sachs. Morgan, Stanley decides to resubmit its bid and approaches the Pepper firm to represent it. Can the Pepper firm accept the representation? Frankel answered in the negative.

Frankel and Wolfram were in agreement on several points. Rule 1.9(a) is "prophylactic"; its application does not depend on proof that the former client's confidential information has, in fact, been disclosed. Wolfram agreed with Frankel's position that head-to-head competition meets the rule's "materially adverse" requirement. The practical difference between the two came down to this: does the rule cover situations like the present case which lie between very broad, sometimes national competition (General Motors versus Ford) and head-to-head competition where only one can win. To repeat, Wolfram said that it does. Frankel first conceded that "at some point between the only-one-can-win [situation] and Adam Smith's marketplace where you have a million competitors there may be a problem with two competitors." When pressed by Judge Gafni, however, Frankel stated that the rule only applies to head-to-head competition.

The case before the court was closer to head-to-head competition than to the world of Adam Smith. Maritrans and the New York companies were competing in one market area, New York harbor, with a limited number of potential customers. There was direct competition for some of the biggest customers, notably oil companies like Mobil and Sun. The unwillingness of executives from the New York towing companies to disclose information provided graphic evidence of real competition with Maritrans.

Judge Gafni's Decisions

On April 21, 1989, two years after the Pepper firm began representing Maritrans's New York competitors, Judge Gafni rendered his decision from the bench. He found that the Pepper firm had "become intimately familiar with Maritrans operations in the course of rendering legal services, including detailed financial and business information," and that some of that information "is still current and would be useful to Maritrans competitors if it were disclosed to them."

Judge Gafni dealt with "adversity" and "substantial relationship" as closely related issues. He held that "the mere possession of Maritrans confidential information by Pepper does not bar Pepper from representing economic competitors of Maritrans. Standing alone, the interests of Maritrans are only *generally adverse* with respect to its New York competitors (italics added)." Moreover, the fact that both representations involved negotiations with the same labor union would not, in Judge Gafni's view, have been enough to create a substantial relationship. He reached the same conclusion where, as in this case, the two representations involved different unions. Those scenarios lacked significant facts in common. Although the judge did not refer explicitly to the testimony of Maritrans's expert Wolfram who had found "substantial relationships" in similar situations, he implicitly rejected Wolfram's approach.

Judge Gafni turned to the November 5 meeting of Pepper's D'Angelo and Haller with the Maritrans officers who were seeking advice on the company's options for responding to the impending strike in New York harbor. Judge Gafni found: "At that point, a link was established between the simultaneous representations of Maritrans and the New York competitors." The opposing parties became "competing economic enterprises" with interests "more than merely generally adverse. Rather, their interests became *directly adverse* as specific counsel was being sought from Pepper as to how Maritrans might directly compete with the New York companies." The competition had, in Frankel's phrase, become head-to-head.

On November 5, Pepper's representation of Maritrans had not yet been terminated; Pepper was concurrently representing the New York companies with the consent of Maritrans, pursuant to the short-lived compromise agreement of November 3. That consent, however, had been limited by a Chinese wall provision to insulate Maritrans information from Messina. Judge Gafni ruled: "Pepper breached the limited consent of Maritrans when it subsequently allowed the information from the November 5 meeting to be conveyed to Messina in late December at the meeting called by Hearn. Such breach was a violation of Rule 1.7(a) of the Pennsylvania Rules of Professional Conduct." The later December disclosure to Messina, in effect, vitiated the consent Maritrans had given. The judge rejected Pepper's argument that all obligations under the compromise agreement lapsed on December 1, when Pepper ceased to represent Maritrans. As he saw it, obligations under the Chinese wall continued indefinitely to protect whatever sensitive information had been disclosed in reliance on it.

Judge Gafni went on to find a violation of Rule 1.9(a), the "former client" rule, but on a narrow ground. He noted that D'Angelo, the Pepper partner designated to work for Maritrans under the short-lived compromise, had later joined Messina as an attorney for the New York competitors and was participating in their labor negotiations. The linkage necessary for a "substantial relationship" under the rule was supplied by the November 5 meeting in which information about Maritrans's plans for responding to the impending New York harbor strike had been disclosed to D'Angelo—the same linkage which supplied the "directly adverse" element under Rule 1.7(a).

Having found violations of the Pennsylvania Rules of Professional Conduct, Judge Gafni turned to "the more difficult problem" whether a preliminary injunction should be granted, a remedy which he characterized as "extraordinary, to be granted only after careful deliberation." The judge attempted to weigh the harm that would result from denying Maritrans an injunction against the harm to the Pepper firm and its New York clients if an injunction were to be granted. D'Angelo of the Pepper firm had testified that an injunction would have "a devastating effect" on their labor law practice, in Philadelphia and beyond.

Judge Gafni focused once more on the disclosures that had occurred in the late December meeting about Maritrans's plans for getting new business during the strike against its competitors. "Since the strike has been ongoing for over fourteen months, it is likely that [Maritrans's] plans have already been implemented" and probably are not "of present-day importance." The judge concluded: "Hence, the future injury to Maritrans cannot be deemed to be irreparable." He gave no explicit consideration to harm that might flow from future disclosures by Messina or other Pepper lawyers. Maritrans's request for an injunction was denied.

Five days later, on April 26, 1989, Judge Gafni called the lawyers back to court to tell them he had changed his mind; he was going to issue an injunction, after all. As he explained: "This is one of those rare situations where I started to look back and to have a sense of disquiet and a lack of ease about whether I had done the right thing." The judge had come to believe that his decision "did not fully account for the special relationship between attorney and client and the comfort level and confidence to which a client is entitled both during and subsequent to his representation by an attorney." Judge Gafni referred once more to Hearn's lack of candor on the witness stand and to the "absence of sensitivity" by D'Angelo and Haller to issues of ethics in the late December meeting with Hearn. Most important, he had not given full weight to the fact that "Rule 1.9(a) is prophylactic in nature. As information was disclosed casually once before, so may it be disclosed in the future. The possibility of disclosure, even inadvertent, is a significant concern."

On May 1, 1989, Judge Gafni enjoined the Pepper firm from representing Maritrans's competitors in collective bargaining negotiations and from communicating Maritrans information to any successor counsel for the New York competitors. Pepper sought a stay of the injunction pending appeal that was denied. Pepper appealed to the Superior Count of Pennsylvania, the Commonwealth's intermediate appellate court.

The case was argued before a three-judge panel of the Superior Court in December 1989 and decided in March 1990. Its opinion was remarkably obtuse. Noting the Judge Gafni had based his decision on violations of the Pennsylvania Rules of Professional Conduct, the court held that those rules are not themselves a basis for injunctive or other civil relief. So far, so good; the rules themselves so state. It is, however, the practice of courts to look to rules of ethics as evidence of the content of general legal obligations—such as the fiduciary obligations of lawyers. That, as he had made clear, was what Judge Gafni had done. There remained the question whether injunctive relief could be justified on some other legal basis, apart from the rules of ethics. The Superior Court rejected that possibility perfunctorily, stating that: "Our independent review of the record reveals no basis upon which an injunction could have been issued."

Maritrans filed a petition for review with the Supreme Court of Pennsylvania. It acquired a powerful ally in Geoffrey Hazard, a Professor at Yale University School of Law and formerly Reporter for the Kutak Commission's Model Rules, who filed an amicus curiae brief in support of Maritrans's position. Hazard pointed out that the Superior Court "badly confused the relationship between duties under the rules of ethics and legal rules that create actionable liabilities apart from the rules of ethics. The court [incorrectly] held that the trial judge's reference to violations of the rules of *ethics* somehow negated the existence of a *legal* duty by the Pepper firm to its former client." In so doing, "it stood the correct analysis on its head." Hazard called for correction of "the egregious and unprecedented error committed by the Superior Court."

On January 29, 1992, the Pennsylvania Supreme Court decided the case in Maritrans's favor, reversing the Superior Court in a sometimes scathing opinion. "The Superior Court emasculated common-law principles, turning the ethics rules governing lawyers into a grant of civil immunity which has been condemned from time immemorial." The Supreme Court borrowed, at length and verbatim (but without attribution), from Hazard's amicus brief, observing that the Superior Court had "badly confused" the relationship between ethics rules and legal rules and had "stood the correct analysis on its head." The Supreme Court agreed with Hazard that, long before modern ethics rules were adopted, "the common law recognized that a lawyer could not undertake a representation adverse to a former client in a matter substantially related to that in which the lawyer had previously served the client." The Court stopped short of creating a blanket rule that a lawyer may not represent the economic competitor of a former client. On the facts of this case, however, "it was perfectly reasonable to conclude that Maritrans' competitive position could be irreparably injured if Pepper and Messina continued to represent its competitors." The Court reinstated Judge Gafni's injunction, five years after the Pepper firm undertook representation of Maritrans' New York competitors.

In November 1992, the Pepper firm agreed to pay $3 million to Maritrans—somewhat less than Maritrans's legal fees in the case—in settlement of its conflict of interest claim and Maritrans agreed to dismissal of its lawsuit.

Comments and Questions

1. The *Maritrans* case is a complex example of the "former client" rule, originally judge-made and codified in 1983 as Rule 1.9(a) of the Model Rules. The classic formulation of the rule is found in Judge Weinfeld's opinion in *T.C. Theatre Corp. v. Warner Brothers Pictures, Inc.*, 113 F. Supp. 265, 268–69 (S.D.N.Y. 1953):

> I hold that the former client need show no more than that matters embraced within the pending suit wherein his former attorney appears on behalf of his adversary are *substantially related* to the matters or cause of action wherein the attorney previously represented him, the former client. The Court will assume that during the course of the former representation confidences were disclosed to the attorney bearing on the subject matter of the representation. It will not inquire into their nature or extent. Only in this manner can the lawyer's duty of absolute fidelity be enforced and the spirit of the rule relating to privileged communications be maintained (emphasis added).

Judge Posner elaborated on the Weinfeld formulation in *Analytica, Inc. v. NPD Research, Inc.*, 708 F.2d 1263 (7th Cir. 1983), shortly before State and Federal courts began to adopt the Model Rules. According to Posner, "substantially related" means:

> [I]f the lawyer *could* have obtained confidential information in the first representation that would have been relevant to the second. It is irrelevant whether he actually obtained such information and used it against his former client (emphasis added).

Interpreting Rule 1.9(a) in *Maritrans*, the expert witnesses and Judge Gafni agreed that the rule is "prophylactic"—that neither actual receipt nor subsequent disclosure of confidential information from the first representation need be shown. Factual inquiries into receipt of information and its possible disclosure would be time-consuming, perhaps more time-consuming than the merits of the case. Furthermore, as Judge Posner pointed out in *Analytica*, inquiry into receipt and disclosure may result in revealing the very information the rule is designed to keep confidential.

2. Nevertheless, considerable time was devoted to proving that confidential information *had* been received by the Pepper lawyers, perhaps because proof of *access* to information—required for a "substantial relationship"—can often be proven only through evidence implicating receipt. However, proof of subsequent *disclosures* of confidential information is clearly not required under Rule 1.9(a). Disclosures are separately prohibited by Rules 1.6 and 1.9(c). So why did Judge Gafni attach such significance to incidents of disclosure in *Maritrans*—especially the disclosures to Messina at the late December meeting. Was it because he viewed entitlement to an injunction as a question separate from a proven violation of Rule 1.9(a)? Or is this an example of facts being more important than law? Recall Hearn's evasive testimony about the late December meeting and the casual attitudes of the other Pepper lawyers in attendance toward their obligations to keep Maritrans's information confidential. If a judge ceases to trust witnesses for one side, that loss of confidence may be more significant to the outcome than abstract legal elements.

3. Maritrans involved both a conflict with a present client under Rule 1.7(a) and a former client under Rule 1.9(a). Attention focused on the former-client conflict since the Pepper firm had terminated its representation months before the lawsuit was filed. Maritrans still might have argued that it was a present client because Pepper had represented it consistently on many matters for ten years, even though it may not have been working actively for it when the dispute arose, and that it could not drop Maritrans like a "hot po-

tato" when more lucrative clients came its way. *See Unified Sewerage Agency v. Jelco, Inc.,* 646 F.2d 1339, 1345 n.4 (9th Cir. 1981).

During the 1980s, several large companies had an arrangement with Joseph Flom of Skadden, Arps, Slate, Meagher & Flom under which they paid an annual retainer to Skadden, in part to be assured of his services if faced with a hostile takeover, but primarily to prevent Skadden from representing other companies that might want to launch a takeover attempt against them. The arrangement drew criticism and Skadden eventually discontinued it. *See* Caplan, *Skadden: Power, Money, and the Rise of a Legal Empire* 81–86 (1993).

4. Model Rule 1.6, "Confidentiality of Information," prohibits disclosure of "information relating to representation of a client." It would have prohibited the Pepper lawyers' disclosure to the New York competitors of information they learned in representing Maritrans. Judge Posner noted in *Analytica*: "This prohibition has not seemed enough, by itself, to make clients feel secure about reposing confidences in lawyers, so a further prohibition has evolved." Why not? Shouldn't Pepper's duty to abide by Rule 1.6 allow the firm to take competing businesses as clients? But is it realistic to expect that lawyers could completely block out information from a former client that would be useful to a competitor?

5. The existence of a substantial relationship is generally understood to depend on a commonality of facts between the former and a subsequent representation. Identity of legal theories or objectives is usually not required. For example, in the *Analytica* case Judge Posner was faced with a situation in which the former representation involved restructuring a company's stock—a non-litigation setting—followed by representation of the same company's opponent in an antitrust case. Despite the different legal contexts, Judge Posner found a substantial relationship because the information the lawyer could have received in the stock restructuring matter "might have been relevant" to the antitrust case. The overlap of facts should be substantial, but may be much less than complete. Judge Posner's *Analytica* opinion for the Seventh Circuit represents a broad approach to former-client disqualification questions. Courts take varying approaches to these questions, however. In *Government of India v. Cook Industries, Inc.,* 569 F.2d 737, 739–740 (2d Cir. 1978), the Second Circuit took a narrow approach to disqualification based on a former representation, saying that it would be granted only when the issues in both cases were "identical" or "essentially the same." What are the likely advantages and disadvantages of a broad versus a narrow approach to former-client disqualification in promoting clients' feelings of loyalty and confidence in their lawyers? From the lawyers' perspective, how do those dif-

fering approaches affect their ability to represent new clients? According to expert witness Frankel, a member of the Kutak Commission which drafted the Model Rules: "We were aware that lawyers commonly represent competitors, especially if they are specialists, and we were not about to include adversity between competitors." And from the judge's perspective, which approach would better avoid protracted litigation over collateral issues?

6. At the time of Judge Gafni's decision, the Model Rules and most jurisdictions did not recognize "Chinese Walls" as a mechanism for avoiding present—or former—client disqualification problems. That has changed. Rule 1.10 was amended in the 2008 Model Rules to avoid former client disqualifications if: "the disqualified lawyer is timely screened from any participation in the matter"; "written notice is promptly given to any affected former client"; and "certifications of compliance with these Rules and with the screening procedures are provided to the former client by the screened lawyer and by a partner of the firm, at reasonable intervals upon the former client's written request and upon termination of the screening procedures." Although not every jurisdiction has adopted the 2008 Rules, in those that have, what practical effect might the endorsement of Chinese Walls have on conflict cases? Certainly, even in a jurisdiction that recognizes Chinese Walls, they must be better constructed and observed than the short-lived wall in *Maritrans*. For a description of a well-constructed Chinese wall, *see Cromley v. Board of Education*, 17 F.3d 1059 (7th Cir. 1994).

7. As expert witness Wolfram stated, the key concepts in Rule 1.9(a)— "substantially related" and "materially adverse"—are closely related and tend to turn on the same facts. His testimony stressed a substantial relationship between Pepper's representation of Maritrans and its competitors for New York harbor business. Frankel, the opposing expert, emphasized a lack of "material adversity" between the two. In his oral decisions, Judge Gafni seemed to equate the two concepts. Verbal formulas aside, the practical heart of the experts' disagreement was on whether a law firm should be allowed to successively represent two competitors in a market in which competition is sometimes (or usually) not head-to-head, but much more direct than in an "Adam Smith," *Ford v. General Motors*, market of virtually infinite customers. How did Judge Gafni resolve that disagreement? Under his ruling, how free would other law firms be to represent competitors of former clients; to represent competitors of present clients under Rule 1.7(a)?

The value of professional independence—in this context, the freedom of lawyers to take on new clients, including clients who compete to some degree with present clients—is in some tension with an expansive reading of conflict of interest. The issue is not simply that expansive conflicts rules would make it economically harder to practice. It is also that powerful private interests should not be able to monopolize access to legal services by invoking conflict rules to prevent lawyers from representing actual or potential competitors. This appears to be the concern that underlies comment [6] to Rule 1.7: "[S]imultaneous representation in unrelated matters of clients whose interests are only *economically adverse, such as competing economic enterprises,* do not require the consent of the respective clients." However, it is sometimes difficult to draw the line. Should the *Maritrans* case have been decided differently if the parties had been competing all along the East and Gulf Coasts in addition to New York harbor? What about representation of different clients in a fledgling industry with a small number of firms, as in some high-tech areas? In some practice areas, such as patents and bankruptcy, the bar is specialized and relatively small. Bankruptcy judges tend to treat potential conflicts leniently in order to avoid conflicting out the relatively few available lawyers experienced in large-scale corporate bankruptcies.

Conflicts of interest are becoming more of a problem as law firms become larger, with more branch offices, and corporations merge, establish multiple subsidiaries, and enter into alliances, such as joint ventures. These trends are giving rise to complex and Byzantine conflicts in which the stakes are high.

8. The Pennsylvania Supreme Court reinstated Judge Gafni's injunction, relying on a common-law principle that "a lawyer could not undertake a representation adverse to a former client in a matter substantially related" to that of the former client. Without attempting any greater specificity, and without reference to Judge Gafni's rationale, the court found a violation of that principle on the facts of the *Maritrans* case. Principles of legal ethics are supposed to provide helpful guidance to lawyers in problems they commonly confront. A departure from earlier ethics codes which were largely cast in generalities like the Pennsylvania Supreme Court's decision, the Model Rules of Professional Conduct represent an attempt at a mature statement of rules—based on the common law, practical experience, the sometimes competing needs of lawyers and clients, and the biases of the drafters—with as much specificity as the subject allows. Are lawyers better served by the specificity of the Model Rules, or by common-law principles and a case-by-case approach?

Theory aside, lawyers are in greater danger of being sued under a common-law, fiduciary theory than for malpractice based on violations of ethics rules. The causation standard for breach of fiduciary duty is often applied more leniently than the malpractice standard and, in many states, neither causation nor injury need be proved to obtain disgorgement of fees.

Chapter 7

Vegas Judge Gone Wild[1]

"Some judges are in office for an entire career and do not accumulate the type of dismal professional history that the record in this case establishes."

—Nevada Judicial Disciplinary Commission after presiding over a formal hearing against Judge Elizabeth Halverson

For many, a judgeship represents the stuff of dreams. A bold aspiration only a select few ever realize, the bench commands great reverence as it signifies the culmination of hard work and sacrifice and symbolizes the height of public service. The judiciary is also a powerful political force in the American landscape. Yet, with the prestige of the position and the awesome power to interpret the law comes the potential for incalculable abuse.

Indeed, although most judges treat their judicial office with due regard, others have on occasion brought great shame to their profession. After all, judges are, first and foremost, human, and they are susceptible to the same temptations and impulses as everyone else. Short of egregious misconduct and impropriety, however, it remains quite difficult to dislodge a judge from office. The analysis that follows aims to illustrate the scope of authority administrative judges enjoy, the duties judges owe to the profession upon discovering judicial impropriety, and the type of professional misconduct our justice system will not tolerate.

How a Battle Between Two Judges in Vegas Becomes a Full-Fledged War

Most reasonable people would agree that animosity among fellow employees in the workplace should be handled internally and, ideally, be defused before it interferes with the flow of work. Unfortunately, however, for two judges in Nevada, the opposite proved true. From their judicial cham-

---

1. This chapter is based on the original research and writing of **Stephanie L. Varela.**

bers in the Eighth Judicial District Court of Clark County, Nevada, Chief Judge Kathy Hardcastle and District Judge Elizabeth Halverson wielded their power either to rectify wrongs committed by the other, or to settle scores— depending on one's point of view. The plot thickened with each escalating counterattack, attracting media attention, stunning most spectators, and ultimately resulting in the removal of one of the two from the bench.

In this saga, most blogs, news reports, and personal accounts portrayed Elizabeth Halverson as a morbidly obese, disabled, cruel, and inept jurist abusing her power in retaliation for wrongs that she believed Kathy Hardcastle had previously committed against her. Those close to Halverson, however, vouched repeatedly and consistently as to her brilliance. Halverson depicted Hardcastle as an iron-fisted, overbearing authoritarian who used her judicial position to destroy Halverson on a personal and professional level.

The acrimonious feud between the two began in 2004 while both sat as judges in Clark County. A former supervisor recounted Halverson coming from a "working class Italian family in San Francisco."[2] Her academic prowess was evident early on. The University of Southern California admitted Halverson into its law school when she was just 19 years old,[3] and granted her a J.D. degree in 1980.[4] Following graduation, Halverson did some work for the federal government.[5] She passed the Nevada Bar Exam in 1992 and was sworn-in as a Nevada lawyer in December of that same year.[6] In 1995, Halverson began working at Nevada's Eighth District court as a law clerk for Judge Don Chairez.[7]

Chief Judge Kathy Hardcastle received her J.D. from Texas Tech University Law School in 1978. She completed a judicial clerkship in Reno after graduation and became a Washoe County Deputy District Attorney. In 1983, Hardcastle moved to Las Vegas to become a Deputy Attorney General in charge of the Insurance Fraud Unit. Additionally, she served as legal counsel for Southern Nevada mental health agencies, the Nevada Equal Rights Commission, and the State Board of Architecture. Five years later, Hardcastle entered private practice. Beginning in 1991, she served as Deputy Public De-

---

2. Stacy J. Willis, *The Trials of Elizabeth Halverson: Is a Disciplinary hearing for the embattled judge about conduct or conformity?*, LAS VEGAS WKLY., Aug. 14, 2008, *available at* http://www.lasvegasweekly.com/news/2008/aug/14/trials-elizabeth-halverson/.

3. Judgepedia, Elizabeth Halverson, *at* http://judgepedia.org/index.php/Elizabeth_Halverson#Biography (last visited Apr. 10, 2009).

4. Willis, *supra* note 2.

5. Judgepedia, *supra* note 3.

6. *Id.*

7. Willis, *supra* note 2.

fender in Las Vegas until she took the bench in Clark County in January 1997.[8]

For nine years, Halverson clerked for several judges, undertook some major projects, and trained new law clerks.[9] From the beginning, Halverson rubbed some of her co-workers the wrong way. For example, although she seemed perfectly capable of walking around the courthouse, Halverson sought and obtained a handicapped parking space due to her weight.[10] This caused measurable resentment, as parking at the courthouse was hard to come by. Halverson, however, paid little attention to her coworkers' sentiments. Her former boss, Judge Chairez, attributed her "fighting attitude" to her father's death and stated further, "She's like Mike Tyson—she will swing back."[11] According to Chairez, Halverson was "brilliant."[12] Nevertheless, Halverson's tenure as a law clerk came to an abrupt end soon after Kathy Hardcastle became chief judge in April 2004.[13] Hardcastle justified the termination as routine, pointing to the temporary nature of law clerk positions. Most individuals serve as a judge's clerk for only one or two years.[14]

By all accounts, Hardcastle intended for the termination to be a gradual one, giving Halverson roughly 90-days notice.[15] But just weeks after being advised that her legal services were no longer necessary, Halverson struck back by declaring her candidacy for judicial office.[16] Her opponent was none other than incumbent judge Gerald Hardcastle, the chief judge's husband.[17] Days after this announcement, battle lines hardened when a court bailiff greeted Halverson and her husband at the courthouse's loading dock and prohibited them from entering the building.[18]

---

8. Clark County, Nevada District Court, Biography of Judge Kathy A. Hardcastle, *at* www.clarkcountycourts.us/ejdc/courts-and-judges/biographies/Kathy%20A%20Hardcastle.pdf.

9. Application for Writ of Quo Warranto at 5, Halverson v. Hardcastle, 123 Nev. 29 (Nev. 2007) (No. 49453).

10. Willis, *supra* note 2.

11. *Id.*

12. *Id.*

13. Terry Carter, *You're Not the Boss of Me*, A.B.A. J., Aug. 2007, *available at* http://abajournal.com/magazine/youre_not_the_boss_of_me/.

14. K.C. Howard, *No More: Halverson Will Get Only Civil Cases Until She Gains Experience*, LAS VEGAS REV.-J., Apr. 25, 2007, *available at* http://www.lvrj.com/news/7183401.html.

15. Carter, *supra* note 13.

16. Application for Writ of Quo Warranto at 5, Halverson v. Hardcastle, 123 Nev. 29 (Nev. 2007) (No. 49453); Carter, *supra* note 13.

17. Application for Writ of Quo Warranto at 5, *Halverson* (No. 49453); Howard, *supra* note 445.

18. Application for Writ of Quo Warranto at 5, *Halverson* (No. 49453).

Hardcastle then placed Halverson on paid administrative leave.[19] This only fueled the fire. Halverson responded by filing a complaint against Gerald Hardcastle with the Committee on Judicial Ethics and Election Practices.[20] In the complaint, Halverson took issue with Kathy Hardcastle's involvement in her husband's judicial campaign. Halverson pointed to Nevada Judicial Canon 5A(1)(b), which forbids a judge from publicly endorsing another candidate for political office; 5A(1)(d), which prohibits a judge from soliciting funds for a political candidate; and 5C(1)(b)(i), (iii), and (iv), which provide that a sitting judge may solicit, advertise, or distribute campaign literature only on his or her own behalf and may express public opposition only to candidates running for the same judicial office.[21]

Halverson's allegations also took aim at Gerald Hardcastle's conduct. She claimed he had encouraged another judicial candidate to distribute promotional bags on his behalf and permitted her to include her own campaign literature in them.[22]

Finding some merit in the complaint, the Judicial Ethics Committee issued an advisory opinion that chastised Kathy Hardcastle for distributing campaign paraphernalia on her husband's behalf.[23] It reprimanded incumbent jurist Gerald Hardcastle for not urging his family to adhere to the standards expected from judges and judicial candidates.[24] It found insufficient evidence, however, to support Halverson's allegations regarding Hardcastle's solicitation of funds and public opposition to Halverson's candidacy.[25]

Despite victory in these skirmishes, Halverson lost the race against Gerald Hardcastle. But she was not deterred for long. Although she was now maneuvering through the courthouse with the aid of an electric scooter and oxygen tank, Halverson mounted a second campaign for judicial office in the fall of 2006 and, this time, she won. She ascended the bench in the Eighth Judicial District Court, Clark County, in January 2007.[26]

---

19. Sam Skolnik, *Judges Step Up Feud, Courthouse Cringes*, LAS VEGAS SUN, May 29, 2007, *available at* http://www.lasvegassun.com/news/2007/may/29/judges-step-up-feud-courthouse-cringes/.

20. Application for Writ of Quo Warranto at 5, *Halverson* (No. 49453).

21. *In Re* Unfair Election Practice, No. 04-2 (Nev. Comm'n on Jud. Ethics Oct. 27, 2004), *available at* http://judicial.state.nv.us/scjeepdecision0423new.htm.

22. *Id.*

23. Application for Writ of Quo Warranto at 5, *Halverson* (No. 49453).

24. Carter, *supra* note 13.

25. *Id.*

26. *Id.*

Halverson's Gloves Come Off:
Makes Headlines as Allegations Surface

The worst was yet to come. Rough around the edges before, Halverson turned into something of a monster once she earned her robes. Her surly temperament, outrageous conduct, and downright malicious personality quickly offended the court employees who worked for her and the lawyers who appeared in her courtroom. Local media captured every sordid detail as reporters described the insiders' dismay with Halverson's judicial performance. In the brief time that she served on the bench, Halverson managed to accumulate an extensive list of wild accusations, ranging from ordering massages from court employees, to chastising attorneys for failing to contribute to her campaign, to falling asleep during several trials.[27] Halverson's conduct not only drove several court staffers to seek employment elsewhere, but it also led to the filing of at least two separate complaints against her, including a discrimination claim[28] and a defamation claim.[29]

More specifically, bailiff Johnny Jordan complained that Halverson ordered him to massage her back and feet, pick up after her, change oxygen bottles for her tank, prepare her lunch from inside her foul-stricken chambers restroom, and place her shoes on her feet. Halverson also expected Jordan to wait by the courthouse entrance daily at 7:30 a.m. to open the door for her, even though Halverson would often arrive past 8:30 a.m.[30] According to Jordan, Halverson would also deliberately throw items on the floor and order him and other staffers to pick them up. During a visit to her daughter's chambers, Halverson's mother asked the judge whether Jordan was her servant. Jordan, an African American, witnessed that comment; he later filed a discrimination claim against Halverson.[31]

In another bizarre twist, at one point Halverson ordered a clerk to swear-in fellow staffers so the judge could interrogate her staff under oath. The point of the inquiry was to ascertain precisely what staffers had disclosed to other judges about their boss. In addition, Halverson habitually used derogatory nicknames for court employees, among them " 'the elf,' 'the evil one,'

---

27. Skolnik, *supra* note 19.
28. Carter, *supra* note 13.
29. K.C. Howard, *Judge Sued by Spoor: Halverson's Ex-Aide Says She Has Been Defamed*, LAS VEGAS REV.-J., May 25, 2007, *available at* http://www.lvrj.com/news/7683897.html.
30. Carter, *supra* note 13.
31. *Id.*

'bitch,' and 'the Antichrist.'"[32] Staffers were not the only ones subjected to these antics. Halverson allegedly berated her husband in front of her staff. She once allegedly went so far as to swear-in her husband to inquire whether the house would be clean in time for a visit from her mother.[33]

During her first criminal trial as district judge, Halverson allegedly fell asleep during witness testimony. Indeed, the judge apparently fell asleep so frequently during the course of several trials that court personnel developed a system to signal each other to wake her up.[34] Worse yet, Halverson spoke with criminal juries outside the presence of lawyers on multiple occasions.[35] During one trial, Halverson "chatted" alone with jurors to answer their questions about criminal procedure, reliability of witnesses, and evidence.[36] At least once, prosecutors felt compelled to extend an excessively generous plea offer to a defendant because of the judge's conduct.[37] Chief Judge Hardcastle removed Halverson from the criminal docket in late April 2007,[38] but not without protest.[39]

What Is a Chief Judge to Do?

As accusations mounted, Chief Judge Hardcastle felt compelled to act. First, Hardcastle approached several veteran judges and asked them to mentor Halverson.[40] As one mentor put it at the time, "we're here to help a colleague improve."[41] Later, Hardcastle appointed three judges to a panel and

---

32. *Id.*

33. *Id.*

34. *Id.*

35. *Id.*

36. *In re* Halverson, 169 P.3d 1161, 1166 (2007); Final Order of Interim Suspension at 15, *In re* Halverson, 123 Nev. 48 (No. 2007-053), *available at* http://www.nvsupremecourt.us/documents/cases/InterimSuspensionOrder.49876.pdf.

37. Carter, *supra* note 13; *see also* Howard, *supra* note 14.

38. Application for Writ of Quo Warranto at 8, Halverson v. Hardcastle, 123 Nev. 29 (Nev. 2007) (No. 49453); Skolnik, *supra* note 19; *see also* Howard, *supra* note 14. Hardcastle based her decision to remove Halverson from the criminal docket on a panel recommendation.

39. *See* Howard, *supra* note 14. Halverson released the following statements through a spokeswoman: "It is totally unnecessary to change my caseload. I am up to date on everything.... There is no reason to do this. I believe this is just more of the ongoing punitive measures I have had to endure. I am not being treated with respect. Clearly the media knows more than I do. Apparently there are people who cannot get over the election results." *Id.*

40. Skolnik, *supra* note 19.

41. Howard, *supra* note 14.

asked them to meet with Halverson, which they did on April 6, 2007. Panel members attempted to address the complaints that had been received concerning Halverson's conduct. According to a memorandum of the meeting written by the court's human resources manager, Halverson was less than receptive to any criticism; she fired back at the panel with fast responses.[42]

For instance, the panel chastised Halverson for berating lawyers who failed to contribute to her judicial campaign. Her response was that "she had not discriminated against any of them because no lawyer had contributed to her campaign."[43] She turned the allegation that she ordered her bailiff to give her messages on its head, claiming that she "told the bailiff to stop being 'too familiar.'"[44] When pressed about ordering the bailiff to prepare her lunch, she explained that the bailiff expressed concern about her and wanted to ensure she ate.[45] With respect to Halverson's outward hostility toward her husband in front of court personnel, she insisted that she would simply put an end to his visits.[46]

The memo also recorded pleas from two of the judges urging her to seek professional help. Halverson agreed to do so—in a fashion. She remarked that a business coach would facilitate better communication between her staff and herself.[47]

The panel scheduled another meeting with Halverson for April 12, 2007, which Halverson failed to attend. Through a messenger, she informed the panel that she would be in trial for the remainder of the afternoon. The panel waited until six that evening before leaving. Later, they discovered that Halverson had simply lied to avoid them. The panel rescheduled the meeting for the following morning but, once again, Halverson did not show up.[48]

For her part, Halverson recounted the details of the April 6th panel meeting somewhat differently. In an action she filed against Hardcastle, Halverson claimed that the panel ignored objections she made regarding the presence of court personnel at the meeting. The judges not only berated her, but also refused to entertain any explanations that she could provide regarding her alleged conduct.

Halverson retained counsel on April 11. He quickly advised the court administrator that Halverson would no longer attend "accusatorial meetings"

---

42. Carter, *supra* note 13.
43. *Id.*
44. *Id.*
45. *Id.*
46. *Id.*
47. *Id.*
48. *Id.*

without the presence of counsel.[49] Halverson insisted that the chief judge relay any further information or instruction to her counsel from that point forward.

The judicial panel eventually concluded that, given Halverson's refusal to cooperate, it could not effectively provide her with the guidance that Hardcastle had envisioned. It recommended the reassignment of Halverson's criminal caseload—a recommendation Hardcastle immediately adopted.[50]

Hardcastle was not alone in attempting to confront Halverson about her disturbing conduct. Two Nevada Supreme Court justices paid Halverson a visit and expressed concern over her alleged treatment of court personnel.[51] After this meeting, courthouse public information officer Michael Sommermeyer stated, "I [saw] the two justices walk[ing] away shaking their heads because Judge Halverson made it clear to them she's smarter than they are. They were chastised."[52]

Battle Lines Harden Between the Two Judges

Early in May, Halverson fired her judicial executive assistant, Ileen Spoor. She sent a written request to the court administrator asking him to notify Spoor of her termination and directed that Spoor be prohibited from returning to the judge's chambers.[53] But Spoor had left a few personal belongings behind and, because of the judge's order, had difficulty retrieving them.

On May 9, Chief Judge Hardcastle directed several court staffers, including a videographer, the court administrator, an assistant court administrator, and armed bailiffs, to escort Spoor to her office to collect her things. Two unauthorized private bodyguards greeted this entourage at the entrance to Halverson's chambers. Halverson later explained that, because court security had been available to her only while court was in session, she had taken additional personal security measures.[54] In any case, she refused to leave the office and claimed that the court staffers were conducting an illegal search. Eventu-

---

49. Application for Writ of Quo Warranto at 7, Halverson v. Hardcastle, 123 Nev. 29 (Nev. 2007) (No. 49453).

50. *See id.*

51. Carter, *supra* note 13.

52. *Id.*

53. Application for Writ of Quo Warranto at 8, *Halverson* (No. 49453).

54. *Id.* at 9.

ally, Halverson called the police. A transcript of this call reveals the exchange between the dispatcher and Halverson. When the dispatcher inquired as to the fired employee's age, Halverson quipped, "Oh, about, I don't know; she looks like she's about 80, but I think she's 52 or 53."[55]

The chief judge was at her wit's end. Immediately following this incident, Hardcastle changed the locks on the doors to Halverson's chambers,[56] and prohibited Halverson and her personal bodyguards from setting foot inside the courthouse until she agreed to meet with the judicial panel and pledge that her unruly behavior would cease.[57] Hardcastle issued an administrative order to this effect and pointed to Halverson's recent actions in support of it.[58] Hardcastle justified the order as necessary to preserve public safety and to prevent further disruption with the courthouse's business operation and administration of justice.[59]

Specifically, after conferring with the judicial panel, Judge Hardcastle concluded that Halverson's decision to hire personal security without prior notification posed potential danger to judges, court personnel, and the public. The order also expressed Hardcastle's belief that threats to security and troublesome judicial conduct would continue given Halverson's "repeated expressions of distress, her repeated claims that 'everyone is against her, and her repeated claims that she cannot trust anyone in Court Administration."[60] Halverson claimed that she only learned about being barred from the building through news reports.[61] She also claimed she never received notice or service of process regarding the termination of her judicial office.[62]

Which Judge Acted Out of Line?

Debate ensued as Halverson questioned Hardcastle's authority. Through proxies, both Halverson and Hardcastle exchanged a series of statements and responses. Writing on Halverson's behalf, attorneys Dominic Gentile and

---

55. Carter, *supra* note 13.
56. *Id.*
57. Skolnik, *supra* note 19.
58. Application for Writ of Quo Warranto at 10, *Halverson* (No. 49453).
59. *Id.*
60. *Id.*
61. *Id.*
62. *Id.*

William Gamage opined, "summarily removing a judge's entire caseload because of some perceived error or misstep is punitive. Ejecting a judge from the very courtroom where she must work to serve her duties as a District Court judge is punitive and amounts to a total usurpation of Judge Halverson's elected office."[63] They argued that the authority to impose judicial discipline, censorship, or removal rested solely with the Judicial Discipline Commission.[64] Moreover, they asserted that a chief judge's responsibilities, as defined by the Eighth District Court rules, do not encompass "extra-judicial power over the actions of other District Court judges."[65]

Many sided with Hardcastle and applauded her actions as consistent with the strong chief judge model adopted in Nevada in the 1990s; this model confers broad, centralized administrative power on the chief judge. For example, Chief Solicitor General Daniel Wong and Hardcastle's attorneys contended that Hardcastle's actions toward Halverson were well within her scope of authority. They pointed to the Eighth District Court rules, which charge a chief judge with wide administrative authority "to facilitate the business of the court" and assure the timely, orderly and proper performance of the court's functions and duties.[66] Consistent with the spirit of prescribed court rules, they claimed, the chief judge properly put the jurist panel together to avoid further personal conflict with Halverson. The actions she took against Halverson were appropriately based on the panel's recommendations and security concerns.[67]

In explaining her actions, Chief Judge Hardcastle made some remarks to local media regarding Halverson's disruptive behavior. Halverson took issue with these comments and blamed Hardcastle for sparking public attacks on her conduct. In May, she fought back by filing a petition with the Nevada Supreme Court for a writ of quo warranto against the chief judge. In the petition, Halverson pressed for justification of Hardcastle's act in prohibiting an elected public official from entering the courthouse.[68] The petition also sought justification for two other allegedly "ultra vires" acts of Hardcastle: ordering Halverson to appear before a jurist panel to determine her compe-

---

63. Skolnik, *supra* note 19.

64. *Id.*

65. *Id.*

66. Eighth Jud. Dist. Ct. of Nev., L.R.1.30, *available at* http://www.leg.state.nv.us/court rules/EighthDCR.html (last visited Apr. 27, 2009).

67. *See, e.g.*, Howard, *supra* note 14.

68. Carter *supra* note 13; *See* Application for Writ of Quo Warranto, Halverson v. Hardcastle, 123 Nev. 29 (Nev. 2007) (No. 49453).

tency, and removing her criminal caseload and reassigning it to other judges.[69] The petition characterized these acts as "inappropriate punishment."

Halverson's petition made some compelling arguments. Citing Nevada statutory law and local court rules, Halverson took the position that a chief judge is indistinguishable from any other judge. The rules merely charge the chief judge with additional responsibility to ensure the business of the court operates smoothly, and these duties are strictly administrative in nature.[70] The law does not go so far as to imbue the chief judge with the power to assess another judge's conduct.[71] Moreover, the junior judge pointed to Neveda Revised Statutes (NRS) §3.220, which read in pertinent part: "The district judges shall possess equal coextensive and concurrent jurisdiction and power." Because all judges enjoy equal coextensive and concurrent jurisdiction, Halverson contended, Hardcastle's judicial panel lacked the power to review her acts.[72] Should improper conduct come to the chief judge's attention, the proper course of action would be to report the alleged behavior to the disciplinary commission.[73]

Ultimately, the Nevada Supreme Court rejected Halverson's position. The Court concluded that its rules, supplemented by local rules of Nevada courts, confer significant, centralized administrative power in the hands of the chief judge.[74] As long as a judicial panel does not impinge on the disciplinary commission's power to formally discipline judges or interfere with a questioned judge's ability to independently decide cases, the Court stated, the creation of such a panel is within the chief's authority.[75] Stripping the criminal case docket from Halverson was also proper because the chief judge articulated justifiable reasons of "convenience or necessity" to do so.

But the Court cautioned that a chief judge's sphere of influence is not absolute. Although the Court affirmed that a chief judge maintains broad administrative authority to ensure that the court operates properly,[76] and that the formation of a panel of review judges is within the scope of this authority, it also held that ordering a colleague to meet with such a panel is not.[77] Therefore, Hardcastle had erred in prohibiting Halverson from entering the

---

69. Application for Writ of Quo Warranto at 1–2, *Halverson* (No. 49453).
70. Carter, *supra* note 13.
71. *See* Application for Writ of Quo Warranto at 15, *Halverson* (No. 49453).
72. *See id.*
73. *Id.*
74. *Id.* at 33.
75. *Id.* at 35.
76. *See id.*
77. *Id.*

courthouse unless she agreed to meet with the assigned panel. Because a chief judge's power does not extend to removal of a judge from the bench,[78] the Court permitted Halverson to return to her chambers just a few days later.[79]

Diversion Efforts Fail—Miserably

Perhaps not surprisingly, Halverson continued to strike back. In particular, the junior judge began gathering documentation allegedly demonstrating Spoor's involvement in a ticket-fixing scheme.[80] A temporary assistant to the judge handed over a large manila folder belonging to Spoor labeled "Quick Fix."[81] The file reportedly contained a large volume of tickets.[82] Both Spoor and courthouse officials denied any illegality. Some court employees contended that Halverson simply wanted to stir trouble and divert attention away from her own alarming behavior.[83]

For her part, Spoor filed a defamation claim soon after her termination, alleging that Halverson had lied about her to the media. In addition to other things she had said about Spoor, Halverson claimed that Spoor had assisted prospective jurors in avoiding jury duty.[84] Spoor maintained her innocence, stating that she merely assisted individuals with scheduling conflicts to postpone their jury service.[85] Eventually, the attorney defending Halverson in the defamation case withdrew, contending that Halverson owed him more than $6,000 in back legal fees.[86]

The Disciplinary Commission Begins Building Its Case Against Judge Halverson

Near the same time that Chief Judge Hardcastle took measures into her own hands, Halverson's case drew the attention of Nevada Disciplinary Commission General Counsel David Sarnowski. Sarnowski filed an informal writ-

---

78. *Id.* at 25.

79. *See generally id.*

80. Carter, *supra* note 13.

81. Howard, *supra* note 19.

82. *Id.*

83. Carter, *supra* note 13.

84. Howard, *supra* note 19.

85. *Id.*

86. *Halverson Attorney Calls it Quits*, Las Vegas Now, Mar. 3, 2008, *at* http://www.lasvegas now.com/global/story.asp?S=7959662.

ten complaint against Halverson with the Commission on April 25, 2007. Pursuant to statutory law, the Commission examined the complaint, launched an investigation into Halverson's conduct,[87] and voted to oblige Halverson to take physical and mental examinations.[88]

The Commission is a small appointed body charged with the duty to investigate judicial misconduct or disability. The Commission can subject violators of the judicial canons to various disciplinary measures, ranging from reprimand to permanent removal from office.

After some delay, the Disciplinary Commission held a hearing on the Halverson matter in July 2007. Transcripts from the July hearing reportedly revealed new and quite frightening allegations made by Halverson's former bailiff, Johnny Jordan. Jordan testified that Halverson ordered him to pull out his gun and fire at Halverson's husband, Ed. Jordan intimated that Halverson's orders were not made in jest. When Jordan refused, Halverson remarked, "See, he don't even do what I say." Jordan claimed that when Ed departed the room, Halverson explained that she would get rid of Ed's body herself.[89]

Jordan also testified that Halverson:

(1) directed Jordan to cover her with blankets as she rested in her chambers;
(2) scolded Jordan and publicly ridiculed him;
(3) personally embarrassed Jordan by telling his fiancée at one point, "By day he's mine, and by night, he's yours";
(4) denied Jordan training opportunities;
(5) used expletive language to refer to her husband and court personnel;
(6) demanded that Jordan work long hours even when there was no jury for him to take charge of;
(7) required Jordan to spy on other court staffers;
(8) required Jordan to forego lunch hours and other breaks so that he could tend to her personal tasks;
(9) ordered Jordan to escort her to her vehicle;
(10) required Jordan to wait with her after work hours until Halverson's husband picked her up from the courthouse;

---

87. *See In re* Halverson, 123 Nev. 48 (2007).

88. Final Order of Interim Suspension, *In re* Halverson, 123 Nev. 48 2007) (No. 2007-053), *available at* http://www.nvsupremecourt.us/documents/cases/InterimSuspensionOrder.49876.pdf.

89. Sam Skolnik, *Bizarre Allegations Come to Light*, LAS VEGAS SUN, Aug. 16, 2007, *available at* http://www.lasvegassun.com/news/2007/aug/16/bizarre-allegations-come-to-light/; Ashley Powers, *Judge Elizabeth Halverson Courts Trouble in Las Vegas*, L.A. TIMES, Mar. 31, 2008, *available at* http://articles.latimes.com/2008/mar/31/nation/na-judge31.

(11) touched Jordan inappropriately behind his neck as he drove her to a work-related event;[90] and

(12) directed the court reporter to remove portions of the record on occasion after the judge made "ill-considered remarks."[91]

Spoor, Halverson's former executive assistant, testified that the relationship between the two began rather amicably. Spoor supported Halverson's judicial campaign and even worked on it. Soon after, however, things turned sour. Halverson often made derogatory remarks about other judges, shouted inappropriate statements to Spoor and other court personnel, and prohibited Spoor and other employees from speaking with any attorneys. Spoor further testified that Halverson made ethnic slurs, including calling Spoor a "faux Jew" for not attending temple services regularly, and frequently used profane language in Spoor's presence.[92]

Judge Stewart Bell, one of the judges who served on Hardcastle's panel to review Halverson's judicial performance, testified that the panel's efforts proved fruitless because Halverson either cast blame on her staff or minimized the panel's concerns.[93] Bell testified that he specifically advised Halverson to stop communicating with juries ex parte, but to no avail.[94] Bell also testified that, based on his investigation, most attorneys found Halverson difficult to work with.[95] The district's Court Administrator, Charles Short, also provided telling evidence on this point. Pursuant to Nevada Supreme Court Rule 48.1, counsel on either side of a civil case may exercise one peremptory challenge of the judge assigned to the case. The lawyer exercising the challenge is never made known to the judge and does not have to provide a reason for exercising the challenge. The case is then reassigned to another judge.[96]

As part of his job, Short kept track of statistics for the court. Short testified that, in just six months, various lawyers had made a total of 199 peremptory challenges against Halverson. The judge with the second highest number of challenges received only 48.[97] Short noted that newer judges typically re-

---

90. Final Order of Interim Suspension at 19–20, *Halverson* (No. 2007-053), *available at* http://www.nvsupremecourt.us/documents/cases/InterimSuspensionOrder.49876.pdf.

91. *See In re* Halverson, 169 P.3d 1161, 1167 (2007); Powers, *supra* note 89.

92. *Halverson*, 169 P.3d at 1168.

93. *Id.*

94. *Id.* at 1167.

95. *Id.*

96. *Id.* at 1170 n.13.

97. *Id.* at 1170.

ceive a larger number of challenges and that judges lack any control over peremptory challenges. Still, as Short testified, the number of peremptory challenges Halverson accumulated in such a brief time hindered the court's administrative efficiency and smooth operation.[98] Short also testified to Halverson's staff turnover, noting that many temporary employees resisted working for the judge. Short acknowledged, however, that Halverson did not fall behind on rendering orders and decisions.[99]

Other claims found throughout various court documents include the following: bringing jurors cookies and dining with them inside the courtroom during the course of a trial;[100] berrating lawyers publicly for failing to contribute to her judicial campaign; disparaging lawyers with sarcasm; and subjecting staffers to menial tasks such as requiring them to remove lint from her robe, ordering feet and back massages, and fetching her lunch.[101]

Although Halverson did not testify at the hearing, she did provide an explanation for some of the allegations made against her. For example, in an affidavit Halverson submitted to the Disciplinary Commission, she explained that she had diabetes and that low blood sugar would arise when she failed to eat, causing her tremendous fatigue. Halverson claimed that low blood sugar had led on one occasion to her dozing off during a trial.[102]

Four court staffers testified for Halverson. These staffers only worked for the judge briefly between late April and mid-July. Some testified they never witnessed any of Halverson's alleged egregious behavior such as falling asleep during trial, using profane language, shouting at staff, conducting herself in an unprofessional manner, or requiring staff to complete personal tasks like preparing her lunch or massaging her neck.[103] To the contrary, these witnesses testified to Halverson's professionalism and courtesy toward staff, attorneys, and litigants.[104]

After reviewing the complaint and considering the totality of circumstances, the Commission drew upon its constitutional and statutory authority to temporarily remove Halverson from the bench pending a final determi-

---

98. *Id.*

99. *Id.*

100. *Id.* at 1167; *See generally* Final Order of Interim Suspension at 15, *In re* Halverson, 123 Nev. 48 (2007) (No. 2007-053), *available at* http://www.nvsupremecourt.us/documents/cases/InterimSuspensionOrder.49876.pdf.

101. Carter, *supra* note 444.

102. *See Halverson*, 169 P.3d at 1169.

103. *Id.*

104. *Id.*

nation in a judicial proceeding. Though the Commission rarely invoked this power, the disciplinary body deemed it necessary after finding that Halverson "posed a substantial threat of serious harm to the public and to the administration of justice."[105]

The Commission based its order on the following grounds: insufficient legal ability to preside over criminal trials; abusive conduct directed at court personnel to the extent that she posed a serious threat to the administration of justice; failure to execute judicial duties by falling asleep during a trial; and failure to cooperate with court staffers and fellow judges.[106] Pending a full-scale disciplinary proceeding, the Commission's ruling resulted in Halverson's immediate but temporary removal from the bench. In the meantime, however, the order, which became effective on July 25, 2007, provided that Halverson would continue to receive her $130,000 annual salary.

Shortly after the Commission issued the suspension order, two former assistants came to Halverson's defense, claiming Halverson was "unfairly targeted."[107] In a local interview, the two shared their displeasure with the Commission's decision and expressed disdain toward the disciplinary proceedings. Although law clerk Sally Owen had not testified before the Commission, executive assistant Linda John said she was appalled because it apparently paid little attention to her testimony. The news report duly noted that court administrators discharged the two employees when the Commission temporarily suspended Halverson's judicial duties. The report also indicated that judges may hire whomever they wish for these assistant positions.[108]

Formal Charges Bring New Allegations to Light

The Judicial Disciplinary Commission reportedly gathered over 2,000 pages of documents in support of its case against the judge.[109] Many of the allegations in the Halverson saga that circulated through the media and formed the basis for the temporary suspension resurfaced when the Commission filed for-

---

105. *See id.* at 1166.

106. Mark Sayre, *Commission Suspends District Court Judge Halverson*, Jul. 25, 2007, http://www.klas-tv.com/Global/story.asp?s=6840409; *see also* Final Order of Interim Suspension, *Halverson* (No. 2007-053).

107. Mark Sayre, *2 Former Employees of Judge Halverson Speak Out*, Las Vegas Now, Jul. 30, 2007, *at* http://www.klas-tv.com/Global/story.asp?S=6861751.

108. *Id.*

109. *New Developments in Judge Halverson Case*, Las Vegas Valley, Feb. 12, 2008, *at* http://www.lasvegasvalley.com/Global/story.asp?S=7862218&nav=168XMeHv.

mal charges against Judge Halverson on January 7, 2008.[110] The accusations included: falling asleep during trial; interacting with jurors outside the presence of counsel; hiring private, unauthorized bodyguards; lying to reporters; refusing to communicate with Chief Judge Hardcastle; disparaging and shouting at court personnel; ordering massages; and using profanity in the presence of employees. Once again, Halverson denied the bulk of the charges. She did admit, however, to eating with jurors during deliberations. Because a family style meal was served in the courtroom, Halverson believed there was no impropriety in this ex parte interaction.[111] On prior occasions, Halverson had suggested that she had engaged in these interactions so jurors would grow fond of her.

But the complaint also brought new allegations to light. The Commission alleged, for example, that Halverson attempted to gain unauthorized access into the county's computer system so that she could read mail or other input of employees.[112] It also alleged that the judge made public comments to local reporters during a child molestation trial that could have influenced the result in the case.[113]

In an interview, Halverson dismissed many of the accusations, suggesting most were either untrue or "rookie mistakes," and contended that she was simply being "singled out."[114] Her attorney, Michael Schwartz, stated in an interview that Halverson may have misbehaved but that her actions hardly amounted to judicial misconduct. "People can make mistakes, that's not misconduct. People can do things that are unintentional, that's not misconduct. People can end up having illness affect them, that's not misconduct."[115]

Despite her temporary suspension and negative publicity, Halverson ran for reelection.[116] In the meantime, the Disciplinary Commission ordered the judge to undergo a psychiatric evaluation no later than July 18, 2008. If she failed to do so, the Commission would preclude her from relying on her disability or other

---

110. Mark Sayre, *Formal Charges Filed Against Judge Halverson*, Las Vegas Now, Jan. 7, 2008, *at* http://www.lasvegasnow.com/Global/story.asp?S=7590881.

111. *See* David Kihara, *Judge Denies Charges, Political Enemies Responsible For Misconduct Allegations, Halverson Says*, Las Vegas Rev.-J., Aug. 6, 2008, *available at* http://www.lvrj.com/news/26330399.html.

112. Sayre, *supra* note 110.

113. Sean Whaley, *Judge Faces Misconduct Charges: Complaint Alleges Halverson Fell Asleep On The Bench, Harassed Employees*, Las Vegas Rev.-J., Jan. 8, 2008, *available at* http://www.lvrj.com/news/13522177.html.

114. Powers, *supra* note 89.

115. *Vegas Judge in Jeopardy*, CBS News, Aug. 4, 2008, *at* http://www.cbsnews.com/video/watch/?id=4318870n%3fsource=search_video (Last visited Apr. 19, 2009).

116. Powers, *supra* note 89.

health concerns to advance her defense during her August 2008 hearing.[117] Halverson protested the Commission's demands, arguing that she had already provided a medical report prepared by a therapist. The therapist had diagnosed Halverson with depression, anxiety, and an adjustment disorder. Halverson cited to the Americans with Disabilities Act and contended that the Commission should not require additional medical information concerning her disabilities.[118]

Halverson Finally Gets Her Day in Court

More than a year after the Commission issued a temporary suspension against the first-term judge, Halverson received a full hearing. But the process was hardly smooth. After several delays, Halverson's attorneys moved to withdraw their legal representation. The Commission granted the request so as to enable Halverson to proceed with the hearing without further conflict.

The Disciplinary Commission scheduled the hearing to last a full week. The hearing did not proceed without interruption, however. Early in the week, Halverson filed a complaint against the disciplinary commission in federal court claiming that the Commission had violated her due process rights.[119] Halverson's complaint alleged the Commission had withheld information from the judge she deemed necessary for her defense, impairing her constitutional right to a fair hearing.[120] During the federal proceeding, she requested to represent herself but the judge denied her request.[121] Halverson's attorneys later requested that the federal judge temporarily suspend the state inquiry—a request he denied as well.[122] Ultimately, Halverson's stall tactic failed, and the commission hearing got underway.

To succeed, commission rules required Special Counsel to prove the allegations against Halverson by clear and convincing evidence.[123] Johnny Jordan,

---

117. *Double Whammy for Judge Halverson This Week*, LAS VEGAS Now, Jul. 3, 2008, *at* http://www.lasvegasnow.com/Global/story.asp?S=8618274.

118. *Id.*

119. Mark Sayre, *Judge to Decide if Halverson's Due Process Rights Violated*, LAS VEGAS Now, Aug. 6, 2008, *at* http://www.lasvegasnow.com/Global/story.asp?S=8794396.

120. Kihara, *supra* note 111.

121. Willis, *supra* note 2.

122. Kihara, *supra* note 111; *Federal Judge Rules on Judge Halverson Case*, LAS VEGAS Now, Aug. 6, 2008, *at* http://www.lasvegasnow.com/global/story.asp?s=8799032.

123. Final Order of Interim Suspension at 5, *In re* Halverson, 169 P.3d 1161 (2007) (No. 2007-053), *available at* http://www.nvsupremecourt.us/documents/cases/InterimSuspension Order.49876.pdf.

the judge's former bailiff, became the main witness on the first day. He broke down in tears on the stand.[124] "I am doing everything to keep my composure here. I can't stand what she did to me.... If you guys allow her to be in office after all of this, what does it say about all of you ... ? I was up here, robbed of my rights, my dignity. How would you feel if it happened to you?"[125]

Things turned uglier the following day when Chief Judge Kathy Hardcastle testified. Hardcastle dismissed any notion that she had singled out Halverson and subjected her to unfair treatment.[126] Hardcastle explained that Halverson's reputation deterred many court staffers from wanting to work alongside her. Moreover, Halverson required personnel to spend a vast amount of time handling complaints waged against her. Jurors and other district judges noted her unruly behavior, and judges often dodged scheduled meetings if they expected Halverson to attend.[127] As a reporter later recounted, Hardcastle's bottom line was that the drawn-out Halverson saga "had been disruptive to the court system."[128]

Later that same day, Halverson took the stand in her own defense. She denied Jordan's accusations and blamed her predicament on political enemies seeking to unseat her.[129] When the prosecutor noted the stark difference between the testimony of Halverson and Jordan, Halverson called Jordan a liar. She then explained that while there may have been some truth to Jordan's testimony, Jordan's account was misleading.[130] As part of her defense, Halverson and her attorney attempted to demonstrate that court personnel engaged in a conspiracy to remove her from the bench.[131] During the junior judge's testimony, both she and the Commission's special prosecutor yelled over one another.[132] When the prosecutor referred to Halverson as former judge, Halverson quipped, "I'm still a sitting judge now. I'm just suspended. I'm not going to be denigrated."[133]

---

124. Mark Sayre, *Disciplinary Hearing Held for Judge Halverson*, LAS VEGAS Now, Aug. 4, 2008, *at* http://www.lasvegasnow.com/global/story.asp?S=8785085.

125. *Id.*

126. David Kihara, *Judge Halverson Kicked off the Bench*, LAS VEGAS REV.-J., Nov. 17, 2008, *available* at http://www.lvrj.com/new/breaking_news/34593399.html.

127. *Id.*

128. Sayre, *supra* note 124.

129. Kihara, *supra* note 126.

130. *Judge Defends Herself on the Stand*, Aug. 8, 2008, *at* http://insession.blogs.cnn.com/2008/08/08/judge-defends-herself-on-the-stand/.

131. Mark Sayre, *Hearing for Judge Halverson Wraps Up*, LAS VEGAS Now, Aug. 16, 2008, *at* http://www.klas-tv.com/Global/story.asp?S=8849824.

132. Kihara, *supra* note 126.

133. *Id.*

The Commission also placed Halverson's former court reporter on the stand. He discussed Halverson's foul language, incessant tendencies to belittle him in the presence of others, and the unpleasant work environment she created for him and others.[134] Ileen Spoor testified next. Spoor recalled Halverson's sleeping tendencies during trial. "I called her name several times and she was snoring away."

The proceedings came to an abrupt halt on the last day originally scheduled for the hearing when Halverson suffered a hypoglycemic attack.[135] The Commission's decision was delayed further after the judge wound up hospitalized when her husband beat her with a frying pan.[136] This was not a staged event. Authorities charged Edward Lee Halverson with attempted murder and battery with a deadly weapon. He later entered a guilty plea to battery with a deadly weapon and, in exchange for his cooperation, the prosecutor dropped the attempted murder charge. In the meantime, Halverson's re-election bid did not fare well. She came in a distant third in the primary election against two other judicial candidates.[137] Constituents evidently had had their fill of the Halverson fiasco and voted her off the bench.

Commission Removes Halverson From the Bench — Permanently

Halverson learned her fate on November 18, 2008. The Judicial Discipline Commission permanently removed Halverson from the bench and barred her from ever serving as a judge again in Nevada. One could fairly characterize the tone of the Commission's 38-page opinion as harsh and unsympathetic. In it, the Commission stated, "the damage resulting from [Halverson's] antics and willful misconduct will be felt by the judicial system

---

134. *Halverson Hearing Enters Third Day*, LAS VEGAS Now, Aug 7. 2008, *at* http://www.lasvegasnow.com/Global/story.asp?S=8805578.

135. Brian Eckhouse, *Halverson Loses Bid to Stay on Bench*, LAS VEGAS SUN, Aug. 13, 2008, *available at* http://www.lasvegassun.com/news/2008/aug/12/advance-halverson-embattled-beyond-primary-election/.

136. David Kihara, *Judge Halverson Kicked off the Bench*, LAS VEGAS REV.-J., Nov. 17, 2008, *available at* http://www.lvrj.com/news/breaking_news/34593399.html.

137. *Judge Halverson Gets Extension in Dismissal Proceedings*, LAS VEGAS Now, Sept. 11, 2008, *at* http://www.lasvegasnow.com/Global/story.asp?S=8993076.

for a significant future period of time."[138] According to the Commission's findings, Halverson's conduct both on and off the bench not only frustrated public confidence in the state judiciary but also demonstrated that she was unfit to hold office.[139] Not surprisingly, Halverson's attorney timely filed an appeal.

Analysis

Despite having some counts dismissed before the end of the evidentiary hearing, Special Counsel succeeded in proving certain allegations by clear and convincing evidence.[140] In the end, the Commission found Halverson's unprofessional behavior violated twelve different rules under various state judicial canons. To begin with, Canon 1 of Nevada's judicial code states: "a judge shall uphold the integrity and independence of the judiciary."[141] A host of Halverson's acts violated this canon. For example, the judiciary's integrity became compromised after Halverson repeatedly engaged in ex parte communications with jurors in criminal and civil proceedings.

This conduct also violated a number of other judicial canons, including: Canon 2(A), which requires a judge to "respect and comply with the law and [] act at all times in a manner that promotes public confidence in the integrity and impartiality of the judiciary";[142] Canon 3(B)(7), which prohibits a judge from initiating, permitting, or considering communication outside the presence of counsel except under limited circumstances;[143] and Canon 3(B)(8), which requires a judge to dispose of all judicial matters fairly.[144] As the Commission so pithily opined: "Eating or chatting with a deliberating

---

138. Findings of Fact, Conclusions of Law and Imposition of Discipline at 23, *In re* Halverson (Nev. Comm'n on Jud. Discipline 2008) (No. 0801-1066), *available at* http://judicial.state.nv.us/decisionsofncjd3new.htm.

139. *See generally id.*

140. *Id.*

141. NEV. CODE OF JUD. CONDUCT CANON 1 (2007). Though Nevada has not adopted the ABA Model Code of Judicial Conduct verbatim, the Nevada Code of Judicial Conduct reflects the spirit of the Model Rules. Generally, the two codes differ only in structure and organization. The Nevada Judicial Code of Conduct may be accessed online at http://www.leg.state.nv.us/CourtRules/SCR_CJC.html. The 2007 ABA Model Code of Judicial Conduct is also available online at http://www.abanet.org/judicialethics/approved_MCJC.html.

142. NEV. CODE OF JUD. CONDUCT CANON 2(A) (2007).

143. *Id.* CANON 3(B)(7).

144. *Id.* CANON 3(B)(8).

jury and answering their law-related and case-related questions in an ex parte setting is so fundamentally wrong that even a first-year law clerk should know better, much less someone who had several years of experience as a law clerk within the court system."[145]

Along similar lines, Halverson made improper public comments to the media while one case was pending.[146] This directly contravenes Canon 3(B)(9), which prohibits a judge from making "any public comment that might reasonably be expected to affect its outcome or impair its fairness" during a pending proceeding.[147] In a post-trial interview with the media, Halverson also falsely stated that an attorney participating in one case had "conned" Halverson into engaging in improper contacts.[148]

Halverson's tendencies to fall asleep during various portions of three separate trials directly violated Canon 2(A).[149] Rather than promoting public confidence in the integrity and impartiality of the judiciary, Halverson accomplished the exact opposite. During trial, a judge's undivided attention is paramount. A judge must be able to hear and decide motions and objections as they arise at various times throughout a proceeding. Inattention on the judge's part, however brief, impairs any chance for fairness to litigants and can yield harmful repercussions, including a possible mistrial.

The Commission's decision noted that once Halverson became aware of her sleeping tendencies, she had a duty to pursue measures to prevent or minimize any chance of falling asleep again.[150] Yet, Halverson failed to assume this duty. In fact, she denied the existence of any such problem, as she often did with other complaints against her.

Although the Commission found that Special Counsel had failed to meet the clear and convincing burden regarding every alleged instance of ill treatment Halverson displayed toward court staffers, it did find the burden had been met with respect to Halverson's derogatory references to other employ-

---

145. Findings of Fact, Conclusions of Law and Imposition of Discipline at 9, *Halverson* (No. 0801-1066).

146. *Id.*

147. Nev. Code of Jud. Conduct Canon 3(B)(9) (2007).

148. Findings of Fact, Conclusions of Law and Imposition of Discipline at 9, *Halverson* (No. 0801-1066).

149. Nev. Code of Jud. Conduct Canon 2(A) (2007). The rule provides: "A judge shall respect and comply with the law and shall act at all times in a manner that promotes public confidence in the integrity and impartiality of the judiciary." *Id.*

150. Findings of Fact, Conclusions of Law and Imposition of Discipline at 7, Halverson (No. 0801-1066).

ees in her bailiff's presence and orders for massages.[151] Special Counsel also met this burden in proving Halverson's use of profanity and verbal abuse of others in her judicial assistant's presence.[152]

As a result, Halverson violated Canon 2(B), which requires judges to refrain from engaging in behavior that undermines the prestige of judicial office.[153] Because the judiciary functions independently of the executive and legislative branches, maintaining this prestige is paramount.[154] Comments that follow this canon suggest that judges should maintain the prestige of judicial office in all their activities, not only while on the bench.[155]

Halverson also violated Canon 3(B)(5), which bars a judge, in the performance of judicial duties, from manifesting bias or prejudice through words or conduct;[156] Canon 3(C)(2), which calls upon judges to abstain from showing bias or prejudice in the performance of official duties;[157] and Canon 4(A), which instructs judges to conduct every extra-judicial activity in ways that neither demean the judicial office nor hamper the proper performance of judicial duties.[158] As the Commission artfully stated: "Staff members are paid by the taxpayers to discharge the lawful directives of judicial officers, not to put up with loud, offensive and boorish conduct by someone who believes that donning the judicial robe absolves them from behaving badly."[159] In addition, the Commission chastised Halverson's efforts to divert its attention from Halverson and on to Spoor's alleged ticket-fixing scheme.[160]

Hiring two private, unauthorized, and unqualified bodyguards without previously informing court administrative officials defied the canons mentioned above as well. Halverson failed to follow court rules and proper protocol for seeking and hiring from a pool of qualified court bailiffs. Moreover, local court rules did not authorize Halverson to hire private guards who had not cleared the court's security screening process.[161] Halverson

---

151. *Id.* at 11.

152. *Id.* at 13.

153. Nev. Code of Jud. Conduct Canon 2(B) (2007).

154. *See id.* Canon 2(B) cmt.

155. *Id.*

156. *Id.* Canon 3(B)(5).

157. *Id.* Canon 3(C)(2).

158. *Id.* Canon 4(A).

159. Findings of Fact, Conclusions of Law and Imposition of Discipline at 13, *In re* Halverson (Nev. Comm'n on Jud. Discipline) (No. 0801-1066), *available at* http://judicial.state.nv.us/decisionsofncjd3new.htm.

160. *Id.*

161. *Id.* at 14.

had also failed to place these guards on the court's hiring rolls as the rules required.[162]

In addition, under Nevada's chief judge system, local court rules charge the chief judge and court's appointed administrator with the responsibility to coordinate and oversee security activities. This system, however, does not call for other judges to implement their own personal security measures. The Commission casted Halverson's need for protection from court personnel as "wholly fanciful."[163] By bringing in her own security, Halverson singlehandedly defied court rules, breached the court's security system, and unnecessarily created potential security risks for all those in the courthouse.[164]

The Commission also found that, in her failure to cooperate with court administrators, refusal to communicate directly with Chief Judge Hardcastle, and attempt to declare the presence of court personnel in her chambers an illegal search, Halverson had once again violated the state's judicial canons. Rather than contribute positively to the operation of the court system and reduce the huge workload of others, Halverson's actions impeded court operations; added more paperwork as court administrators had to sift through mounds of complaints; frustrated work relations; deterred others from wanting to work with her; and ultimately drove court staffers away.

Postscript

This case is not yet over. Immediately after the Disciplinary Commission rendered its decision, Halverson's attorney timely appealed the Commission's decision to the Nevada Supreme Court. Because the decision left her permanently unemployed, Halverson filed an Emergency Motion to Proceed in Forma Pauperis on March 16, 2009. The Nevada Supreme Court received Halverson's initial brief the next day. Other court filings included: a Motion to Dismiss Appeal and To Impose Sanctions; a Motion for Order Shortening Time; and a Response in Opposition to Emergency Motion to Proceed In Forma Pauperis. On April 17, 2009, the Commission issued an Order Denying Motion to Proceed In Forma Pauperis without prejudice. The Nevada Supreme Court has not yet ruled on the Motion to Dismiss Appeal.[165]

---

162. *Id.* at 15.

163. *Id.* at 16 n.13.

164. *Id.* at 16.

165. E-mail from Kathy Schultz, Management Analyst, Commission on Judicial Discipline (Apr. 20, 2009, 10:50 a.m. EST) (on file with author).

Comments and Questions

1. Given Halverson's interactions with criminal jurors and inexperience with criminal procedure, it appears that Hardcastle had justifiable reasons for reassigning her criminal docket and assigning only civil cases to her. Once she was reassigned to civil cases only, do you believe that Halverson continued to pose a threat to the administration of justice? Note that no attorneys or parties were called by the Commission to testify against Halverson. Should that be taken as a sign of her competence as a judge, at least in the civil arena? Or does the statistical evidence regarding the number of civil attorneys who chose to "strike" Halverson when her name came up reveal something different?

2. One observer applauded the Nevada Commission on Judicial Discipline for its swift actions against Judge Halverson. Rather than spending a year attempting to unravel complaints filed against the judge, the Commission shielded the public from probable future harm while simultaneously preserving her financial status pending a full hearing on the allegations waged against her by suspending her prior to the fall hearing.[166] Do you agree that this was the right step to take?

3. The judicial antics on display in the Halverson saga helped revive calls for judicial reform[167] and raised serious questions about the election of state court judges. Specifically, in 2006, a series of articles in the *Los Angeles Times* rejuvenated efforts to move toward a system of merit-based judicial appointment so candidates would not have to raise money for their campaigns.[168] Do you believe judges should be appointed rather than elected? What are the advantages and disadvantages to each method? Are constituents sufficiently knowledgeable on judicial candidates to vote responsibly? Should judges be insulated from public opinion?

4. What do you think about judicial candidates raising money from lawyers expected to appear before them if they win? What about incumbent judges raising campaign funds from lawyers with pending cases? Can elected judges really remain judicially independent and impartial? Or are these judges unduly influenced by the contributions they receive toward their campaigns?

---

166. Sherman Frederick, *When Judges Go Bad*, Las Vegas Rev.-J., Aug. 12, 2007, *available at* http://www.lvrj.com/opinion/9112626.html.

167. Carter, *supra* note 13; *Series on Las Vegas Judges Renews Calls for Reform*, L.A. Times, June 14, 2006, *available at* www.latimes.com/news/politics/la-na-judges14jun14,1,4762430.story.

168. *Series on Las Vegas Judges Renews Calls for Reform, supra* note 600.

5. One commentator opines that a judicial disciplinary commission serves as a necessary check on the state's system of justice.[169] How so? Do you believe it does so effectively?

6. In its written order, the Commission suggested that one occasion of falling asleep does not, on its own, warrant a temporary suspension. However, Halverson's sleeping tendencies, when combined with other conduct, did form part of the basis for the Commission's decision to suspend Halverson temporarily. Do you think occasionally falling asleep merits removal from the bench? After all, millions of Americans fall asleep during the most inopportune times. No one, including prominent leaders of our country, is immune from this natural tendency. Consider former President Bill Clinton. He fell asleep during a ceremony commemorating Martin Luther King. Former Vice President Dick Cheney reportedly fell asleep during cabinet meetings. One of President Obama's chief economic advisors recently fell asleep at a summit. How should falling asleep weigh in the totality of circumstances standard?

7. Nevada's disciplinary commission proceedings are sealed from the public. Allegations and many of the documents become public only after the case reaches the state supreme court. Is it in the state's best interest to keep these proceedings a secret?[170] Do taxpayers and the voting public have a right to be aware of charges brought against elected officials?

---

169. Frederick, *supra* note 166.
170. Sayre, *supra* note 512.

Chapter 8

Lights, Camera, Malfeasance[1]

"Wow this is wild. Has Gary Crossen, a formal federal prosecutor and partner at Foley Hoag, read too many John Grisham novels?"

—David Lat, *Above the Law*

In August 1995, Kevin Curry heard opportunity knock.[2] For Curry, a former assistant attorney general and longtime defense attorney, the tapping first began while gossiping with his friend and client, George Macheras,[3] a lawyer in Lowell, Massachusetts.[4] During these conversations, Macheras informed Curry that a friend felt that he was "getting screwed" in court.[5] The "friend," it turned out, was none other than Telemachus Demoulas, a self-made billionaire who had monopolized the Boston media for the previous few years in a public wrangle with his brother George over their family's supermarket chain, an empire worth an estimated 1.5 billion dollars.[6] When Curry learned a short time later that the judge presiding over the *Demoulas* litigation had issued a decision that cost Telemachus' branch of the family hundreds of millions of dollars, he was ready to pounce. For Curry, the knock of opportunity had grown deafening, and he was poised to answer. Neither professional ethics, nor even general morals, would stand in his way.

Two weeks after Judge Maria Lopez issued her *Demoulas* decision, Curry —with the help of Ernest Reid, a private investigator—made his first move. Not wanting to be too aggressive with someone he had never met, Curry kept his first contact with the Demoulas family indirect. He chose to introduce himself to Telemachus via letter, suggesting that Telemachus meet with him and Ernest Reid to discuss "a matter of importance and confidence."[7] As

---

1. This chapter is based on the original research and writing of **Mindy Yergin**.
2. *In re Curry*, 880 N.E.2d 388, 394 (Mass. 2008).
3. *Id.* at 395 n.8.
4. Gerard O'Neill, *The Demoulas Trap*, BOSTON MAG., December 2006, *available at* http://www.bostonmagazine.com/articles/the_demoulas_trap/.
5. *Curry*, 880 N.E.2d at 395 n.8.
6. O'Neill, *supra* note 4.
7. *Curry*, 880 N.E.2d at 394.

Curry well knew, at the time that Telemachus received this letter, his life, and those of his family members, had been consumed by their very own Greek tragedy. For more than a decade, the Demoulas family had engaged in an epic war over its larger than life grocery store chain. Battles raged in Massachusetts courtrooms, and the carnage regularly splashed across the front pages of the *Boston Globe*. It was in this charged atmosphere that Telemachus accepted the meeting with Curry and Reid and arranged for his second in command and son, Arthur T., to stand by his side.[8]

At the meeting in early September, Telemachus, Arthur T., and the other family members who were present hung onto Curry's every word. They had been stung by Judge Maria Lopez's decision to give a controlling interest in the supermarket chain to the other side of the family. They listened intently as Curry told them that their case had been "over before it began." He informed them that Judge Lopez had been bribed before, and that their case was not the first one she had fixed. For good measure, Curry also commented on Judge Lopez's private life, suggesting that her character off the bench matched that of her character when wearing robes. Notably, even though Reid had thoroughly investigated Judge Lopez before this meeting, nothing he uncovered supported Curry's disparaging remarks. But, proof or no, Curry's accusations were like music to the family's ears.[9]

Curry's performance resulted in exactly the reaction he sought. The family, horrified at having "been had," asked what options were open to them. Curry explained that to right the wrongs Judge Lopez had committed, they would need to expose her malfeasance to the media. He warned them, however, that before justice could be achieved, the family needed hard evidence of Judge Lopez's misconduct. "Selflessly," Curry offered his and Reid's services for gathering this evidence. One week after the meeting, Arthur T. took Curry up on his offer and paid him a $25,000 retainer. Eventually, Curry would receive more than $125,000 for his engagement with the Demoulas family.

During the next fifteen months, Reid dug through public records searching for incriminating information on Judge Lopez and the attorneys who worked for Telemachus' brother, George (the winning side of the *Demoulas* litigation). Reid diligently searched for damaging details arising from not only their professional lives, but also their personal ones. Simultaneously, Curry reviewed every decision Judge Lopez had ever written. He hoped to

---

8. *Id.* at 395.
9. *Id.*

discover discrepancies in the writing style that might suggest someone other than Lopez authored the *Demoulas* opinion.[10] In pursuit of this theory, Curry even contacted a law professor whom he suspected of being the opinion's real author. Rather than openly accusing the law professor of the deed, Curry secured an interview with him under the guise of potentially hiring him as an expert witness for a case involving substantial assets. After the interview, Curry remained unsure whether the law professor had ghost-written the opinion.[11]

Opening Act: The Ruse Is Hatched

Curry's big break came in November 1996, when Arthur T. gave him a resumé that Judge Lopez's law clerk, Paul Walsh, had sent to the Demoulases' lawyers during his job search in the fall of 1995. Reid and Curry examined the resumé and deduced that Walsh desired a position in international commercial civil litigation. They decided that they needed to talk to Walsh and trick him into spilling dirt on Judge Lopez. Because they knew that they could not approach Walsh directly, they concocted a plot to fabricate a lucrative employment opportunity—Walsh's dream job—and pretend to interview him for it. To further their plan, Reid refocused his investigation from the judge and opposing attorneys to Walsh himself. He looked for the dirty laundry of not only Walsh, but of his parents, friends, and neighbors as well.[12]

Finally, in April, they were ready. Reid called Walsh and introduced himself as a legal headhunter. He said that he wanted to speak with him about an "attractive opportunity" that existed at a law firm. As expected, Walsh bought the story. They set up a meeting at Walsh's own home on April 9th.[13]

When the day of the meeting arrived, Reid changed his story slightly. Deciding that a fabricated corporate position provided more creative freedom for manipulating Walsh, he discontinued the tale about a law firm. Instead, Reid described his new client as an international corporation in need of in-house counsel. To make this story believable, Reid fabricated numerous details about the phony corporation. He told Walsh that his client's corporate offices were located in Bermuda, Boston, and New York, and that the client

---

10. *Id.*
11. *Id.* at 395 n.12.
12. *Id.* at 395–96.
13. *Id.* at 396.

demanded a candidate with impeccable writing skills. Reid used this last tid-bit to steer the meeting toward his real purpose, gleaning information from the clerk about Judge Lopez and the *Demoulas* case. Specifically, Reid asked Walsh "if he had worked on any 'cases of note' while clerking for the Superior Court."[14] To this, Walsh immediately volunteered, "[w]e wrote the *Demoulas* decision." Although Walsh's statement was not the exact response Reid hoped for, he knew it was a start. With only slightly more manipulation, he elicited the words he came to get. The clerk claimed, "I wrote the decision." And, falsely believing that he was being interviewed for his dream job, Walsh did not stop there. Hoping to impress this headhunter, he began puffing away. Before the interview ended, Walsh confided to Reid that not only had he written the *Demoulas* decision, but that Judge Lopez had read it and not even bothered to edit it.[15]

The very next day, Curry met Reid at their usual haunt, the Forest Hills Cemetery in Jamaica Plains. This location frequently served as their confer-ence room for confidential sessions, and Curry needed privacy today. He wanted to find out what information Reid had extracted from the clerk, and to brainstorm on how they could use it to keep the Demoulas family gravy train heading their way.[16]

On this muddy spring day[17] they plotted their next move. They decided that Reid should set up another meeting with Walsh because they believed that they could squeeze more damaging details about Judge Lopez's conduct in the *Demoulas* case from him. They also needed to find a way to get the clerk to agree to tell others about Judge Lopez's transgressions, or at least record him repeating the allegations. They left the cemetery armed with spe-cific assignments. Curry agreed to call Arthur T. to update him on the situa-tion, and Reid agreed to call the law clerk to convey "that the 'client' was im-pressed with the writing samples, especially the *Demoulas* decision" and to set up another time for them to meet.[18]

On May 4, Reid got together with Walsh for a second time. Delicately balancing his headhunter persona with his true purpose, Reid casually in-quired about the *Demoulas* decision, asking if, in the clerk's opinion, the case had been rightly decided. Walsh responded, "The [Supreme Judicial Court] upheld me, so what does it matter?" Reid was not satisfied—the answer was

---

14. *Id.*
15. *Id.*
16. O'Neill, *supra* note 4.
17. *Id.*
18. *Curry*, 880 N.E.2d at 396.

not strong enough to suit his purposes. Desiring an opportunity to probe deeper, Reid ended the meeting by inviting Walsh to either New York or Halifax, Nova Scotia, for an interview with the client. Coincidentally, both locales allow clandestine tape recording of private conversations as long as one party consents, while Massachusetts does not.[19]

Believing this next step in their scheme to be critical, Reid and Curry invested a lot of time, effort, and creativity in setting the stage for the upcoming ruse. Characters were concocted, lines were scripted, and props were designed. Curry assumed the alias of "Kevin Concave, Director of Operations" for "British Pacific Surplus Risks, Ltd.," (British Pacific) a fictitious "international insurance underwriting business." Curry recruited another private detective, Richard LaBonte, to manage the fake interview with him. This detective assumed the identity of "Richard LaBlanc," another supposed British Pacific employee.[20]

They left no stone unturned and spared no expense. They ordered British Pacific business cards for both "Kevin Concave" and "Richard LaBlanc," complete with an actual address in London, a working facsimile number, and a telephone number manned by a person with a British accent. They gathered documents on Walsh. They scripted interview questions and prepped LaBonte exhaustively. In keeping with their guise of recruiting for a fancy, top-notch corporation, Reid delivered to Walsh roundtrip airfare and $300 in cash "in compensation for missing a day's work."[21]

Scene Two: The First "British Pacific" Interview

On June 5, after a month's preparation, Walsh flew to Halifax and arrived at the Citadel Hotel where he met British Pacific executives Kevin Concave (Curry) and Richard LaBlanc (LaBonte). Handing over his business card, Concave introduced himself as "Director of Operations," and LaBlanc as "the man who puts out the fires."[22] Before grilling Walsh on the *Demoulas* case and Judge Lopez, Curry began the interview with chit chat. No doubt hoping to forge a personal connection with Walsh and thereby disarm him, he commented "[w]e're both a pair of Irishmen."[23] Curry further confided, "[t]he

---

19. *Id.*
20. *Id.* at 397.
21. *Id.*
22. O'Neill, *supra* note 607.
23. *Id.*

last guy Reid sent me weighed 300 pounds, had yellow teeth, and a Dutch-boy haircut. You're a good looking guy. We're going to get along."[24]

As the tempo of the interview picked up, Curry weaved an attractive web of lies about the fake job opportunity. But, despite his early attempts to dis-arm Walsh, the clerk grew nervous and began to stutter during the series of questions and answers. Curry, again attempting to put the clerk at ease, in-formed him that they knew he stuttered, and that his stutter did not detract from his attractiveness to British Pacific. They were mainly evaluating candi-dates for this job based on their writing abilities.[25]

Surprised that his interviewers knew such intimate details about him, Walsh asked how they discovered his stutter before talking to him. In re-sponse, Curry showed the clerk a copy of the recommendation letter an at-torney had written for him as part of his Massachusetts bar admissions appli-cation—a letter that mentioned Walsh's stutter. Upon seeing the letter, Walsh shared with his interviewers another detail about it, one that they did not al-ready know, but which they eagerly seized for later use. Walsh confessed to them that the attorney who wrote the recommendation did not actually know him personally. Rather, the attorney did it as a favor for the attorney whom Walsh had originally asked to be a reference, but who had to decline because of a 'conflict of interest.'[26] Why Walsh volunteered such a compro-mising bit of information about himself remains unclear. Perhaps he thought that if Concave had managed to acquire the bar recommendation letter, he must also be privy to the its unethical underpinnings and was asking about it to test Walsh's honesty. Perhaps he just wasn't thinking clearly under the stress of an interview for a job he desired so intensely. Or perhaps he felt that since Concave had painted himself as a bit of a bad boy earlier,[27] he would win points by sharing that he, too, wasn't always a rule abider. Whatever rea-son Walsh had for divulging this sensitive information, Curry and LaBonte were immediately aware of its potential blackmail value, and carefully stored it away for later use.

As the interview continued, Curry steered the topic toward the impor-tance of writing skills, using the same ploy that had earlier worked for Reid.

---

24. *Id.*

25. *Curry*, 880 N.E.2d at 397.

26. In fact, the attorney who Walsh originally asked to write the letter had his license sus-pended at the time and so was unable to serve as an attorney reference. However, Walsh did not know this.

27. During the introductory phase of the interview, Curry told the clerk he had dodged the draft by fleeing to Canada during the Vietnam War. O'Neill, *supra* note 4.

He segued from this job prerequisite into flattery, complimenting Walsh on his 'writing sample,' the *Demoulas* opinion. Concave told Walsh that he had asked British Pacific's outside counsel, Robert Shaw, to review the opinion and that he had been *very* impressed.[28] Further goading Walsh into spilling dirt on the handling of the *Demoulas* litigation, Concave questioned him as to how, while being a mere law clerk, he had managed to write the entire opinion himself. Walsh defended his earlier claim of authorship of the opinion by replying that Judge Lopez was "lazy."[29] According to Curry, Walsh further added that Judge Lopez was biased and that she informed him before the trial began who were the "good guys" and who were the "bad guys," and who "the winners and losers were going to be." (Walsh would later deny making these statements.)[30]

After the interview concluded, all of the parties returned to Boston with buoyant spirits: Walsh, because he believed there was a great job opportunity on his horizon, and Curry and LaBonte, because they believed they had succeeded in coaxing damaging evidence about Judge Lopez's misconduct on the *Demoulas* case out of the unsuspecting clerk.

Eager to share their good news, Curry reported back to Arthur T. as soon as he returned to Boston, arranging to meet Arthur on a hillside near the *Demoulas* headquarters.[31] During their rendezvous, Curry raved about the information he had tricked Walsh into relaying. "I think we got him," Curry bragged. He also told Arthur T. that the clerk had confirmed that he had written the opinion "word for word" and that Judge Lopez told him how to decide the case before the trial concluded.[32] Curry assumed that his anecdotes of the Nova Scotia meeting had bought him another ticket to continue his ride on the Demoulas' family gravy train. He already had earned approximately $140,000 on the case, and he intended to get his hands on even more of the supermarket mogul's money.[33]

---

28. Although almost every word Curry had spoken at this point was a lie, from his fake name, to his false purpose, to the fabricated corporation he supposedly represented, this lie was arguably even more nefarious than the others because it implicated an innocent individual. Robert Shaw, an attorney in a New York law firm and a friend of the Demoulases, had expressly declined any role in the plot. Far from being an accomplice to the conspiracy, Shaw adamantly refused even to lend an empty conference room in his law firm's office in furtherance of the scheme.

29. O'Neill, *supra* note 4.

30. *Curry*, 880 N.E.2d at 398–99.

31. O'Neill, *supra* note 4.

32. *Id.*

33. *Curry*, 880 N.E.2d at 395 n.11.

Gary Crossen Enters Stage Left

Much to Curry's dismay, rather than securing future fees from Arthur T., his performance on the hillside ended up being his denouement in the De-moulas production. Later that same day, Arthur met with his lead counsel in the *Demoulas* litigation, Gary Crossen, to inform him that he had hired Reid and Curry to investigate Judge Lopez. Arthur T. also filled Crossen in on all of the details of the sham interview in Halifax and on the law clerk's confessions about Judge Lopez's judicial misconduct. He wanted Crossen, his trusted advocate, to take over the lead in this sordid affair.[34]

Thus, on June 8, 1997, Gary Crossen, a prominent and well-reputed Boston attorney, replaced Curry as producer and director of the ruse. Crossen, who joined the Massachusetts bar in 1977,[35] had worked hard to create a re-sumé studded with accomplishments. Beginning as a Suffolk County prosecutor who focused on organized crime, he gained even more name recognition in legal circles when he served as a federal prosecutor from 1983 to 1988.[36] During his tenure with the U.S. Attorney's Office, he was promoted to Chief of the General Crimes Division, and later Chief of the Criminal Division.[37] Eventually, however, he decided it was time to move into the private sector and, in 1988, he accepted a position with the venerable firm, Foley, Hoag & Eliot.[38] As a partner at Foley, Crossen specialized in criminal and civil litigation and worked with big name clients. Not only did he represent the Demoulas super market moguls, but he also acted as ethics counsel to two successive Republican governors, William F. Weld and Paul Celluci.[39] In addition to his work at Foley, Crossen maintained a noted presence in the greater Boston community and in the state, serving as Chairman of the Judicial Nominating Commission,[40] and as a member of the Needham School Committee.[41]

When Arthur T. first shared with Crossen the details of Curry's seamy ruse, Crossen voiced concern. He replied that it was both "troubling" and

---

34. *Id.* at 398.

35. *In re* Crossen, 880 N.E.2d 352, 358 (Mass. 2008).

36. *Id.*

37. *Id.*

38. O'Neill, *supra* note 4.

39. Charles A. Radin, *Panel Wants Lawyers Disbarred*, Boston Globe, October 28, 2006, at B1, *available at* http://www.boston.com/news/local/massachusetts/articles/2006/10/28/panel_ wants_lawyers_disbarred/.

40. *Id.*

41. Christina Pazzanese, *Lawyer Won't Quit*, Boston Globe, May 19, 2005, *available at* http://www.boston.com/news/local/massachusetts/articles/2005/05/19/lawyer_wont_quit/.

"significant."[42] One might assume that as a lawyer serving as ethics counsel to two governors, his concern was with the tactics employed by Curry. Sadly, though, this was not the case. Crossen's concern was not related to the *tactics* used by Curry, but rather with the *quality of the information* Curry had extracted. As Crossen later explained, "[I] did not give a whole lot of thought to the issue of the propriety [of Curry's communications with the law clerk]."[43]

Crossen warmed to his lead role quickly. Conveniently, he had a decade's worth of practice running undercover operations for the government, making him perfect for the job. Although Crossen would later try to minimize his part in the elaborate hoax, nonchalantly claiming that he had simply "inherited the ruse,"[44] in fact he vigorously embraced it, employing a battalion of undercover skills in the attack he led on Walsh.

Richard K. Donahue Enters Stage Right

On June 9, Crossen and Arthur T. dragged yet another well-connected and highly esteemed lawyer from the Demoulas defense team into the scheme, Richard K. Donahue. Donahue, former president of the Massachusetts Bar Association, former chairman of the Board of Bar Overseers (the state's attorney disciplinary committee), former president and chief operating officer of Nike and former assistant and close confidant to President Kennedy,[45] had been hired back in 1995 by Telemachus and his wife Irene to coordinate courtroom strategy and handle PR.[46] Unfortunately for Donahue, his spotless reputation was about to be tainted by his pairing with Crossen in a scheme that would eventually result in the downfall of his legal career.

Arthur T. wanted Donahue to brainstorm with him and Crossen about the best ways to use the muck Curry had uncovered on Judge Lopez.[47] As a group, they considered options ranging from filing affidavits with the Commission on Judicial Conduct, to continuing the subterfuge in another one-party consent jurisdiction so that they could secretly tape record the law

---

42. O'Neill, *supra* note 4.

43. *Crossen*, 880 N.E.2d at 359–360.

44. *Id.* at 365.

45. John R. Ellement, *SJC Blasts 2 Lawyers in Ethics Breach*, BOSTON GLOBE, February 7, 2008, *available at* http://www.boston.com/news/local/articles/2008/02/07/sjc_blasts_2_lawyers_for_ethics_breach/.

46. O'Neill, *supra* note 4.

47. *Curry*, 880 N.E.2d at 399.

clerk's comments.[48] Although Donahue questioned the propriety of the entire undertaking, especially the clandestine taping of a meeting with a judge's law clerk, he eventually yielded to Crossen's judgment.[49] Donahue later defended his acquiescence by asserting that Crossen had reassured him with the claim that "he was having [the ethical issues] looked into, and that he was not concerned with it and that basically I shouldn't be."[50]

Scene Three: Walsh's First Call Back Interview

Team Subterfuge Expands

Once the decision to continue the hoax was made, Crossen jumped into action. He immediately instructed an associate at his law firm to research the laws of jurisdictions that permitted one party to record a conversation without the consent of the other party. Specifically, he told the associate to review the one-party recording laws of Canada and Caribbean islands such as Bermuda and the Bahamas. In order to better determine Curry's credibility, Crossen also ordered the associate to investigate Curry's background.[51]

Over the next few days, Crossen consulted with his team on the details of the ruse. The main co-conspirators were Donahue, Curry, Reid, Arthur T., and two new investigators, Stewart Henry, and Joseph McCain. Crossen recruited the latter two men because he had worked with them previously when investigating another misconduct allegation against Judge Lopez—a claim that during the trial she had dined with an attorney representing the opposing branch of the Demoulas family.[52]

The team decided that Walsh's next interview with "British Pacific" would be at the Four Seasons Hotel in New York, another one-party consent jurisdiction. They assumed that they could trick the law clerk into repeating the allegations against Judge Lopez that he had made to Curry, but this time on tape. Once the investigators-posing-as-interviewers succeeded in eliciting these statements from Walsh, the plan was for Crossen to enter the room and aggressively confront him. They would threaten, intimidate, and harass Walsh until he agreed to work with them against the judge.

---

48. *Id.*
49. *Id.*
50. *Crossen*, 880 N.E.2d at 360.
51. *Id.*
52. *Id.*

Before contacting Walsh, the final details of the interview were ironed out by the subterfuge team. Because they decided that Walsh should be told that the upcoming interview would include a "decision-maker" at British Pacific, they needed a new actor. Crossen hired yet another private investigator to fill this role, this time former United States Secret Service Special Agent-in-Charge Peter Rush.[53] The final plan was for Rush, assuming the identity of "Peter O'Hara, General Manager of British Pacific," to conduct the interview of Walsh alongside LaBonte. Crossen and Stewart Henry would monitor the interview from an adjoining room.[54] From this observation post, Crossen, and Crossen alone, intended to make the decision as to whether the law clerk uttered the "magic words" that would trigger the confrontation.[55] As for Curry, he had been officially written out of the script—he was not invited to accompany the team to New York at all.[56]

Notably, for the *second* time since Crossen took command of the ruse, a member of his team voiced concern regarding the tactics proposed. This time it was Rush, the newest recruit. The former Secret Service agent specifically inquired "whether the New York interview was ethical and legal," before agreeing to participate. He was "particularly concerned to know whether it was permissible for him, as a private citizen, to conduct a sham interview with the law clerk, another private citizen." According to Rush, Crossen assuaged his concerns by responding that "[he] had researched the ethics of it and that it was legal." Rush further testified that Crossen had compounded this first lie with another false reassurance, again in Rush's words, that "it's been cleared by ethics." In this manner, Rush was led to believe that Crossen's firm had an ethics committee that had reviewed and blessed the scenario. Based on Crossen's misrepresentations, Rush prepared to fly to New York for the sham interview.[57]

Reid, the original "headhunter" who contacted Walsh, slipped into his professional job consultant persona yet again. This time, he called Walsh to share exciting news: Kevin Concave and Richard LaBlanc had been so impressed with Walsh in Halifax that British Pacific wanted to fly him to New York to meet with a "decision maker."[58] The interview, Reid assured, would be first class all of the way. For the second time, Reid delivered round trip air-

---

53. *Crossen*, 880 N.E.2d at 361.

54. *Curry*, 880 N.E.2d at 400.

55. *Crossen*, 880 N.E.2d at 361 n.11.

56. *Curry*, 880 N.E.2d at 400.

57. *Crossen*, 880 N.E.2d at 361–62.

58. *Id.*

plane tickets and cash to Walsh, telling him to look out for the chauffeur who would be waiting for him at La Guardia airport.[59] Less than two weeks from the day of the Halifax interview, Walsh's first meeting with the "client," he had received the callback interview he had eagerly anticipated.

Welcome to New York

On June 17, the driver of a black Mercedes limousine greeted Walsh at New York's La Guardia airport and drove him to the Four Seasons. Rush, introducing himself as "Peter O' Hara, General Manager of British Pacific," handed over a business card that matched the others Walsh had received. He then launched into tales about British Pacific, all of which sounded great, and all of which were one hundred percent fabricated. He explained the nature of the company and its reinsurance business, stating, "some of the risks we have out there, particularly the maritime risks are just huge, and we're growing, we've been expanding into ah, ah Europe, and parts of Europe that been behind the ah, you know, the iron curtain for years and there's new opportunities out there, there's going to be a lot of travel, but there's going to be great opportunities."[60]

Rush then maneuvered the conversation toward what he called the "Demopolis" case by using the segue strategy that Curry and Reid had perfected —flattery aimed at Walsh's writing skills. O'Hara congratulated Walsh, telling him that Robert Shaw, the lawyer Curry had falsely presented as "British Pacific's outside counsel" in Halifax, had been "very laudatory" about the law clerk's writing ability. Walsh patted himself on the back once again by telling his interviewers that he wrote the decision on his own. But, this time, he added an unexpected caveat. He explained to his interviewers that he was able to write the opinion on his own because he had attended the whole trial, and Judge Lopez had deliberated with him about the witnesses at the end of each day. This remark, among others Walsh made throughout the interview concerning Judge Lopez's predisposition, were decidedly more equivocal and weaker than what Curry had represented Walsh's Halifax remarks to be.

For example, although Walsh stated, "She probably knew from the start who was going to win...," the conversation continued:

Rush: Did she really?

Walsh: I, I, dunno. I mean she had seen an earlier trial with the
            same ... people.... I think that the evidence and the

---

59. O'Neill, *supra* note 4.

60. *Crossen*, 880 N.E.2d at 362 n.20.

correspondence over the … years, … just showed … who was telling the truth, and who's lying.

Rush: So [Judge Lopez], she had been the Judge in the first trial and she was just waiting to take to take a piece out of 'em in the second trial (laughs).

LaBonte: And when this [trial] ends you spent 84 days (laugh). Listening to what was already known or felt …

Walsh: Well you know …

LaBonte: … predetermined.

Walsh: I don't, I don't, I don't, know if it was predetermined so … I'd like to think that she kept some sense of, of open-mindedness.… She, she, um probably prior to the, to the trial starting. But, ah, as I said, I felt she kinda kept somewhat of an open mind, so …

Rush: And, and she just told you from the get go … who's the good guys, and who's the bad guys and allow you to write the opinion.

Walsh: Yeah, yeah and support it.[61]

Although Rush had gleaned one apparently helpful comment from Walsh, overall the team had failed to get any firm, unequivocal confession about Judge Lopez's predisposition and misconduct in the *Demoulas* case. Moreover, because the law clerk dissolved into such a stuttering wreck during the inter-rogative portion of the interview, Crossen decided not to give the order to confront him. In fact, Walsh's obvious mental distress caused LaBonte to step out of the interview room and sneak into the adjoining room where Crossen was listening and watching to warn him that "bracing" Walsh "would give the law clerk a 'heart attack.'"[62] Thus, after an hour and a half of questions, Rush concluded the interview and sent a nervous Walsh back to Boston.

NYC Fallout: Warning Bells Ring

Crossen reviewed the tape before calling Arthur T. He relayed to his client that the interview "was a mixed bag," and that he had not braced the law clerk.

---

61. *Id.*
62. *Id.* at 363.

Once he flew back to Boston, he set up a meeting with his investigators Henry and McCain, and with Edward Barshak and Susan Hartnett, two other lawyers on the Demoulas family defense team, both of whom were partners at another Boston law firm. At this meeting, Crossen told them about the sham interview. Their immediate response centered on the ethics of such a ruse. Thus, for the third time, a question was raised about the seemingly unethical nature of the scheme. Crossen responded that he would look into the matter.

Surprisingly, this time Crossen did take the ethical concern seriously enough to look into the issue. On June 20, he asked an associate at his firm to research the propriety of speaking with a former law clerk. However, Crossen did *not* take the ethical concern seriously enough to change his course of action. The associate got back to him later that same day to report that "although he had been unable to find an explicit ban on contacts with former law clerks, a limited privilege may prevail between judges and their clerks, and that even absent such privilege, policy arguments disfavored such contacts." Crossen ignored these findings. And, equally significant, he chose not to probe any further.[63]

June 20, 1997, was a notable date for those entangled in the Demoulas affair for another reason as well. On that date, pursuant to Judge Lopez's order, the long delayed merger of the Demoulas supermarket assets took place. This merger transferred 51% of the stock in the business from Telemachus' family back to rival George Demoulas's family. The stock transfer was valued at upwards of half a billion dollars. Arthur T. wanted something done, and fast.

On June 23, at least a dozen lawyers, all from the most premier Boston law firms, convened to review a motion Barshak had prepared requesting Judge Lopez to recuse herself from the case. At this meeting, which stretched over two and a half hours, many of the lawyers present heard about the Walsh ruse for the first time. While Arthur T. did the explaining, Crossen distributed transcripts of the New York interview with Walsh to the roundtable of attorneys. For the fourth time in this sordid tale, questions were raised about the ethics of the tactics. Barshak, John P. Sullivan, Judith Dein, and Samuel Adams all expressed doubt about the propriety of the conduct and contended that any details of Lopez's misconduct that came from the manipulation of Walsh was "worthless or should not be pursued further." Dein directly asked Crossen "whether it was ethical to 'approach a law clerk who had been on a case you tried." As had become his habit, Crossen reassuringly replied, "[we] had researched that, and, while [there were] issues that related to approach-

---

63. *Id.* at 363–364.

ing a juror, that prohibition did not relate to a law clerk." Crossen then reemphasized his opinion that the material from Walsh was "persuasive" and should be incorporated into the recusal motion.[64] Despite Crossen's recommendation, the majority of the group voted to exclude all of the information obtained from Walsh from the motion and base the request for recusal on unrelated grounds. Almost a month later, Judge Lopez heard and subsequently denied the motion.[65]

Scene Four: Walsh's Second Call Back Interview

Nevertheless, the plot continued to thicken. Despite the other attorneys' insistence that the scheming needed to stop, Arthur T. and Crossen left the recusal motion emergency meeting still hungering for a coup de grâce from Walsh. Arthur T. privately instructed Crossen and Donahue that "he did not want to let the law clerk matter drop." Crossen then proposed the next "logical step"—to set up another encounter with the law clerk, but this time hit him with the truth. Crossen envisioned luring the law clerk back with a final "big pitch" interview and then confronting him with the ruse as well as the consequences of not cooperating with them. Donahue, unable to shake his ethical concerns, approached Arthur T. separately to warn him that Barshak threatened to walk away from the defense team if any of the Walsh material was used. This threat did not deter Arthur T., and its only consequence was that Crossen and Donahue kept all of their future interactions with Walsh concealed from Barshak and Adams.[66]

In accordance with the plan, another Four Seasons hotel room was booked, this time in Boston, for the final "interview." Curry, invited back onto the team, met with the others in Crossen's offices the day before. They decided that the strategy for this last meeting with Walsh should be more of a "free-form interview" designed to "(1) apprise the law clerk of the ruse, (2) serve to determine whether the law clerk would verify the statements attributed to him in Halifax and parts of his New York interview, and (3) gauge the law clerk's willingness to cooperate with defendants' counsel by confirming the statements in an affidavit or otherwise." They also agreed that it would be prudent to place the law clerk under surveillance after the interview in case he attempted to contact either Judge Lopez or opposing counsel.[67]

---

64. *Id.*
65. *Id.*
66. *Id.*
67. *Id.* at 365.

Walsh, both thrilled and nervous, arrived for his final interview dressed in a blue Brooks Brothers suit, one he had bought for the occasion. He arrived early, allowing himself time to rest and gather his thoughts on a bench in the nearby Public Garden. This was it, he thought to himself, he was about to land the job of a lifetime.[68] Just a few minutes later, Walsh was led into the suite in the Four Seasons. Rush greeted him there, and advised him "to listen carefully because he would hear something that would send him on the 'rollercoaster of [his] life' and elicit a range of emotions and 'concern for the future.' But, Rush added, "if you cooperate with us, it will be okay." [69] Rush then told Walsh another fantastic tale, only this time it was the truth. It was the story about how he had been duped.

While Walsh wrestled with the shock from the news, Rush introduced Crossen and Donahue as they entered the suite. His head still spinning, realizations began to strike Walsh like lightning. "No British Pacific? No Peter O' Hara? No job? And just what had he said during those earlier meetings?"[70] The bar application letter! But that was so long ago, could that really harm him now?[71] The prominent veteran attorneys, who had trapped him in this room and in this situation, sure appeared to think so. Crossen, using a good-cop/bad-cop routine, warned Walsh that he could not prevent his clients from using the 'information' they had gathered. His words, according to Walsh, were that if Walsh "did not 'help him' there would be a 'missile' fired 'that's out of my control, and it's off, and I don't know where it goes and what it ends up doing.'" To save Walsh from this missile, Crossen needed to have a "candid conversation" with him "about what really happened here."[72] "We are here to get to the truth [about Lopez]," Crossen emphasized.[73]

Walsh, furious about the squalid tricks played on him, started shouting at Crossen. He was disgusted that a lawyer of Crossen's stature, experience, and background did "nothing to stop the chicanery." Crossen defended himself by stating that he had simply "inherited the ruse"; by the time he arrived on the scene it was out of his control. He also distanced himself from the deceitful tactic of surreptitiously taping the interviews by insinuating that there had been nothing he could do to stop it.

---

68. O'Neill, *supra* note 4.
69. *Crossen,* 880 N.E.2d at 365.
70. O'Neill, *supra* note 4.
71. *Id.*
72. *Crossen,* 880 N.E.2d at 365.
73. O'Neill, *supra* note 4.

Donahue then explicitly laid out for Walsh what had been implied by Crossen—that "if he didn't cooperate with them, the false letter submitted with his bar application would be made public." As they all knew, submitting such false information with an application for admission to the bar was grounds for discipline in Massachusetts. Standing strong in the face of these threats, Walsh contended that he had been "puffing" in the earlier interviews. He informed them that he had not written the entire *Demoulas* opinion and that their clients had received a fair trial in the *Demoulas* case. He further refused to be questioned about Judge Lopez's supposed predisposition.[74]

After another string of threats, Walsh got up to leave. "B-b-bastards!" he shouted at them on his way out the door.[75] As Walsh walked out, a small remnant of professionally responsible conduct surfaced in Crossen. He advised his victim to "retain a lawyer."[76]

Scene Five: The Unraveling—Walsh Fights Back

Now a nervous wreck, Walsh returned to his own firm. He looked so dejected and distraught on his walk through the streets of Boston that McCain, Crossen's crony on surveillance duty, worried that he was suicidal.[77]

Once Walsh reached his own offices he went straight into an empty conference room to be alone. To his embarrassment, that was where Robert Sullivan, the founder of his firm, eventually found him crying.[78]

However embarrassing this moment was, it ended up being the turning point in his crumbling world. Sullivan rapidly sprung into action, getting the best attorney he could think of on the phone: Harry Manion.[79]

Later that same day, Walsh met Manion, founding partner of Cooley Manion Jones, a well respected Boston firm. They talked at Manion's poolside cabana in his back yard—a peaceful setting by any standard. However, the serenity was not enough to calm the distressed clerk. Not only had he just been told that he was going to be blackmailed with information that could cost him his career, but he and his wife had discovered that they were being followed. Guys dressed in Hawaiian shirts with oversized cell phones seemed

---

74. *Crossen*, 880 N.E.2d at 366.
75. O'Neill, *supra* note 4.
76. *Crossen*, 880 N.E.2d at 366.
77. *Id.*
78. *Id.*
79. O'Neill, *supra* note 4.

to be hanging around his apartment, and a "delivery man" had appeared at his home with a pizza that neither he nor his wife had ordered. Crossen was trying to intimidate him, and it was working.[80]

Eventually, Manion succeeded in calming Walsh down. Once he got the clerk to a state of mind in which he could make decisions, he gave him his two choices. "Do nothing and hope it goes away. Or strike back." Walsh chose the latter. Recalling this moment later, Walsh remarked, "Shit, they were going to run me over. I decided ... not to let them."[81]

Before taking on the fight, Manion wanted to make sure that he knew everything. He considered the bar letter and interview puffing that Crossen was holding over Walsh's head to be small potatoes. But before moving forward, Manion needed to know if there was anything else out there, something more damaging to the clerk. "Are there skeletons in the closet to worry about here?" he asked. "I need to know: You got a broad stashed? Doing coke in clubs? I gotta know because they are going to use it against you. They're ruthless and enormously well-financed."

"You're looking at what you've got," Walsh promised. "There's nothing. Some high school beer-drinking. That's it. I can handle anything they've got."

"No turning back," Manion cautioned. "Once the toothpaste is out of the tube, no 'fuhgeddaboudits.' It's become a very serious assault on a sitting judge."[82]

That same weekend, Manion contacted the U.S. Attorney's office. Mark Pearlstein, then first assistant U.S. attorney, directed him to the FBI. By Monday morning, Manion had Walsh discussing the situation with Federal agents. After listening to Walsh and reading through the affidavits that he had prepared for them, the agents explained that there was not enough evidence to make a case. If Walsh wanted to move forward, they told him, he would have to get Crossen to threaten him again, and admit that he had tapes, on record. This time, if Walsh agreed to do it, *he* was going to need to be the one wired. Walsh agreed.

On August 20, Walsh met with Crossen in Foley Hoag's offices. This time, *Walsh* was the one with the body recorder, and *Walsh* was the one making statements artfully designed to elicit specific incriminating responses.[83]

"I think what you guys did to me is despicable, I just couldn't imagine doing something like that to another attorney. If in fact you do have tapes ...

---

80. *Id.*
81. *Id.*
82. *Id.*
83. *Id.*

then I probably am ruined. And I wanna hear what's on the tapes before I can make any kind of decision."

"At some point in time you oughta hear the tapes. Today is not that point in time," replied Crossen.

But soon, Walsh had Crossen where he needed him. "Well, you may not like the way we approached this, but … that's life in the fast lane, Paul.… What I want is a candid conversation with you about, ahem, the predisposition issue … that she decided the case in advance. That's what I want."

Walsh waited patiently, knowing that the threat would follow eventually, just as it had before. And then it came. "If there is a way for Paul Walsh to deal with this, that's, that's, ahem … not harmful to your career, it probably is for you to have the candid conversation with me … an acknowledgement that the judge was way out in front on a determination of the facts here, that she predetermined it."[84] Otherwise, Crossen warned, "the client … might direct the attorney's to use the information [i.e., the tapes] at or before the Appeals Court hearing."[85]

Walsh, now armed with hard proof that Gary Crossen had threatened him, needed to get just one more thing. The other bit of proof that the FBI wanted, proof that tapes of the sham interview existed. Unfortunately, though, this meeting had turned to stalemate. He'd have to try again later.[86] Across the next two days, the deadlock continued during a series of phone calls that went back and forth. Walsh continued to demand to hear the supposed tapes, and Crossen continued to counter with his demand that the clerk publicly accuse Judge Lopez of maintaining a bias throughout the *Demoulas* litigation.

Finally, Crossen caved. He agreed to let the clerk hear a "small segment" of the taped New York interview to prove to him that he had tapes. Coincidentally, the "small segment" that Crossen decided to play for Walsh was the portion in which Walsh foolishly mentioned that his bar recommendation letter contained false information. This was the exact piece of intelligence that Crossen was using to blackmail him. Crossen would later claim that he and Donahue chose this three minute segment from the two and a half hour interview because it "did not involve a matter of substance." In any event, on August 22, Walsh arrived at Crossen's office to hear the tape, wearing an FBI wire. Crossen, Donahue, and McCain played the tape, watching his reaction for signs of defeat.

"You've got tapes," Walsh acknowledged.

---

84. *Id.*
85. *Crossen*, 880 N.E.2d at 367.
86. *Id.*

"We've got tapes," Crossen replied, ignorant to the nail he had just ham-mered into his career's coffin. And believing that he had the upper hand, Crossen threw another daggered innuendo at Walsh. "We're on a fast moving train here … [and] the train is ready to pull out of the station," he said.[87]

The meeting soon concluded, but not before Crossen managed to add yet another veiled threat. "Um, I'm gonna respectfully suggest to you, okay, that you try to block out Monday and come visit us." Walsh acquiesced and walked out the door.[88]

When Monday[89] rolled around, Walsh didn't show up for the scheduled meeting. Instead, he left a voice message for Crossen, claiming that he was out of town. Crossen, angry at being stood up, became even angrier when the investigator tailing Walsh relayed to him that Walsh was actually in Boston that day. He called Walsh, got no answer, and left a message.[90]

Walsh waited until the next day to return the call. When he did, Crossen informed him that he was "a little bit angry" that the law clerk had lied to him about being out of town. Walsh, equally angry, reproached Crossen for put-ting him under surveillance. Crossen quickly denied having Walsh followed, but cautioned "if we don't get something done before" Thursday, he was not "optimistic" that the client "won't insist upon me dropping the hammer, if you will." Resorting to his good cop, bad cop trick yet again, Crossen claimed that he could "no longer keep his client [reined] in."[91]

The Finale

Four days later, on August 29, 1997, the FBI served grand jury subpoenas on McCain, LaBonte, Rush, and Reid.[92] On this same day, Crossen learned that he, too, was the subject of an FBI investigation. But, curiously, no subpoena was ever served on Crossen, the ringleader of the affair, or Curry, its instigator. Indeed, in contrast to the investigators, none of the lawyers connected to the scheme was ever subpoenaed or indicted. Instead, their cases appeared to be mired in bureaucratic tape for years. First, U.S. Attorney Donald Stern recused

---

87. *Id.* at 367–68.
88. O'Neill, *supra* note 4.
89. August 25, 1997.
90. *Crossen*, 880 N.E.2d at 368.
91. *Id.*
92. *Id.*

himself because Crossen had formerly held a high position in the office. Next, the cases got sent to the Department of Justice (DOJ) in Washington, where they seemingly stalled. Though no one knows why, perhaps the fate of the attorneys had something to do with their prior stature in the community. For example, former U.S. Attorney Wayne Budd, former Suffolk County DA Ralph Martin, and Governor Weld of Massachusetts each sent a letter to DOJ on Crossen's behalf. According to Weld, Crossen was "the greatest and the straightest."[93] Eventually, in 2001, the cases were officially dropped when Janet Reno declined to prosecute them in her last days in office.[94]

Fortunately for justice's sake, Crossen, Curry, and Donahue did not get away scot-free. In January 2002, the Massachusetts Office of Bar Counsel filed a three-count petition for discipline against the three attorneys. In Massachusetts, disciplinary matters are investigated and prosecuted by the Office of Bar Counsel, then reviewed by the Board of Bar Overseers (BBO). If the alleged misconduct is grave, a hearing process takes place and a report of the hearing is sent to the BBO along with a recommendation for discipline. The BBO has the discretion to accept or modify the recommendation, and can even hold hearings of its own.[95] Before the punishment goes into effect, it must be approved by a single justice of the Supreme Judicial Court.[96]

In this case, the degree of the alleged misconduct undeniably warranted a special hearing. The BBO appointed M. Ellen Carpenter, a top bankruptcy lawyer and former bar association president,[97] as the special hearing officer. After presiding over 24 days of hearings that involved 21 witnesses, 177 documents, and spanned across an 18 month time period, Carpenter issued her report on May 11, 2005. In a searing 229 page ruling, she denounced Curry, Crossen, and Donahue for their misconduct, describing their "seamy ruse" as a "Potemkin village [created] to gull Walsh into believing he was about to land the job of his dreams."[98] She recommended disbarment for all three lawyers. "I have found no case that deals with facts remotely like those at issue

---

93. *Id.*

94. *Id.*

95. Mass. Bar Assoc., Lawyer and Judicial Discipline, *at* http://www.massbar.org/3798.

96. *Id.*

97. Bryan Marquard, *M. Ellen Carpenter, 52, Top Bankruptcy Lawyer*, Boston Globe, December 12, 2006 *available at* http://www.boston.com/news/globe/obituaries/articles/2006/12/12/m_ellen_carpenter_52_top_bankruptcy_lawyer/.

98. Jonathon Saltzman & Ralph Ranalli, *Disbarrment Urged for 3 in Scheme*, Boston Globe, May 13, 2005 *available at* http://www.boston.com/news/local/massachusetts/articles/2005/05/13/disbarment_urged_for_3_in_scheme/.

in this sordid affair.... [These lawyers] have left what one can only hope is not an indelible impression that lawyers, even very prominent ones, will do almost anything to prevail if money is at stake...."[99] She particularly berated the seasoned attorneys for focusing their plot on Walsh, a "young, innocent, and vulnerable victim" and "treating the young lawyer like some cornered junkie from one of Crossen's criminal cases."[100]

Specifically, Carpenter found that, by (1) planning, executing, and participating in a scheme that lured a former law clerk into his clutches under false pretenses; (2) taping secret conversations with the clerk; (3) attempting to force the law clerk into stating under oath that Judge Lopez had predetermined the *Demoulas* stockholder derivative trial; and (4) denying the law clerk's accurate accusation that he was having him followed, Crossen had violated Canon 1, DR 1-102(A)(2), (4)–(6) and Canon 7, DR 7-102(A)(4)– (7)[101] of the then applicable *Canons of Ethics and Disciplinary Rules Regulating the Practice of Law.*[102]

Carpenter similarly determined that Curry was guilty of violating all of the same Canons, except for DR 7-102(A)(4) and (5)—which were implicated by Crossen's lies to Walsh about the surveillance. She found that Curry had violated his ethical duties by concocting and participating in a scheme to manipulate a former law clerk into disclosing confidential communications with a judge regarding the specifics of a case, by falsely representing his identity and that of his associates, by luring the clerk under false pretenses out of the state in an effort to pry confidential communications from him, and by manipulating the clerk into making damaging statements about a judge intended to force the judge's recusal. Carpenter was especially disturbed by the fact that Curry "viewed his misconduct as business as usual.... This was, he informed me, the kind of investigation he and [a private detective] generally conducted—dredging, as it turns out, for scandalous information and cultivating scurrilous charges to use against others when it suited his purposes."[103]

Crossen, Curry, and Donahue's lawyers all responded to Carpenter's recommendation by maintaining that their clients had done nothing wrong. In

---

99. *Id.*

100. *Id.*

101. *Crossen*, 880 N.E.2d at 368–69.

102. *Curry*, 880 N.E.2d at 401 n.23. The outdated Canons and Disciplinary Rules are cross-referenced with the new Massachusetts Rules of Professional Conduct in Comment 1 following the conclusion of this chapter.

103. Saltzman & Ranalli, *supra* note 98.

fact, according to the lawyers representing the chastised attorneys, their clients' conduct *aligned with* the ethical code. Crossen, Curry, and Donahue's actions simply fulfilled their duty to "zealously represent their clients' interests."[104] "This is one hearing officer's opinion," commented Thomas Kiley, Curry's counsel, "and we obviously disagree with it." Crossen himself vowed, "I will vigorously fight this ruling, which has no legal impact on my current ability to practice law. I believe the ruling is gravely and fundamentally flawed."[105]

Unfortunately for them, the Board of Bar Overseers agreed with Carpenter. After conducting its own hearings, the Board unanimously endorsed the hearing officer's findings. It also approved her disciplinary recommendation of disbarment for Curry[106] and Crossen. For Donahue, however, the Board blunted the blow. Noting Donahue's lesser role in the scheme, it determined that a three year suspension was more appropriate than disbarment.[107]

On February 6, 2008, the Supreme Judicial Court of Massachusetts unanimously adopted the Board's recommendations. Particularly colorful in his commentary on the decision to disbar Crossen, Chief Justice Marshall wrote,

> The record leaves no doubt that Crossen was a willing participant, and at times a driving force, in a web of false, deceptive, and threatening behavior designed to impugn the integrity of a sitting judge in order to obtain a result favorable to his clients. The scope of this misconduct has scant parallel in the disciplinary proceedings of this Commonwealth. This was not conduct on the uncertain border between zealous advocacy and dishonorable tactics, a border about which reasonably minds may differ. It struck at the heart of the lawyer's professional obligations of good faith and honesty.[108]

Crossen's response? Defending his actions to the end, he stated, "I disagree with the result.... I tried to get to the truth about a very serious allegation of judicial misconduct. That was what we attempted to do."

---

104. Ralph Ranalli, *For Demoulas Case Clerk, Vindication*, BOSTON GLOBE, May 16, 2005, *available at* http://www.boston.com/news/local/articles/2005/05/16/for_demoulas_case_clerk_vindication/.

105. Saltzman & Ranalli, *supra* note 98.

106. *Curry*, 880 N.E.2d at 401.

107. Radin, *supra* note 39.

108. *Crossen*, 880 N.E.2d at 357.

Postscript

Since their disbarment, Curry, Crossen, and Donahue have kept low profiles. Crossen professed an intent to concentrate his energies in the coming years in the business sector.[109]

Ironically, Paul Walsh succeeded in landing his dream job, a job that mirrored the fictional one with which Curry and Crossen had teased him. By 2000, he lived and worked in Hong Kong as Far East counsel for a Needham based software company. He and his wife remained happily married with three young sons.

Ironically, Judge Lopez resigned from the bench in 2003, in the midst of an investigation into alleged judicial misconduct. The Massachusetts Commission on Judicial Conduct claimed that Lopez had engaged in a pattern of conduct that was prejudicial to the administration of justice and unbecoming a judicial officer. These accusations, unrelated to her actions and behavior in the *Demoulas* case, stemmed from a case in which she sentenced a transgendered defendant who pled guilty to the kidnapping and sexual assault of an 11-year-old boy to probation. Although a public outcry arose over the lax punishment handed out, the investigation by the Commission focused on her outbursts against the ADA in the case. It questioned whether she abused her power and had the temperament to serve on the bench. The review concluded that Lopez lied under oath and showed bias against prosecutors. Rather than accept her sentence of a six month suspension and a public apology, Lopez resigned from the bench. In a letter addressed to the chief justice she claimed that her admonishment of the ADA was normal and appropriate because of the "media circus" he created.[110]

Lopez did not, however, stay unemployed for long. In 2005, she joined the ranks of Judge Judy with her own syndicated show, which had two successful seasons before going off the air. "She's got an explosive personality and something to say," said Thompson, her LA agent. According to the Boston Globe, the deal just for the pilot was six figures.[111]

As for M. Ellen Carpenter, the special hearing officer who made the initial findings and disbarment recommendation for Curry, Crossen, and Donahue, she passed away just six months after issuing her report.

---

109. Ellement, *supra* note 45.

110. *Judge Maria Lopez Resigns: Judge Was Scheduled for Hearing on June 10*, WCVBTV.COM, May 19, 2003, *at* http://www.thebostonchannel.com/news/2213417/detail.html.

111. Joanna Weiss, *TV Viewers Will be Able to Rule on Lopez*, BOSTON GLOBE, November 1, 2005, *available at* http://www.boston.com/ae/tv/articles/2005/11/01/tv_viewers_will_be_able_to_rule_on_lopez/.

Comments and Questions

1. The Canons that the special hearing officer, Board of Bar Overseers, and ultimately the Supreme Judicial Court of Massachusetts found Curry and Crossen to have violated correspond to Rules 3.3, 3.4, 4.1, 4.4, and 8.4 of the Massachusetts Rules of Professional Conduct,[112] the contemporary standard of ethics governing Massachusetts lawyers since its adoption in 1998. The Massachusetts Rules are based upon, and are more or less consistent with, the ABA's Model Rules of Professional Conduct (Model Rules).[113] With respect to the rules that Curry and Crossen violated, Rule 4.1 ("truthfulness in statements to others") and Rule 4.4, ("respect for rights of third persons") are identical to their Model Rule counterparts, whereas rules 3.3, 3.4, and 8.4 are slightly modified from the original.

2. An addition that Massachusetts made to its version of Model Rule 3.4 ("fairness to opposing party and counsel") seems to be relevant to Crossen's ethical breaches, even though neither the special hearing officer nor the Court referenced the corresponding provision in the old Cannons. This addition, subsection (h), states that a lawyer shall not "present, participate in presenting, or threaten to present criminal or disciplinary charges solely to obtain an advantage in a private civil matter."[114] It would seem that Crossen directly violated this prohibition when he threatened to disclose Walsh's false bar recommendation if he did not cooperate. Instead, the special hearing officer found that Crossen's actions violated the equivalent of Model Rule 3.4(b), which states that a "lawyer shall not ... assist a witness to testify falsely, or offer an inducement to a witness that is prohibited by law." Why do you think this subsection of the rule was used instead? An oversight?

3. Rule 8.4, the general misconduct rule, is the last rule that corresponds to the canons that Curry and Crossen were held to have violated. Specifically, Curry and Crossen violated the equivalent of Rule 8.4(a), (b), (c), (d), and (h). Subsection (h) is the only portion of this rule that does not mirror the analogous Model Rule; however, it is only a very general catchall that forbids a lawyer from "engag[ing] in any other conduct that adversely reflects on his or her fitness to practice law."[115] Although one could imagine situations in

---

112. The Massachusetts Rules of Professional Conduct can be found at http://www.mass.gov/obcbbo/rpcnet.htm.

113. *Curry*, 880 N.E.2d at 401 n.23.

114. MASS. RULES OF PROF'L CONDUCT R. 3.4(h), *available at* http://www.mass.gov/obcbbo/rpc3.htm#Rule%203.4.

115. *Id.* R. 8.4(h).

which a lawyer's misconduct may not precisely fit into the other subsections of 8.4, making subsection (h) necessary to render a sanction, this is not one of them. The behavior of Curry, Crossen, and Donahue very clearly fit into many specifically forbidden areas of misconduct, making the application of subsection (h) to this case superfluous.

4. Did some of the lawyers in this affair engage in ethical violations that were overlooked by the disciplinary authorities? Consider Curry's very first action—writing a letter to Telemachus Demoulas asking to meet about his case. Did this violate Model Rule 7.3(c) regarding the solicitation of clients? What about Curry's apparently unsupported comments that Judge Lopez was corrupt? Check out Model Rule 8.2. Finally, a number of lawyers who found out what was going on refused to participate in the shenanigans, to their credit. But didn't they all violate Model Rule 8.3(a), which requires a lawyer who witnesses professional misconduct to report it? Is there plausible explanation for why these violations were not addressed by the officials or the Court?

5. Crossen and Curry put careful thought into the locations they chose for their respective sham interviews of Walsh because they wanted to make sure that the tapings were legal. Later, Crossen would argue that the legality of what they were doing meant that it could not be unethical. This argument fell on deaf ears. The disciplinary authorities decided, in effect, that lawyers are sometimes held to a higher standard than the law allows. Does this make sense? Is it fair?

6. Curry and Crossen's ruse bears shades of resemblance to "sting" operations carried out by federal prosecutors. In fact, as mentioned earlier, Crossen likely learned many of the tactics he used with Walsh during the years he prosecuted organized crime on behalf of the government. Further, Crossen even raised this as a defense to the charges against him claiming "he reasonably believed at the time that as a private attorney he was empowered to use the same investigative techniques that would have been available to government attorneys." However, Chief Judge Marshall shot down this argument, highlighting an essential difference between the two. "The critical factor distinguishing government and private attorneys is the lack of oversight for the latter. Whatever leeway government attorneys are permitted in conducting investigations, they are subject not only to ethical constraints but also to supervisory oversight and constitutional limits[,] ... constraints that do not apply to private attorneys representing private clients."[116] Do you think this is a legitimate distinction? Are there any additional reasons why government prosecutors should get more leeway to supervise undercover stings than private counsel?

---

116. *Crossen*, 880 N.E.2d at 377–80.

Chapter 9

The Nefarious "Zinkster"[1]

"A signed baseball by a football player doesn't mean anything to me."
—Panel Judge, Oral Arguments, *In re Brian Zink*

This chapter considers the sometimes fine line between zealous advocacy and illicit conduct, and explores how a "joke" between friends can escalate into a conflict of interest between a prosecutor's personal desires and his professional duties. It is, in the end, a sordid tale of bribery and lies.

The "Negotiation"

In May 2006, Mary Hart was charged with three counts of felony forgery in the Circuit Court of St. Charles County, Missouri. Hart contacted attorney and named partner David Dalton II of the Lake St. Louis law firm of Dalton Coyne Cundiff & Hillemann, P.C. Dalton had previously represented Hart in an unrelated civil matter, so Hart was familiar with him. Dalton took Hart's case, retained supervisory authority over it, and assigned it to fifth-year associate Brian Zink because of Zink's expertise in criminal defense.

The case against Hart was assigned to Charles County Assistant Prosecutor Matthew Thornhill.[2] Long before this case was initiated, Zink and Thornhill had established a friendship that extended well beyond their professional relationship.[3] Even when they interacted in a professional capacity, their communications were often very casual. For example, the letter that Thornhill wrote to Zink communicating his initial sentencing recommendation for Hart opened with the salutation "Dear Zinkster."[4] Despite this familiarity,

---

1. This chapter is based on the original research and writing of **Loren J. Beer.**
2. *See* Mo. Sup. Ct. Disciplinary Hearing at 2, *In re* Zink, Jan. 7, 2009 (No. SC89623) (whole paragraph).
3. Thornhill even had Zink's picture hanging on the wall in his office from a golf tournament in which the two had played together.
4. Letter from Matthew Thornhill, Assistant Prosecuting Attorney, St. Charles County, to Brian Zink, Attorney, Dalton, Coyne, Cundiff & Hilleman (Jun. 16, 2009) (on file with author).

Thornhill's position on the proper outcome of the case was tough. He informed his friend that he opposed probation for Hart and was going to recommend a six year jail sentence. If Hart were to obtain a probationary sentence despite his recommendation, Thornhill told Zink that he would ask for five years of intensive supervision preceded by sixty days "shock treatment" in the county jail, as well as restitution and court costs. The letter closed with the invitation: "If you have any questions, please give me a jingle."

Zink rejected Thornhill's offer as unduly "severe." He told Thornhill that Hart had cooperated with the St. Charles County Regional Drug Task Force.[5] Hart's cooperation, Zink maintained, was significant and should be considered as a mitigating factor on her behalf. Thornhill responded: "You know, I don't really care about that; most of the people I'm dealing with say they have done some work with the Drug Task Force, so that is not going to get you a whole lot of mileage, Brian."[6] Thornhill then revealed that Major Jeff Finkelstein, a supervising officer of the Drug Task Force, had authored a memorandum for Hart's case file that instructed Thornhill not to grant Hart any leniency.[7]

Seeing that the plea negotiations were going nowhere, Zink opted for an alternate approach. Playing on his friend's love for sports, Zink told Thornhill that retired Pittsburgh Steelers quarterback, Terry Bradshaw, was Hart's godfather. In the same breath, Zink suggested that this relationship should be a basis for a reduction in Hart's sentence. Rather than responding negatively to Zink's insinuation, Thornhill expressed disbelief that Hart and Bradshaw were related. The two argued back and forth about Hart's claim until Thornhill suggested a method of verifying it.[8] The conversation continued:

Thornhill: If you are so convinced Brian, I tell you what, why don't you have Terry Bradshaw autograph a baseball and send it down here as confirmation....

Zink: You got it. Consider it done.[9]

Perhaps not so coincidentally, at the time of this negotiation, Thornhill had a variety of sports memorabilia in his office, including a collection of au-

---

5. Disciplinary Panel Hearing Decision at 3, *In re* Thornhill, Jul. 3, 2009 (No. SC89421).

6. Transcript of Disciplinary Panel Hearing at 91, *In re* Thornhill (No. SC89421).

7. *Id.*

8. Thornhill's lawyer, Christopher McGraugh, would later explain the oddity of the baseball request by highlighting the ease with which an individual could acquire a signed *football* by a *football* player. "But a baseball, that's different. A baseball signed by a football player would compel direct contact with Bradshaw." Telephone Interview with Christopher McGraugh, Attorney, Leritz, Plunkert & Bruning, P.C. (Mar. 19, 2009).

9. *Id.*

tographed baseballs.[10] His collection included baseballs signed by rock star Chuck Barry and baseball players Brian Jordan, Bob Gibson and Tommy Lasorda.

Zink went back to the firm and relayed the details of his conversation with Thornhill to Dalton. Zink told Dalton that Thornhill would reduce Hart's charges if she could get a baseball signed by Bradshaw.[11] The two agreed that the next logical step was to find out if Hart could deliver. Dalton called Hart and requested the baseball.[12] After this and other conversations with Zink and Dalton, Hart believed, rightly or wrongly, that the baseball was a *quid pro quo* for a reduction of her sentence.

The FBI Investigation and Arrival of the Baseball

In early July 2006, Hart contacted the St. Charles County Drug Task Force. She explained that her attorneys had advised her that the prosecuting attorney in her forgery case had agreed to accept sports memorabilia in exchange for a reduction of her charges. Hart questioned whether this was legitimate and elaborated that her attorneys had encouraged her cooperation and urged her to produce the ball. The Task Force, in conjunction with the Federal Bureau of Investigation, initiated a criminal investigation to explore the validity of Hart's bribery allegation.[13]

Chief of Police Robert Noonan of the Drug Task Force contacted Jack Banas, head of the St. Charles County Prosecutor's office and Thornhill's boss, regarding Hart's allegations. They met in mid-July, at which time Noonan played for Banas a taped conversation between Dalton and Hart that confirmed Hart's story and implicated Dalton, Zink, and Thornhill. Noonan left Banas with the impression that the matter was under investigation by the Drug Task Force in conjunction with the FBI. Banas, of course, made no mention of this conversation to Thornhill or anyone else in the office. Rather, Banas secretly monitored Thornhill and the Hart case.[14] "The [FBI and Banas waited] to see if the ball would be transferred."[15]

---

10. *Id.* at 123.

11. Brief for the Informant at 8, *In re* Zink, Oct. 27, 2008 (No. SC89623).

12. *Id.*

13. *See id.*

14. *See* Transcript of Disciplinary Panel Hearing at 17–23, *In re* Thornhill (No. SC89421) (whole paragraph).

15. Telephone Interview with Christopher McGraugh, Attorney, Leritz, Plunkert & Bruning, P.C. (Mar. 19, 2009).

With the cooperation of Hart, the FBI continued to record telephone conversations between Hart and her attorneys. In one such conversation, Zink told Hart that her felonies would be "taken care of" if she could produce a baseball signed by Bradshaw.[16] As part of the sting, Hart agreed to produce the coveted item. The FBI did not record any conversations between Zink and Thornhill, and presumably Dalton and Thornhill never spoke.

In late July, Hart delivered on her promise and gave Zink a baseball purporting to have Terry Bradshaw's signature on it. Zink called Thornhill and proudly proclaimed that Hart had produced the autographed baseball, just as he knew she would. Thornhill was taken aback; "never in his wildest dreams" did he ever imagine Hart would come through.[17] After a lengthy conversation about the authenticity of the ball, Thornhill finally said, "[L]isten, Brian, if it's really real, it is going to be worth something. And you keep it."[18] After they decided that Zink would keep the baseball, Thornhill assured Zink that he would speak with the law enforcement officials who opposed leniency and see if he could garner their approval for a reduction in Hart's sentence.[19] Thornhill said that the baseball "created an opportunity for him to investigate further."[20]

About two and a half weeks later, Thornhill contacted Lieutenant Paul West, an officer with the St. Charles County Drug Task Force and inquired about Hart's good deeds. West told him that Hart had been involved in the biggest arrest the Task Force had made the prior year. West expressed a favorable opinion of Hart, but did not recommend or request that Thornhill reduce Hart's charges to misdemeanors. He did, however, react favorably to the idea when Thornhill brought it up. Thornhill then contacted Major Finkelstein, who was considerably less enthusiastic about Hart. He told Thornhill that she was "the biggest liar in town."[21] Nevertheless, the Major said that he would defer to West's judgment with regard to the evaluation of Hart's cooperation.[22] With the baseball in the picture, Hart's cooperation with the Drug Task Force, which Thornhill once said would not get Zink "a whole lot of mileage," was apparently now going to form the basis of leniency for her.

The St. Charles County Prosecutor's Office had a longstanding policy that all sentencing recommendations, all changes in such recommendations,

---

16. *See* Reply Brief for the Informant at 11, *In re* Zink, Dec. 23, 2008 (No. SC89623).
17. *See* Transcript of Disciplinary Panel Hearing at 141, *In re* Thornhill (No. SC89421).
18. *Id.*
19. *Id.* at 144.
20. *Id.* at 153.
21. *Id.* at 149.
22. *Id.* at 147.

and any other change to a case file, must receive approval from a superior in the office. As an Assistant Prosecuting Attorney, Thornhill was required to follow this policy, and he had done so for the first thirteen years of his career. Indeed, he had obtained authorization for his original sentencing recommendation in the Hart matter. But, on August 24, 2006, Thornhill deviated from his typical "by the book" behavior: he changed his recommendation in Hart's case *without* the consent of his supervisor.[23] Thornhill reduced Hart's charges from three felony forgery charges, which carried a six year prison sentence, to three misdemeanor charges that carried no jail time whatsoever and a trivial monetary penalty.[24] Thornhill relayed this change to Zink and told him that he thought it "was fair."[25] Zink agreed and Hart's charges were accordingly reduced.[26]

Then the sky came crashing down. On August 31, 2006, the FBI appeared at Zink's office to interview him about his representation of Hart. Initially, Zink thought that the FBI had contacted him to seek Hart's assistance in future drug cases. But the conversation soon took an ominous turn: the federal agents began asking pointed questions about the role a Terry Bradshaw autographed baseball had played in the plea negotiations surrounding Hart's forgery case.

Zink told the FBI that the baseball was a joke and that the only point of negotiation between him and Thornhill was Hart's past cooperation with law enforcement, namely through her participation with the St. Charles County Drug Task Force. Zink stated that he never even remotely insinuated to Hart that her felony charges would be reduced if she produced the autographed ball.[27] Some days later, Dalton was interviewed by the FBI and said the same thing. Unfortunately for the two defense attorneys, the FBI had recorded conversations between them and Hart that directly contradicted the majority of their statements.

Around this time, Thornhill received a phone call from Steven Hillemann, a named partner at Zink and Dalton's law firm. Hillemann warned Thornhill that Zink had been contacted by the FBI about the Hart case. Hillemann thought Thornhill "should know what was going on" in the event that

---

23. *Id.* at 115.

24. *Id.* at 93.

25. *Id.*

26. Disciplinary Panel Hearing Decision at 5, *In re* Thornhill, Jul. 3, 2009 (No. SC89421).

27. Oral Argument by Chief Disciplinary Counsel, Alan Pratzel, *In re* Zink, Jan. 7, 2009 (No. SC 89623), *available at* http://www.courts.mo.gov/SUP/index.nsf/0/5edfd60e27b1799686 257506007da88f/.

the FBI tried to contact him. After recognizing the implications of Hille-mann's warning, Thornhill called him back and rescinded his misdemeanor recommendation:

> Listen Steve, if this gal has told even one person that this baseball is the basis for a plea deal … that is not correct, and that's not why this rec-ommendation was changed. So I hate to tell you, but there is no rec anymore. It has got to go back to the original.… [S]o you tell Zink, if you see him, that the deal is off.[28]

Thornhill never directly communicated his change-of-mind to Zink or Dal-ton personally. He later claimed that, in his mind, "telling one [partner in the firm] was telling the firm."[29] Then, without conferring with his direct super-visor or Banas, Thornhill transferred the case to a junior prosecutor in the of-fice,[30] hoping "he could clear it up and that would be the end of it."[31]

As Hillemann had predicted, the FBI contacted Thornhill on September 11, 2006. The FBI told Thornhill that someone at Zink's firm had told Hart that an autographed baseball could be exchanged for a reduced sentence and asked Thornhill to speculate why someone would say something like that if it were not true. Thornhill did not deny the baseball's existence to the FBI, nor did he deny that getting the baseball from Hart was his idea. But he immediately at-tempted to dispel any suggestion that the baseball was a *quid pro quo* for le-niency. He adamantly rejected the notion that the baseball affected his handling of the case, maintaining that the baseball was merely a joke between friends.

Later that same day, Thornhill told Banas about the FBI's visit. Thornhill assured Banas that he was only joking about the baseball. He claimed that he was trying to test Hart's credibility to see whether Bradshaw would really "go to bat for her" if she were to obtain probation. Banas was not convinced. He asked why Thornhill had not simply asked Hart to obtain a letter of recom-mendation from Bradshaw, which would have achieved the very same goal. Thornhill responded that he was concerned that Hart might forge such a let-ter. Although this made little sense—she could forge a signature on a base-

---

28. Transcript Disciplinary Panel Hearing at 107, *In re* Thornhill (No. SC89421).

29. *Id.* 108–09.

30. The date of the transfer is in dispute. The record indicates Thornhill made inconsistent statements concerning this event. Thornhill now contends he transferred the file the same day he spoke with Hillemann, but on a previous occasion, when speaking to Banas, Thornhill revealed he transferred the file after September 11, 2006, the day the FBI contacted him. The discrepancy in dates is about one to two weeks but was not considered significant by the Panel in their determination.

31. Transcript of Disciplinary Hearing at 111, *Thornhill* (No. SC89421).

ball just as easily—Banas left it at that. He did not want to interfere with the FBI investigation.[32]

Shortly thereafter, Zink was interviewed for a second time, this time by Assistant United States Attorney Hal Goldsmith in addition to the FBI. Zink essentially repeated his prior assertions that the ball was a joke and was only intended to demonstrate the credibility of his client to Thornhill. He insisted that he had never told his client otherwise. At this point, AUSA Goldsmith confronted Zink with the conversations that the FBI had taped between him and Hart. Cornered, Zink acknowledged his previous false statements.[33] When later questioned about the nature of his misstatements to the federal authorities, Zink responded:

> In the course of my conversations with the federal agents, I told the agents that the ball was a joke between Mr. Thornhill and myself [sic]. And in the course of that interview, in essence, the ball was a part of the deal, and it wasn't just a joke or a game between me and Mr. Thornhill, and that that was [sic] the false statements.[34]

Essentially, Zink admitted that the baseball was "part of the deal" between him and Thornhill. Dalton similarly acknowledged his prior false statements to the FBI after being confronted with his recorded conversations. Zink and Dalton were informed that they had violated 18 U.S.C. § 1001 by lying to the FBI. Section 1001 makes it a crime to knowingly and willfully make a false statement "in any matter within the jurisdiction of any department or agency of the United States."[35] The stage was set for criminal proceedings against the two.

Zink and Dalton's "Voluntary" Abstention from the Practice of Law

On June 1, 2007, Zink and Dalton entered into a pretrial diversion agreement with the United States Attorney's Office in an effort to avoid federal

---

32. *See id.* at 32–33 (whole paragraph).

33. *See* Brief of the Informant at 9, *In re* Zink, Oct. 27, 2008 (No. SC89623).

34. Oral Response at Disciplinary Panel Hearing, Brian Zink, *In re* Zink, Jun. 26, 2008 (No.SC89623).

35. Section 1001 of Title 18 provides: "Whoever, in any matter within the jurisdiction of any department or agency of the United States knowingly and willfully falsifies, conceals or covers up by any trick, scheme, or device a material fact, or makes any false, fictitious or fraudulent statements or representations, or makes or uses any false writing or document knowing the same to contain any false, fictitious or fraudulent statement or entry, shall be fined not more than $10,000 or imprisoned not more than five years, or both."

prosecution. As a condition of the agreement, they were required to abstain from the practice of law for a period of twelve months. Additionally, both pledged not to violate any state or federal laws, not to drink alcoholic beverages to excess, to work at a lawful occupation, and to remain within the judicial district unless given permission to travel by a pretrial services officer.[36] They were also required to cooperate fully with the Missouri Supreme Court and the Missouri State Bar Disciplinary Commission in any future disciplinary proceedings against them. That same day, Dalton and Zink reported their misconduct to the Missouri Bar. In accordance with their agreements, Zink and Dalton abstained from the practice of law from June 25, 2007, through June 26, 2008.[37]

Matthew Thornhill and the Disciplinary Panel

The Missouri Bar caught wind of the way that Thornhill had handled Hart's case when Banas filed a disciplinary complaint against him. The Bar responded by charging Thornhill with professional misconduct under Rules 4-8.4(d),[38] 4-1.11(e),[39] and 4-8.4(a). Rule 4-1.11(e) prohibits a lawyer who also holds public office[40] from engaging in activities in which the lawyer's "personal or professional interests are or foreseeably could be in conflict with his or her official duties or responsibilities."[41] According to the Bar, Thornhill violated this rule when he agreed to accept sports memorabilia in exchange for a sentencing reduction. Given that Thornhill handled Hart's case in a manner contrary to the disciplinary rules, the Bar charged that he violated Rule 4-8.4(a), which states that it is professional misconduct for a lawyer to "violate or attempt to violate the Rules of Professional Conduct, knowingly assist or induce another to do so, or do so through the acts of another."[42] This

---

36. Allison Retka, Two Lake St. Louis Attorneys Take Suspension of Practices, St. Louis Daily Record & St. Louis Countian, Jul. 5, 2007, *available at* http://findarticles.com/p/articles/mi_qn4185/is_20070705/ai_n19353704.

37. *See* Brief for Informant at 9, *In re* Zink, Oct. 27, 2008 (No. SC89623) (whole paragraph).

38. The Missouri Rules of Professional Conduct, for the most part, mirror the Model Rules of Professional Responsibility. Any applicable Missouri variation is duly noted.

39. In the Missouri Rules effective July 1, 2007, Missouri added Rule 4-1.11(e)(1) and (e)(2) to what was otherwise identical to Model Rule 1.11.

40. It can be assumed that a prosecutor is a "lawyer who holds public office" for the purposes of this rule.

41. Mo. Rules of Prof'l Conduct R. 4-1.11(e).

42. *Id.* R. 4-8.4(a).

conduct, the Bar alleged, was "prejudicial to the administration of justice" in violation of Rule 4-8.4(d).[43] Thornhill denied all of these rule violations and was tried before a Disciplinary Panel on April 9, 2008.[44]

The Bar's Legal Position

According to the Bar, Thornhill's request for the baseball served no legitimate purpose and his explanations did nothing to alleviate the Bar's concern that it was a *quid pro quo*. The Bar pointed to the fact that Thornhill already had a collection of special baseballs and an autographed Terry Bradshaw baseball would be a prized addition to that.[45] It described Thornhill's initial unenthusiastic reaction to Hart's cooperation with the Drug Task Force and noted that it was not until *after* Zink told him that he had obtained the baseball that he agreed to speak with Task Force agents on her behalf.[46] The Bar proffered that the *only* reason Thornhill did this was to create a paper trial. "[Thornhill knew] he [couldn't] go from a felony recommendation to a misdemeanor recommendation without something in the file explaining the basis for that, something other than, 'I got a ball.'"[47]

The Bar then questioned Thornhill's truthfulness by comparing three inconsistent statements he had made to explain his request for the baseball.

Bar Counsel:	At various times when you have been asked about the incident, you have given different explanations for why you asked for the ball. Is that fair to say?
Thornhill:	I have described it differently.... I have used different words to describe what I was doing.
Bar Counsel:	You've said that you asked for the ball as a joke?
Thornhill:	I used that phrase, yes.
Bar Counsel:	Okay. You said that you asked for the ball to see if Terry Bradshaw would support Mary Hart?
Thornhill:	Yes.

---

43. *See id.* R. 4-8.4(d).

44. In Missouri, a Disciplinary Hearing Panel consists of two lawyers from the community and a member of the general public. The Panel issues an advisory opinion to be affirmed or rejected by the Missouri Supreme Court.

45. Transcript of Disciplinary Panel Hearing at 199, *In re* Thornhill (No. SC89421).

46. *Id.* at 96.

47. *Id.* at 208.

| Bar Counsel: | Okay. And you said you asked for the ball to test Hart's credibility? |
| Thornhill: | Yes, I have said all of those things.[48] |

According to the Bar, Thornhill's lack of candor bore directly on his duties as a prosecutor.

The Bar also pointed to Thornhill's failure to obtain supervisory approval of the sentence reduction as further evidence of his ill motive. It rejected his various explanations for this failure: that he (a) didn't know how strictly enforced the policy was; (b) wasn't getting along with his supervisor; and (c) was planning on getting to it "eventually." Finally, the Bar contended that Thornhill should have immediately alerted a supervisor or withdrawn from the case once Zink called him about receipt of the ball. Rather, Thornhill had admitted saying that the baseball was an "opportunity for further negotiation." According to the Bar, Thornhill's handling of the Hart matter was egregiously improper and merited a serious sanction.[49]

Thornhill's Legal Position

Throughout the proceedings, Thornhill stuck to his guns. He flatly denied the baseball was a *quid pro quo* for a reduction in sentencing.[50] He claimed that it was simply symbolic of Hart's veracity. Thornhill asserted that Zink had told him that Bradshaw would be "willing to do anything for [Hart] and would get involved with her life and make sure she goes straight."[51] Thornhill honestly believed that "if someone of [Terry Bradshaw's] influence and financial wherewithal [got] involved with this gal, [then she would have some] hope of actually turning herself around." Thornhill said the baseball allowed him to make certain assumptions and inferences about how far Bradshaw was "willing to go" for Hart. "So if she asked him [for the baseball and he delivered,] the inference would be [that] if she asked him to help her out and give her a place to live, get her out of the state, whatever it may be, I could assume that he would go with it."

Thornhill admitted that he had made a mistake and acknowledged that his actions resulted in an appearance of impropriety, but he insisted that he never elicited the baseball for his own personal interest. He admitted that his

---

48. *Id.* at 114.
49. *See id.* (whole paragraph).
50. *Id.* at 201.
51. *Id.* at 92.

actions were "stupid" and if he could do it all over again he would have never made the request, let alone not informed his superiors of the status of the case. But he insisted that it really was all very harmless:

> It [was] just two friends, one making an outrageous claim that he said he believed; the other one, that is me, saying I can't believe that you are foolish enough to believe what this gal is telling you. And getting egged up enough to say, I will tell you what; I'm going to make an outrageous demand. And that I never, in my wildest dreams, expected it to come to fruition.[52]

The Panel Determination

The Panel determined that Thornhill's actions violated Rule 4-1.11(e)(1) and consequently, Rule 4-8.4(a) because Thornhill "failed to recognize his involvement in prosecuting and negotiating a reduction of charges with Hart's counsel was marked by a conflict of interest, which should have caused [Thornhill] to withdraw from the case in August 2006 if not earlier."[53] Rule 4-1.11(e)(1) prohibited Thornhill from engaging in activities in which his personal or professional interests were, or foreseeably could be have been, in conflict with his official duties or responsibilities.[54] The Panel also concluded, however, that Thornhill did not demonstrate an intention to engage in "conduct that [was] prejudicial to the administration of justice" and therefore did not violate Rule 4-8.4(d).

This latter conclusion resulted from the Panel's failure to find that Thornhill had arranged a *quid pro quo* exchange of the autographed sports memorabilia for a reduction of Hart's felony charges. Apparently, it thought that the evidence on this specific point was too weak. After all, Thornhill never did take possession of the ball. Nevertheless, it held that Thornhill's actions had created an appearance of impropriety. Upon receiving a telephone call from Zink informing him that the autographed ball had arrived, Thornhill had failed to alert his supervisors or transfer the case to another prosecutor. In fact, although the timing was disputed, Thornhill did not transfer the case until after being visited by the FBI.

The Panel wrestled with the proper sanction for Thornhill because "the situation arose from Thornhill's personal interest in sports memorabilia, an

---

52. *Id.* at 131.
53. Disciplinary Panel Hearing Decision at 7, *In re* Thornhill, Jul. 3, 2009 (No. SC89421).
54. Mo. Rules of Prof'l Conduct R. 4-1.11(e).

area not covered in the Rules of Professional Conduct."[55] It determined that, although Thornhill's actions were no doubt negligent, the actual aftermath of Thornhill's conduct was minimal because the charges in Hart's were eventually dropped for entirely unrelated reasons. As additional mitigating factors, the Panel considered Thornhill's clean disciplinary record, cooperative attitude, and his exhibited remorse.

The Panel concluded that Thornhill "did not act dishonestly and did not seek to profit from his handling of the Hart matter." In conflict of interest cases, the Missouri Supreme Court had held that when a lawyer is "merely negligent in determining whether representation may be materially affected by the lawyer's own interests," the appropriate sanction is a public reprimand.[56] The Panel recommended that Thornhill receive a public reprimand. Neither the Missouri Bar nor Thornhill objected to the Panel's determination and so, on June 23, 2008, the decision became final. Thornhill received a public reprimand; his license to practice law remained in good standing. This sanction, as Zink's attorney Paul D'Agrosa described it, was nothing more than "a slap on the wrist."[57]

Brian Zink and the Disciplinary Panel

Zink stood before the Disciplinary Panel on June 26, 2008. While Thornhill was charged with only three rule violations, Zink could hardly say the same. The Missouri Bar did not take well to the fifth-year associate and alleged that Zink had violated Rules 4-1.4(a)(3), 4-4.1(a), 4-3.5(a), 4-8.4(c), 4-8.4(d), and 4-8.4(e). Out of this laundry list of rule violations, Zink conceded that he had violated Rule 4-8.4(c), which prohibits a lawyer from "engag[ing] in conduct involving dishonesty, fraud, deceit, or misrepresentation,"[58] and also Rule 4-4.1(a), which prohibits making false statements of material fact to third persons. Zink admitted that he violated these rules when he made false statements to the FBI and the U.S. Attorney's Office.

---

55. Allison Retka, *St. Charles Judge Fined by Missouri Supreme Court in Alleged Bribe*, St. Louis Daily Rec. & St. Louis Countian, Oct. 2, 2008, *available at* http://findarticles.com/p/articles/mi_qn4185/is_20081002/ai_n29496654/.

56. *See In re* Howard, 912 S.W. 2d 61, 64 (Mo. 1995).

57. Telephone Interview with Paul D'Agrosa, Attorney, Wolff & D'Agrosa (Feb. 17, 2009).

58. Mo. Rules of Prof'l Conduct R. 4-8.4(c).

Zink went three for six with the Disciplinary Hearing Panel, which ultimately determined:

(1) Zink violated Rule 4-1.4(a)(3) because Zink failed to consult with Hart regarding relevant limitations on Zink's conduct when Zink knew Hart expected assistance not permitted by the rules of professional conduct;

(2) Zink engaged in misconduct involving dishonesty, fraud and deceit in violation of Rule 4-8.4(c) when Zink made false statements of material fact to the FBI and the United States Attorney's Office;

(3) Zink violated Rule 4-8.4(e) by communicating to Hart an ability to reduce or eliminate her charges in exchange for improperly influencing the prosecutor using sports memorabilia;

(4) Zink did not engage in conduct prejudicial to the administration of justice, and therefore did not violate Rule 4-8.4(d);

(5) Zink's untruthful statements were not in violation of Rule 4-4.1(a), even though Zink admitted to a violation of the Rule in his answer, because the statements were not made during the course of Zink's representation of Hart;

(6) Zink did not violate Rule 4-3.5 because it could not be proved by a preponderance of the evidence that Zink sought to influence an official (Assistant State Attorney Thornhill) by means prohibited by law.

The Panel concluded that "[t]he facts in this case convincingly demonstrate [Zink] engaged in misconduct which violated the rules of professional conduct.... [Zink's] serious misconduct warrants a severe sanction."[59] The Panel recommended retroactive suspension, which essentially gave Zink credit for "time served" under his pretrial diversion agreement with the United States Attorney's Office. Crucial to the Panel's relatively lenient recommendation was Zink's "full and free disclosure to the Disciplinary Hearing Panel," and Zink's admissions in his Answer. Zink gladly accepted the recommendation, but the Missouri Bar rejected it and filed an appeal with the Supreme Court of Missouri.[60] So, unlike Thornhill, Zink's case was about to go into extra innings.

---

59. Brief for the Informant at 11, *In re* Zink, Oct. 27, 2008 (No. SC89623).

60. In Missouri, the determinations of a Disciplinary Hearing Panel are advisory and the Supreme Court reviews all cases *de novo*. The Court is free to reject, in whole or in part, the recommendations of the Disciplinary Hearing Panel. *See In re* Belz, 258 S.W.3d 38, 41 (Mo. 2008).

Zink's Final Inning: The Missouri Supreme Court

On January 7, 2009, the Supreme Court of Missouri convened a three judge panel to determine Zink's fate. Unlike the Disciplinary Panel, the Court held that Zink had violated all six rules alleged by the Bar. The Court also found that the Panel's recommendation of retroactive suspension failed to adequately address the egregiousness of Zink's conduct and did not take sufficient account of the Court's authority to regulate the practice of law. As a result, the Supreme Court indefinitely suspended Zink's license with leave to reapply in six months.[61] It distinguished Zink's "appropriately harsher" sanction from Thornhill's public reprimand on the ground that Zink intentionally lied to the United States Attorney's Office and the FBI and obstructed a pending criminal bribery investigation.[62]

David Dalton's Disciplinary Hearing

Of the three men, Dalton fared the worst. Although Dalton's conduct throughout the entire ordeal seemed minimal compared to that of Thornhill and Zink, Dalton faced the largest number of rule violations. This is because he was Zink's supervising attorney in the matter. As a result, Dalton was charged with everything Zink had been charged with, plus violations of Rules 4-5.1(b) and 4-5.1(c). Dalton's hearing was held on January 4, 2008.[63]

At the hearing before the Panel, Dalton admitted that he informed Hart that if she produced a signed Terry Bradshaw baseball, the baseball would be given to Thornhill in exchange for Thornhill's promise to reduce her pending criminal charges. Unlike Dalton, Zink had never made this direct admission. The Panel determined that Dalton had failed to explain to Hart that the baseball was not a *quid pro quo* for a sentence reduction, but rather a symbol of Hart's credibility. The Panel held that Dalton should have corrected any mis-

---

61. Under Supreme Court Rule 5.28, if an applicant for reinstatement is suspended indefinitely with leave to reapply in a period of six months or less and is not on probation, the applicant's license "shall be reinstated as a matter of course 30 days after the application for reinstatement is referred to the chief disciplinary counsel for report and recommendation." If, "within that 30-day period, the chief disciplinary counsel files a motion to respond to the application for reinstatement, the license shall not issue and the matter shall proceed in the normal manner."

62. *See* Mo. Sup. Ct. Disciplinary Hearing at 6, *In re* Zink, Jan. 7, 2009 (No. SC 89623) (whole paragraph).

63. *See* Disciplinary Hearing Panel Decision at 1–8, *In re* Dalton, Jan. 4, 2008 (No. SC89104) (whole paragraph).

guided notions his client may have had about the relationship between the baseball and any reduction in her sentence.[64]

According to the Panel, Dalton was directly answerable for Zink's actions because he maintained direct supervisory authority over him. As the senior partner in the matter, it was Dalton's responsibility to ensure that Zink's actions conformed to the Rules of Professional Conduct. Instead, by ratifying and even joining in Zink's unethical behavior, the Panel determined that Dalton had violated Rules 4-5.1(b) and (c). Of import, Dalton freely admitted that his conduct was in violation of these rules and expressed remorse. Nevertheless, the Panel recommended that Dalton be suspended from the practice of law for a period of one year. The Bar and Dalton accepted the Panel's recommendation and the Supreme Court of Missouri affirmed. Dalton was suspended from the practice of law from March 6, 2008 until March 6, 2009.[65]

Postscript

In November 2008, Dalton filed a hardship application with the Supreme Court of Missouri to stay his suspension. On December 16, 2008, the Court granted this motion and lifted the suspension; at that time Dalton had been barred from practice for just over nine months. Dalton was placed on probation through December 31, 2009.[66] Dalton based his hardship application on his purported inability to provide for and support his four children without the ability to practice law or pursue other gainful employment.[67]

Dalton Coyne Cundiff & Hillemann is now Coyne Cundiff & Hillemann and neither Zink nor Dalton is associated with the firm. Dalton is now a sole practitioner at the Dalton Law Firm, P.C., located in Troy and St. Peters, Missouri.[68] Dalton's website states: "David has practiced law in the community for over 18 years and has made a commitment to providing exceptional service and quality results. Excellence in advocacy is the foundation of the law firm."

In early December 2006, Banas informed Thornhill that he had no choice but to fire him. Rather than accept the inevitable, Thornhill resigned

---

64. *Id.* (whole paragraph).

65. *Id.* (whole paragraph).

66. *See* Order Confirming Suspension Stayed, *In re* Dalton, Dec. 16, 2008 (No. SC89104).

67. *See* Hardship Application for Probation of the Respondent, *In re* Dalton, Dec. 4, 2008 (No. SC89104).

68. Website for Dalton Law Firm, *at* http://www.daltonlegalhelp.com/ home.

his position as Assistant State Attorney. But this outcome is not nearly as grim as it sounds for Thornhill. Notably, his resignation came *after* he had been elected to serve as an Associate Circuit Judge for St. Charles County in November 2006. Thornhill took office in January 2007 and remains an Associate Circuit Judge today. However, Thornhill handles only civil matters because Banas disqualifies him whenever he is assigned to a criminal case. In defense of this practice of automatic disqualification, Banas has stated, "It is clearly an internal conflict and always has been and always will be as long as I'm sitting prosecutor. Frankly, in my mind it is a matter of trust. That is not going to change."[69] Thornhill continues to maintain his innocence despite his former boss's apprehension. "My family and I have been deeply saddened by the accusations leveled against me by my former employer.... I am proud of my service to the people in that office. I am completely innocent of the improper conduct of which I have been accused."[70]

Brian Zink lives at home with his wife and plans to apply for reinstatement of his license in July 2009.[71]

Mary Hart's case was ultimately dismissed after the victim decided not to prosecute. Her whereabouts are not known.

Comments and Questions

1. Thornhill promised Zink that he would contact Major Finkelstein and Lieutenant West to discuss Hart's cooperation with the Drug Task Force and determine whether her participation warranted leniency. Thornhill made this promise to Zink and presumably Zink's client Hart at the end of July. A few days after Zink's conversation with Thornhill, Zink and Thornhill ran into each other at the courthouse and Zink asked Thornhill if he had contacted "those guys yet?" Thornhill responded he had not and was not planning to right away. "[L]isten, Brian, I got bigger fish to fry. I got this primary, which is—basically, my life is on hold until I get past that. I will ... call these guys, but it's going to be after that primary election." At the time, Thornhill was

---

69. Steve Pokin, *Judge Denies Wrongdoing Before Disciplinary Panel*, St. Charles (Mo.) J., Jul. 12, 2008, *available at* http://stcharlesjournal.stltoday.com/articles/2008/07/15/news/sj2tn 20080712-0713stc-judge0.ii1.txt.

70. Steve Pokin, *Allegation of Attempted Bribery Cost Lawyer His License*, St. Charles (Mo.) J., Mar. 29, 2008, *available at* http://stcharlesjournal.stltoday.com/articles/2008/03/30/news/ sj2tn20080329-0330stc-pokin0.ii1.txt.

71. After Zink abstained from practicing law, but before his license was suspended, he worked as a process server.

running for Circuit Judge and the primary election was August 8, 2006. Although Thornhill and Zink spoke about contacting the Drug Task Force in the end of July, it was not until August 15th or 16th that Thornhill began to make the initial contacts.[72]

Assume that Zink accepted Thornhill's explanation for this delay because Thornhill was a friend whom he wanted to see on the bench. Assume further that Hart wanted her case disposed of as quickly as possible. Would Zink's conduct in not pushing Thornhill harder violate Rule 4-1.3, which requires that a "lawyer shall act with reasonable diligence and promptness in representing a client"? Comment 3 to Rule 4-1.3 requires a lawyer "act with reasonable promptness." In this context, Rule 4-1.0(h) defines "reasonable" as "the conduct of a reasonably prudent and competent lawyer." Surely, tolerating delay due to personal friendship is not reasonable, is it? On the other hand, a two or three week lapse in the movement of a case is not a long time in the practice of law. Should Zink's motivations be relevant?

2. David Dalton believed that Rule 1.6's Duty of Confidentiality[73] was implicated when he was questioned by the FBI about the Hart case.[74] Do you think it was? Rule 1.6 states: "A lawyer shall not reveal information relating to the representation of a client unless the client gives informed consent [or] the disclosure is impliedly authorized to carry out the representation." Comment 3 to the rule states that "[t]he confidentiality rule ... applies not only to matters communicated in confidence by the client but also to all information relating to the representation." Comment 4 elaborates a bit more: "[t]his prohibition also applies to disclosures by a lawyer that do not in themselves reveal protected information but could reasonably lead to the discovery of such information by a third person." Put another way, the ethical duty applies to all information that relates to the representation of the client, regardless of whether (a) it is privileged, (b) the client asks for it to be kept in confidence or (c) revealing the information might harm the client.

---

72. Transcript of Disciplinary Panel Hearing at 145–46, *In re* Thornhill (No. SC89421) (whole paragraph).

73. Missouri's Rule 1.6 differs from the Model Rule in that effective July 1, 2007, Missouri omitted 1.6(b)(2) and (b)(3). This omission has no bearing on this analysis.

74. On March 15, 2009, Loren J. Beer contacted David Dalton and asked if he would agree to let her interview him. Dalton declined the request, but before his denial, he stated that he believed that Rule 1.6 was implicated during his conversations with the FBI. Dalton said he thought he was bound by a duty of confidentiality not to reveal client confidences when approached by the FBI. This comment explores Dalton's theory, a theory that was never argued during either Dalton or Zink's disciplinary proceedings.

Recall that Zink initially thought that the FBI contacted him to discuss Hart's past cooperation with certain drug task forces. Zink thought that the FBI was interested in working with Hart. Therefore, initially, Zink was impliedly authorized to reveal certain confidential information to the FBI in order to settle his client's matter. In other words, such disclosure was "appropriate to carry out the representation." But what about when the FBI asked if Zink ever had a conversation with his client about a Terry Bradshaw baseball being used as a *quid pro quo* for a reduction in sentencing? Wouldn't this matter fall within the crime-fraud exception to the attorney-client privilege? If so, would that permit Zink to answer the FBI's questions? Or would that still be a violation of Rule 1.6's duty of confidentiality?

Regardless of your answers to these questions, one crucial fact remains: the rules do *not* give lawyers the right to lie to the FBI, the tribunal, or any other third party in an effort to preserve client confidentiality. If the rule applies, they must stand silent.

3. Thornhill phoned Hillemann to inform him the "deal was off the table." Thornhill, however, never communicated this message directly to Zink even though Zink was the attorney representing Hart. Hillemann had no relation to the case other than the fact that he worked at the same law firm as Zink and Dalton. When Thornhill was questioned as to why he did not contact Zink directly, he stated: "Well, I mean, I assumed that they—that telling one was telling the firm."[75] Later he added, "I believe telling [Hillemann] was equivalent to telling Zink in many ways."[76] When asked to describe the significance of telling Hillemann versus Zink that the misdemeanor recommendation had been withdrawn, Thornhill replied:

> [I thought] I'd better call Hillemann back, because if I call Zink and I tell him that the rec is withdrawn and we're talking about the case, if [the FBI] ever interview[s] me, that I was calling him and trying to confirm my testimony to—with him. You know, let's get our stories straight ... I didn't want any inference of that.... I thought I had better just call Steve back and tell him, you tell Brian that the deal is off.[77]

Did Thornhill have an obligation under the rules to expressly inform Zink he was withdrawing his sentencing recommendation? Comment 2 to Rule 4-1.10 provides:

---

75. Transcript of Disciplinary Panel Hearing at 109, *In re* Thornhill (No. SC89421).
76. *Id.* at 160.
77. *Id.*

The rule of imputed disqualification ... gives effect to the principle of loyalty to the client as it applies to lawyers who practice in a law firm. Such situations can be considered from the premise that a *firm of lawyers is essentially one lawyer* for purposes of the rules governing loyalty to the client or from the premise that each lawyer is vicariously bound by the obligation of loyalty owed by each lawyer with whom the lawyer is associated (emphasis added).[78]

Does this rule apply to non-conflict situations? If so, does this comment suggest, as Thornhill proposes, that telling one layer in a law firm something is the same as telling every individual lawyer?

4. It was not disputed that Zink and Dalton's actions violated 18 U.S.C. § 1001. To establish a violation of this section, the government must prove Zink and Dalton knowingly and willfully made false and material statements within the purview of a government agency's jurisdiction. The United States Supreme Court held in *United States v. Rodgers*, 466 U.S. 475, 479 (1984), that the FBI qualifies as a "department or agency of the United States." As for the "materiality" requirement, a statement is "material if it has a "natural tendency to influence or [be] capable of influencing" any governmental action or objective.[79] Do you think Zink and Dalton's statements were material? It could be argued Zink and Dalton's false statements were material because they hindered the FBI's investigatory efforts and influenced the FBI's ongoing investigation of the bribery. Do you agree with this characterization?

5. Thornhill seemed to skate through this case relatively unscathed. Do you agree that there was insufficient evidence of a *quid pro quo*? Was Thornhill simply lucky in that Hart could not credibly make phone calls to him directly (because a prosecutor would expect to negotiate with counsel, not the defendant)? Are you bothered by the fact that Thornhill now serves as an Associate Circuit Judge in St. Charles County?

---

78. Mo. Rules of Prof'l Conduct R. 4-1.10 cmt 2.
79. Kungys v. United States, 485 U.S. 759, 770 (1988).

Chapter 10

Death of a Client-Confessor[1]

I believe Mr. Hunt is factually innocent of these crimes—these terrible crimes. I think he is doing life in prison for a crime he didn't commit. And I've never, ever, ever before violated a client's confidence, never. But Jerry's dead. My disclosure can't hurt him and I have to weigh that disclosure against the continuing harm against this man.[2]

> —Staples S. Hughes, former attorney to Jerry Dale Cashwell, testifying to Lee Wayne Hunt's innocence

For over twenty years, North Carolina Appellate Public Defender Staples S. Hughes agonized over whether to reveal a former client's confidences that he thought would free an innocent man from prison. After his former client died in prison in 2002, Hughes believed that the law allowed him to tell what he knew. He also believed that disclosing his former client's confidences was both "ethically permissible and morally imperative." The North Carolina State Bar may or may not have agreed with Hughes, but the North Carolina courts did not.

It all began in 1985, when Hughes was a young public defender representing Jerry Dale Cashwell, an indigent defendant on trial for a double homicide in Fayetteville. Cashwell confessed multiple times to Hughes and his co-counsel, stating specifically and unequivocally that Cashwell had acted *alone* in planning and committing the execution-style murders.[3] However, even though he pleaded guilty, Cashwell never admitted his *sole* guilt to anyone but his attorneys. They kept his confession secret pursuant to their ethical duties of loyalty and confidentiality, even while another man, Lee Wayne Hunt, was on trial as Cashwell's accomplice. They stood mute as a jury con-

---

1. This chapter is based on the original research and writing of **Ann Hove.**

2. Petition for Rule 2 Review for Petitioner, North Carolina v. Hunt, 659 S.E.2d 6 (2008) (No. 565P07) [hereinafter Petition] (citing transcript of hearing on Motion for Appropriate Relief at 25–26).

3. John Solomon, *The End of a Failed Technique—but Not of a Prison Sentence*, WASH. POST, November 18, 2007, at A15.

victed Hunt on two counts of first degree murder and two counts of conspiracy to commit murder, for which he was sentenced to two life terms plus two consecutive ten year terms in prison.

Over the next twenty years, Hughes remained silent about Hunt's innocence, despite internal torment over what he believed to be the wrongful conviction and sentencing of an innocent man. "It bothered me most ... when Mr. Hunt was being tried," Hughes said in an interview more than two decades later. "And it's bothered me ever since. There wasn't anything I could do about it.... I knew they were trying a guy who didn't do it."[4]

After Cashwell's suicide in prison in 2002, Hughes' obligation to keep Cashwell's confession a secret became less clear. Ordinarily, an attorney's ethical duty of confidentiality and his client's evidentiary attorney-client privilege both survive the latter's death. But, under the unique facts of this case, Hughes believed otherwise. Based on recent case law in the controlling jurisdiction, on a broad interpretation of the exceptions to the confidentiality rule, and on his own internal sense of ethics and morality, Hughes would in fact reveal his former client's confession. Like many quandaries of legal ethics, Hughes' dilemma involved not only the North Carolina professional ethics rules, but also ethics *qua* ethics, in the abstract sense of right versus wrong. Hughes's disclosure of the confessions of a dead client dealt not only with his duty of confidentiality, but also with his deeply-felt moral obligation to help free an innocent man from prison.

Murders of Roland "Tadpole" and Lisa Matthews

On March 7, 1984, authorities found Roland "Tadpole" Matthews and his wife Lisa shot and stabbed to death in their living room. Tadpole was seated in a chair while his wife Lisa was on her knees, slumped over a coffee table. Their two-year-old child was unharmed in a bedroom.[5] Tadpole had been involved in a marijuana trafficking operation in Fayetteville, North Carolina. An investigation uncovered the involvement of other men in that operation, and led to the arrest of Jerry Dale Cashwell, Lee Wayne Hunt, and Kenneth West as suspects for the Matthews murders. These men, and others, were involved in a widespread drug trafficking operation throughout Cum-

---

4. *Id.*

5. North Carolina v. Hunt, 381 S.E.2d 453, 455 (1989); North Carolina v. Cashwell, 369 S.E.2d 566, 567 (1988).

berland County. Hunt led the drug ring from his fortified home, a place his cohorts called the "barn" or the "bunkhouse."[6]

Later, during Hunt's murder trial, the State granted Gene Williford, another man involved in the operation, full immunity from criminal charges in exchange for his testimony. According to Williford, Tadpole had "ripped off" fourteen to fifteen pounds of marijuana from Hunt about two weeks prior to the murders. Early in the morning of March 6, 1984, Williford was present at Hunt's home along with Hunt, Cashwell, West, and another man named Terry Lofton. Williford testified that Hunt told the men about Tadpole's theft and said he wanted to "'teach Tadpole a lesson' that nobody could steal pot from him."[7] He further testified that Hunt instructed Cashwell to go to Tadpole's place of work, wait for him, and accompany him home. Williford would take Hunt and West to Matthews's home later that night, at which time Hunt was going to confront Tadpole about the theft. According to Williford, nothing was said in his presence about *how* Hunt intended to "teach Tadpole a lesson."[8]

Later that night, Williford drove Hunt and West to a location near the Matthewses' residence. Williford testified that Hunt had a nine millimeter pistol and West had a .38 or .357 caliber pistol and a hunting knife. Hunt directed Williford to pick them up in thirty minutes. Williford left, and when he returned, he found West, Cashwell, and Hunt running up to the car. West was carrying a green trash bag full of the "stolen" marijuana. Williford noticed that West and Hunt "looked like they had blood on them." Hunt told Williford to "shut up and get out of there quick."[9]

Williford then drove to Hunt's house, where the men went inside to change clothes and clean up. About fifteen minutes later, West, Cashwell, and Hunt came back outside with two green trash bags. They told Williford that they would "stash the pot and get rid of the clothes." Hunt told Williford to go home, be careful, and get with him later.[10] Several days later, while they were standing outside Hunt's residence, Hunt told Williford that he and West were going to Florida for a couple weeks until "all this blew over." Hunt also warned Williford not to say anything about being near the Matthewses' residence or seeing Hunt "that night."

---

6. Order of Superior Court Denying Hunt Motion, at 14, North Carolina v. Hunt, 659 S.E.2d 6 (No. 85 CRS 16651-54) (2007) [hereinafter Order].

7. *Hunt*, 381 S.E.2d at 455.

8. *Id.* at 456; *Cashwell*, 369 S.E.2d at 566–67.

9. *Hunt*, 381 S.E.2d at 456; *Cashwell*, 369 S.E.2d at 567.

10. *Id.*

Later, Williford returned to Hunt's residence. Cashwell, West, and Terry Lofton were also there. One of them asked what had happened. To this, West responded that the "fat bitch begged us not to kill her too" and that he "was surprised ... how easy it had gone over that they got the pot back." Williford also testified, over Hunt's objection, that after each of these statements, the conversation ceased, and Hunt gave West "a long glance like he had better shut up."[11]

Authorities did not arrest Cashwell, Hunt, West, and Williford in connection with the murders until more than a year later. The state did not charge Williford, who had secured full immunity in exchange for his testimony against the others.[12] Because the State's case was weakest against West, he was able to plead out to the lesser felonies of accessory after the fact and conspiracy,[13] and he signed a statement of facts that state attorneys composed implicating the others. Cashwell and Hunt were not as fortunate.

Faced with overwhelming evidence against him, Cashwell pleaded guilty to the murders. He did not, however, admit in his plea colloquy that he had committed the murders alone. This was critical because, based on the predicate assumption of Hunt's shared responsibility for the murders, Cashwell was able to bypass capital sentencing and avoid the death penalty. As zealous advocates, Hughes and the other attorneys representing Cashwell concealed Cashwell's admissions for precisely this reason, also honoring their professional obligation to conceal confidential client statements connected with the representation.

During his trial, Hunt's attorneys subpoenaed Hughes and his co-counsel to support their theory of Hunt's innocence: that Cashwell had acted alone. Of course, Hughes and Cashwell's other attorney asserted Cashwell's attorney-client privilege and did not testify. Several other witnesses did testify, however, that Cashwell had told them how he had killed the victims alone. Hunt also testified on his own behalf to the same effect.

The Superior Court of Cumberland County rejected all of this testimonial evidence as inadmissible hearsay. It reasoned that because Cashwell was not a party in Hunt's trial, none of Cashwell's out of court statements regarding his sole guilt was admissible. The jury convicted Hunt, and he was sentenced to two life terms plus a term of years. It was the harshest sentence in the case.

---

11. *Hunt*, 381 S.E.2d at 385.

12. *Cashwell*, 369 S.E.2d at 569.

13. Order, *supra* note 6; NORTH CAROLINA CRIMES: A GUIDEBOOK ON THE ELEMENTS OF CRIME 37 (Robert L. Farb ed., 5th ed. 2001).

The evidence against Hunt was mostly circumstantial, and was questionable at best. Williford's testimony contained serious inconsistencies with the fact statement in West's plea agreement. For example, Williford testified that West carried a knife when Williford dropped him off with Hunt near the Matthewses' residence on the day of the murder, and that thirty minutes later, West raced back to Williford's car with blood on him. In contrast, West asserted that he never entered the Matthewses' residence that evening, but instead remained outside.

Fellow jail cell inmates of both Hunt and Cashwell testified for the state against Hunt, but only in exchange for sentence reductions. According to inmate Jeffrey Dale Goodman, Hunt told him that he was charged with two counts of first degree murder regarding a couple that was "killed over drug money," but that "all they had was just two dead bodies, no witnesses" and that "they would never find the gun." Goodman claimed that Hunt described the murders to him, stating that the man was shot first, the woman jumped up and was shot in the head, their throats were cut, and a baby, who was too small to relate what happened, was put in a back room; although full of accurate detail, Goodman's testimony conveniently mimicked the story that had run in all the local newspapers when the murders took place the year before.[14] Moreover, Goodman's testimony may have implicated Hunt's guilt as an accessory after the fact, but it nowhere squarely inculpated Hunt as having planned or perpetrated the murders.

The state also offered testimony from Samuel Thompson, one of Cashwell's fellow jail inmates. Thompson's description of the murders differed from Goodman's. Thompson claimed that when Hunt and West showed up at the Matthewses' house, Cashwell let them in, Hunt handed Cashwell a gun, and Cashwell then shot Tadpole twice in the head, after which Hunt shot Lisa. Cashwell and West thereafter stabbed both Lisa and Tadpole.

Thompson's story would clearly implicate Hunt in the murders, if there were no reason to question its reliability. Gregory Weeks, the assistant public defender who represented Thompson, had testified in an earlier case that, when Weeks tried to plea bargain for Thompson in 1985, Thompson never mentioned having information on Cashwell—which would have been a very useful bargaining chip. It wasn't until a year later, the week that Cashwell's case came to trial, that Thompson informed state prosecutors that he was willing to testify against Cashwell. At that point, attorney Gerald Beaver, who

---

14. Pat Reese, *Murders Remain Unsolved*, FAYETTEVILLE (N.C.) NEWS & OBSERVER, June 8, 1984, at 1A.

also represented Thompson, negotiated on Thompson's behalf. He testified that Thompson "wanted to get out of jail" and that Thompson believed his testimony would secure his release in about three months.[15]

The Superior Court in Hunt's trial also admitted evidence of FBI bullet lead testing that experts used to link Hunt to the Matthews murders. The FBI later discredited this type of analysis as scientifically invalid and susceptible to false or misleading results. Lead matching, which a former chief metallurgist at the FBI now calls "junk science," was the only physical evidence the State used against Hunt.[16]

Despite the unreliability of the testimonial and physical evidence in the case, the jury convicted Hunt of both murders. This conviction withstood appeal all the way up to the North Carolina Supreme Court.[17] Hunt was in prison when Cashwell committed suicide in 2002, and he remains there today.

The Real Story?

Back in 1985, Staples S. Hughes was an assistant public defender in Fayetteville. The state appointed Hughes and fellow attorney Stephen Freedman to assist public defender Mary Ann Tally in representing Jerry Dale Cashwell in the Matthews case.[18] Other lawyers were assigned to represent Hunt and West. As time progressed, Hughes and his co-counsel began to suspect that Cashwell had committed the Matthews murders alone.

Cashwell's Confidential and Privileged Confession

During an initial interview with Hughes and Freedman, Cashwell "histrionically" denied having anything to do with the Matthews murders.[19] How-

---

15. Whether these attorneys were within the applicable state ethics rules here is (relatively) beyond the scope of this chapter.

16. Solomon, *supra* note 3; Petition, *supra* note 2. The FBI first used this "bullet-lead-matching" technique while investigating the assassination of John F. Kennedy, trying to match bullet fragments discovered at Dealey Plaza with bullets found in Lee Harvey Oswald's rifle. *Evidence of Injustice* (CBS television broadcast Nov. 18, 2007). For over forty years, Bureau scientists conducted analysis based on this now-debunked technique to help state and local prosecutors convict defendants, like Hunt, around the country. *Id.*

17. Hunt also filed a motion for new trial *pro se* in 1994, which the Superior Court also denied. *See* Petition, *supra* note 2.

18. *Id.* at 4.

19. *Id.*

ever, preliminary investigation indicated that Cashwell was prone to fits of rage and violent outbursts related to his developing deafness. This fact, together with information from potential witnesses and other aspects of the investigation, pointed to Cashwell as the sole perpetrator. When Hughes asked Cashwell why others might implicate him as the only person responsible for the double homicide, Cashwell's response, after hesitation, was, "I guess because I did it."[20]

Cashwell then spilled the entire story of how he murdered Tadpole and Lisa Matthews. He recounted how he spent the entire day with them, and described how he alone shot and stabbed both of them. Cashwell explained that his dispute with the Matthewses started as a minor tiff about turning up the television, but then escalated into murderous violence. As Hughes recalled, "the phrase that [Cashwell] used was that he just 'lost it.'[21] [The murders] had nothing to do with drugs."[22]

"It was ... one of those moments that stops you completely still," Hughes later said. "[M]y client [was] saying, 'Not only did I kill two people, but these other folks didn't have anything to do with it. The state's case [was] a lie ... a fabrication.'"[23]

Cashwell was clear that he had no interest in shielding West or, especially, Hunt, whom Cashwell blamed for spreading the word about his guilt. However, according to Hughes, Cashwell was consistently clear, throughout the representation and over the two decades thereafter, that he was singularly responsible the Matthews murders, and that Hunt and West had no involvement until after the fact.[24]

Cashwell's confession seriously hamstrung Hughes and his co-counsel, preventing them from engaging in meaningful plea bargaining and limiting their trial strategy to a defense based on reasonable doubt. Consistent with their ethical duties of confidentiality and loyalty to Cashwell as their client, Hughes and his co-counsel had to keep quiet. Disclosing Cashwell's admission of singular guilt would subject him to the death penalty. By keeping it a secret, Hughes and his co-counsel allowed the State, and the courts, to assume Hunt's complicity in the murders. This strategy helped Cashwell secure a life-sentence plea agreement and avoid death row.

---

20. *Id.* at 5.
21. *Id.*
22. Solomon, *supra* note 3.
23. CBS, *supra* note 16.
24. Solomon, *supra* note 3.

Silence Is Golden—and Painful

Despite his certainty that Cashwell alone murdered the Matthewses, Hughes kept quiet about Cashwell's admissions throughout the multiple trials and appeals that followed. But he never forgot about it. After Cashwell's death in 2002, Cashwell's confession haunted Hughes's conscience even more. Still, Hughes continued to keep his mouth shut, even though he was certain that Hunt was serving life in prison for crimes he did not commit.

Distinguishing Cashwell's Attorney-Client Privilege from Hughes's Ethical Duty of Confidentiality

Hughes had no other option but to endure years of torment over this case, because the North Carolina ethics rules on confidentiality, and the evidentiary rule of attorney-client privilege, required his silence. His obligation to keep Cashwell's admission a secret derived from his attorney-client relationship with Cashwell. In general, an attorney-client relationship is a contractual one, with terms implied by custom, and with specific duties and limitations embodied in case-law and in state rules of professional conduct.

As his attorney, Hughes owed Cashwell a duty of loyalty and thus a duty of confidentiality, both during and after conclusion of the representation. Specifically, Rule 1.6(a) of the North Carolina State Bar Rules of Professional Conduct states that "[a] lawyer shall not reveal information acquired during the professional relationship with a client unless the client gives informed consent, the disclosure is impliedly authorized in order to carry out the representation, or the disclosure is permitted by paragraph (b)." This rule essentially mirrors its ABA counterpart, Model Rule 1.6. North Carolina Rule 1.9(c)(2), which also has a Model Rule equivalent, provides that an attorney's duty of confidentiality extends to former clients as well.[25]

A lawyer's ethical duty of confidentiality is very broad. It covers not only direct communications between the attorney and client, but also any and all information related to the case that the attorney learns during the representation. In contrast, the attorney-client privilege is a rule of evidence. It is much narrower than the ethical duty, covering only private communications between attorney and client. It prevents a court, or other governmental tribunal, from using its powers of subpoena or contempt to compel revelation of

---

25. N.C. RULES OF PROF'L CONDUCT R. 1.6 cmt. 1 (2006); *see also id.* R. 1.9(c)(2).

such communications.[26] The privilege may be waived only by the client; thus, attorneys are required to invoke it on their client's behalf unless and until instructed otherwise. Like the duty of confidentiality, the attorney-client privilege must be observed indefinitely, including after the client's death, unless the communication falls into a recognized exception.[27]

The privilege and the duty differ in their exceptions as well. There are four common exceptions to the privilege: (1) during law suits between client and attorney; (2) when the attorney is an attesting witness on a document; (3) regarding basic information related to the representation (i.e., revelation of a fee arrangement or client's identity); and (4) the "crime-fraud" exception, where a client has sought an attorney's services to engage in or assist a future crime or fraud.[28]

Jurisdictions vary on whether a fifth exception to the privilege becomes available following the death of the client. North Carolina, it turns out, recognizes such an exception. In the case of *In re Miller*,[29] the North Carolina Supreme Court carved out an exception to the privilege when the client has died and either: (1) the attorney-client communications in question related solely to a third party; or (2) even if the communications pertained to a right or interest of the client, disclosure of the communications would neither impose civil liability upon the deceased client's estate nor harm the deceased client's reputation or loved ones.

By way of contrast, federal common law is less clear concerning the extent to which it recognizes an exception for deceased clients. The issue was most recently addressed by the Supreme Court in *Swidler v. Berlin*.[30] Although the Court held that the state's interest in investigating crime was insufficient to override the privilege even after a client's death, it noted in *dicta* that the revelation of otherwise privileged communications between attorney and client may be necessary to prevent conviction of an innocent person.

There are typically seven exceptions to the ethical duty of confidentiality, which both the ABA Model Rules and the North Carolina ethics rules list in Rule 1.6(b). These exceptions are: (1) the client gives written informed consent to the disclosure; (2) the attorney is impliedly authorized to make such disclosure; (3) there is a dispute involving the attorney's conduct; (4) the attorney needs to obtain legal advice; (5) disclosure is required by court

---

26. David Luban, Lawyers & Justice: An Ethical Study 187 (1988).
27. Swidler & Berlin v. United States, 524 U.S. 399 (1998).
28. Restatement (Third) of the Law Governing Lawyers §§75, 82–83 (2008).
29. *In re* Miller, 595 S.E.2d 120 (2004).
30. *Swidler & Berlin*, 524 U.S. 399.

order or other law; (6) disclosure is required to prevent reasonably certain death or substantial bodily harm; and (7) disclosure will prevent or mitigate substantial financial harm that may result from the use of the attorney's services.

North Carolina has adopted this list with only minor differences. Significantly, its exception relating to death or bodily harm omits the word "substantial." However, the pertinent comment states that one should interpret the rule's phrase, "to prevent reasonably certain death or bodily harm" as permitting disclosure to prevent "reasonably certain death or *substantial* bodily harm," leaving the interpretation of the exception subject to dispute.

Death and Disclosure

Cashwell's prison suicide occurred in 2002. Initially, Hughes did nothing; at that time, the doctrine that death does not invalidate the attorney-client privilege was well entrenched. But then the *Miller* case started to rise through the North Carolina courts. Hughes followed the case carefully.

In *Miller*, authorities discovered Dr. Eric D. Miller dead from arsenic poisoning. At the time of his death, his wife was involved in a relationship with her co-worker, Derril H. Willard. Shortly thereafter, Willard sought legal counsel from attorney Richard T. Gammon. Within days of meeting with Gammon, Willard committed suicide.[31]

The State subpoenaed the confidential communications between Willard and Gammon. Gammon asserted Miller's attorney-client privilege, but the court overrode the privilege with regard to certain statements after reviewing Gammon's affidavit *in camera*.[32] The Court held that it could override attorney-client privilege after death of a client in only two circumstances. First, the Court stated that the privilege does not exist where a client has died and the communications between attorney and client related *solely* to a third party. Second, the privilege also does not protect communications that transpired between attorney and client even if disclosure could have affected the rights or interests of the client (were he alive), but such disclosure (1) would not subject the deceased client's estate to civil liability, and (2) would not harm the deceased client's reputation or loved ones. Because the communications at issue

---

31. *Miller*, 595 S.E.2d at 120.

32. *Id.* Under "*in camera* review," a court reviews confidential information under video recording to preserve a record of that review without revealing potentially confidential information. BLACK'S LAW DICTIONARY (8th ed. 2004).

in *Miller* had come from a dead client, and related solely to a third party, the court ordered Gammon to disclose these statements to the State.

In light of the dicta in *Swidler* and now the holding of *Miller*, Hughes reviewed his options. He believed that revelation of Cashwell's confession was permissible under the bodily harm exception to North Carolina's confidentiality rule. He knew that Comment 6 to the rule clarified that disclosure could be made even if the bodily harm sought to be prevented was not imminent as long as "there is a present and substantial threat that a person will suffer such harm at a later date if the lawyer fails to take action necessary to eliminate the threat."[33] Hughes believed that, by serving a life sentence in prison for crimes he did not commit, Hunt suffered the kind of harm this rule contemplated. Thus, Hughes was convinced that his disclosure of Cashwell's confessions would not violate Rule 1.6(a).

As to the privilege, Hughes believed his case fit into the four corners of the *Swidler* dicta and the *Miller* holding. Considering the latter, Cashwell had openly pleaded guilty to the Matthews murders while he was alive. Hence, disclosing his private statements of singular guilt would not harm his reputation or his loved ones. Further, Cashwell had been indigent and left no estate to incur civil liability. As Hughes later said, "[h]is estate was a pair of shower shoes and two paperback books." These circumstances appeared to overcome the attorney-client privilege.

After weighing the factors of Cashwell's suicide, the impact of *In re Miller* on the inviolability of the attorney-client privilege, the exceptions to confidentiality in the North Carolina ethics rules, and his personal sense of morality, ethics, and justice, Hughes decided to reveal Cashwell's admissions to vindicate Hunt's innocence. He contacted Professor Richard Rosen, supervising attorney at the Innocence Project at the University of North Carolina School of Law, about Cashwell's confession and its implication for Hunt's innocence. The Project already had a case file for Hunt. So, after Hughes agreed to testify, Rosen filed a Motion for Appropriate Relief (MAR) in the Superior Court of Cumberland County, in Fayetteville, North Carolina, requesting a new trial on Hunt's behalf.

Even a Well-Conceived Plan Can Fail

On January 8, 2007, Hughes took the stand in Hunt's MAR hearing. But before he could barely get out a word, Judge Jack A. Thompson of the Cumber-

---

33. N.C. Rules of Prof'l Conduct R. 1.6 cmt. 6 (emphasis added).
34. Adam Liptak, *When Law Prevents Righting a Wrong*, N.Y. Times, May 4, 2008.

land County Superior Court intervened.[34] "If you testify," Judge Thompson said, "I will be compelled to report you to the state bar. Do you understand that?"

This was the worst case scenario. Rather than ordering him to breach the privilege under the *Miller* exception, Judge Thompson was threatening Hughes with serious professional consequences if he failed to honor it. Nevertheless, Hughes felt certain that he was doing the right thing. He told the judge that he understood the court's position, and then he continued with his testimony.[35] Hughes testified that twenty-two years ago, his former client, Jerry Dale Cashwell, now dead, confessed that he acted alone in committing the double murder of Roland "Tadpole" and Lisa Matthews for which Lee Wayne Hunt was serving a life sentence. After Cashwell died in prison in 2002, "it seemed [to Hughes] at that point ethically permissible and morally imperative that [he] spill the beans." Hughes disclosed this information in testimony to help exonerate Hunt after over twenty years of imprisonment for crimes he did not commit.

The superior court ultimately excluded Hughes's testimony about Cashwell's confession, finding it inadmissible as a breach of Cashwell's attorney-client privilege.[36] Additionally, Judge Thompson stated in his order denying the MAR that "Mr. Hughes ... committed professional misconduct" by breaching the attorney-client privilege of his former client.

The court also found that Hughes's testimony was inadmissible hearsay that did not qualify for treatment as a statement against a penal interest under North Carolina Evidence Rule 804(b)(3). Under North Carolina case law, such statements must *actually* subject a declarant to criminal liability, and corroborating circumstances must insure the trustworthiness of the statement.[37] The court held that, because Cashwell made his admissions to his attorneys during their representation of him, he made such statements confidentially and, therefore, he could not have expected the statements to subject him to criminal liability.[38] Furthermore, the court found that Cashwell's confession lacked corroborating circumstances that would insure its trustworthiness. The court determined that it was physically unlikely that Cashwell could have committed the murders alone and traversed a distance of six miles on foot between locations where other witnesses placed him that

---

35. Telephone Interview with Staples S. Hughes, North Carolina Appellate Defender in Gainesville, Fla. (Mar. 3, 2009); Petition, *supra* note 2, at 8; Liptak, *supra* note 833.

36. Petition, *supra* note 2, at 8; Order, *supra* note 6, at 11.

37. N.C. R. Evid. 804(b)(3); Order, *supra*, note 6, at 11; State v. Singleton, 354 S.E.2d 259, 263 (1987).

38. Order, *supra* note 6, at 12–13; People v. Vespucci, 745 N.Y.S. 2d 391, 399 (2002).

night. In addition, it had been raining, and Cashwell's sister and mother tes-tified that Cashwell's clothes did not appear to be wet from the rain when he came home.

Hunt appealed Judge Thompson's order to the North Carolina Court of Appeals. The appeals court denied Hunt's petition for writ of certiorari, without opinion. Hunt then petitioned the Supreme Court of North Carolina for "Rule 2" review of his MAR denial. In this petition Hunt argued that the superior court had failed to apply the mandatory precedent of *In re Miller*, which stated an exception to the attorney-client privilege in similar situa-tions. Hunt also argued that the court erroneously failed to recognize the newly discovered evidence of Hughes's testimony and of the discredited bul-let lead analysis. Finally, Hunt argued that the court violated his due process rights in failing to admit Hughes's testimony, and by allowing the State to offer materially inconsistent theories of guilt in Hunt's prosecution and West's plea agreement.

The North Carolina Supreme Court summarily rejected Hunt's argu-ments and denied his petition for Rule 2 review, allowing Judge Thompson's order to stand. Despite Hughes's resolute certainty about Hunt's innocence and Cashwell's singular guilt in the Matthews murders, the court of last re-sort in North Carolina has now left the fate of Hunt's release in the hands of the newly-created North Carolina Innocence Inquiry Commission. His case is still pending before this agency.[39] Hunt remains imprisoned, now in this twenty-fifth year, for crimes Staples S. Hughes believes that he did not com-mit.

What Happened in Grievance Committee, Stayed in Grievance Committee

Lawyers have long faced lay criticism for staying quiet about the guilt of their clients.[40] By contrast, Hughes was awarded with a State Bar disciplinary complaint for speaking up about his deceased client's guilt. Although the source of the complaint is confidential, all indications are that it was filed by Judge Thompson.

In any event, in January 2008, the State Bar Grievance Committee dis-missed the complaint without public comment. As a result of the dismissal,

---

39. Liptak, *supra* note 34.
40. *Id.*

the North Carolina State Bar did not conduct a hearing to determine whether Hughes had violated its ethics rules on client confidentiality. In addition, the substance of the complaint and the Committee's rationale in dismissing it remain confidential and inaccessible.[41] Hughes came out unscathed, though his efforts to save Hunt were rebuffed.

Comments and Questions

1. The odd result in this case is that Hughes violated the narrow attorney-client privilege although—judging from the dismissal of the ethics complaint—he did not violate the more encompassing duty of confidentiality. There are several possible explanations for this outcome. One is that it is simply the result of an anomaly in our enforcement system—privileges are interpreted and enforced by the courts, while ethical duties are interpreted and enforced by the Bar. Alternatively, it is possible that the divergence arose from the different exceptions to the two doctrines. After all, while the duty of confidentiality may be breached to prevent serious bodily injury, the same is not true of the privilege.

Also note that the case deals with an area of tremendous gray. Reasonable people could disagree about Judge Thompson's interpretation of the privilege, just as they could disagree about the Committee's apparent interpretation of the exceptions to the duty. The *Miller* factors could have been interpreted to open the door to Hughes's testimony, just as the bodily harm exception to the ethical rule could have been interpreted to keep it out. What do you think? Did Hughes breach the attorney-client privilege? Did he breach his ethical duty of confidentiality?

2. The fact that Hughes acted on his "moral imperative" here points to the elephant in the room of legal ethics—to what extent should an attorney's sense of morality factor into lawyer-client relations? Should lawyers even consider the impact of clients' decisions on others?[42] Under a directive lawyering approach to moral issues in law practice, some legal scholars argue that lawyers can and should act on the basis of their own principled convictions, even when they realize that their view on the issue is not absolute. Under this theory, lawyers' moral obligations should take precedence over professional obligations when they conflict. A lawyer should act to promote "justice" in

---

41. E-mail from Katherine Jean, Counsel to the North Carolina State Bar (Feb. 17, 2009, 17:28:05 EST) (on file with author).

42. Leonard L. Riskin et al., Dispute Resolution and Lawyers 129–32 (3d ed. 2005).

each case, a maxim that connotes basic values of the legal system and other norms ordinarily morality. This theory is problematic, however, because a lawyer's individual sense of morality is far from an objective standard. Such decisions are based on subjective value judgments, which may conflict with the profession's ethical stance or with the client's sense of morality and personal dignity.[43]

Under a more client-centered approach, a lawyer should remain neutral and non-judgmental of a client's decisions that implicate moral issues. This approach presents the potential danger that a lawyer may act merely as a hired gun, and steer a client toward a consequentialist self-serving moral analysis. This approach conflicts with many other moral frameworks that would advocate "doing the right thing" regardless of negative consequences.[44]

Under a collaborative approach, both the lawyer and the client should together conduct a moral discourse regarding decisions related to the representation. In this way, a lawyer would not impose personal morals on a client; rather, the relationship would mirror a friendship in which participants aim toward becoming better people.[45] Moral discourse between lawyers and their clients is possible and can be fruitful.[46] A failure to discuss morals in a representation may risk ignoring the interests of other people.[47] To the extent that a lawyer and client share moral values there is a greater likelihood of mutual understanding and rapport. Also, where lawyer and client have differing moral views, they may gain insight from these differences. Encountering differing moral viewpoints enables one to question and look beyond his or her own perspective.[48] The ABA Model Rules encourage, but do not require, a collaborative approach.[49]

Which approach to morality did Hughes exercise in this case? Would you have done the same thing? Should Hughes have engaged Cashwell in a discussion of the moral ramifications raised by his confidential confession?

3. The duty of confidentiality and the attorney-client privilege are doctrines founded on the utilitarian principle that the justice system works best if

---

43. *Id.*

44. Michael Seigel, *Use of Privileged Information for Attorney Self-Interest: A Moral Dilemma*, BUS & PROF'L ETHICS J., Fall 1983, at 1.

45. RISKIN ET AL., *supra* note 42.

46. THOMAS L. SHAFFER & ROBERT F. COCHRAN, JR., LAWYERS, CLIENTS, & MORAL RESPONSIBILITY 52 (2d ed. 2009).

47. *Id.* at 54.

48. *Id.* at 53.

49. See MODEL RULES OF PROF'L CONDUCT 2.1 ("In rendering advice [to a client], a lawyer may refer not only to law but to other considerations such as moral, economic, social and political, that may be relevant to the client's situation.").

clients can speak to their attorneys freely. Nevertheless, each doctrine recognizes several instances where the importance of disclosure is deemed to outweigh the benefits of confidentiality. Should the death of a client be a factor on the scale? Always, or only under certain circumstances? If the latter, what should these circumstance be?

Index

A

ABA Model Rules. See Model Rules of Professional Conduct
adversity, 123
    substantially related, 126–27
advocacy
    illicit conduct *vs.*, 183–89
Analytica, Inc. v. NPD Research, Inc., 127, 128
attorney competency
    of Steven Glazer, 78–81
attorney sanctions. *See also* disbarment; suspension of license
    public reprimand, 193–94
attorney-client relationships. *See also* conflicts of interest
    morality in law practice, 216–17
    privilege, 216
    privilege, exceptions to, 211
    privilege survives death, 204
    privilege *vs.* confidentiality, 210–12
    sex with clients, 91–108

B

Bannon, Brad, 37
Bell, Stewart, 144
Berlin, Swidler v.
    privilege exception for deceased clients, 211

Bershad, David, 53, 61
Bester, Margot, 4
Bible
    Matthew 6:24, 9
Bishop, Keith, 19
Black, Freda, 19
Board of Education, Cromley v., 129
Bray, Robert, 115
bribery, 185–89
Broomfield, Nick, 87
Brown, Laura, 94–95, 98–99
Burns, John, 115

C

capital cases, 69–79
    attorney competency in, 78–81
    attorney requirements in, 89
    death penalty issues, 84–87
    State v. Smith, 89
Carpenter, M. Ellen, 177–78, 180
Cashwell, Jerry Dale, 204, 206, 208
    confidential and privileged confession, 208–9
    privilege *vs.* confidentiality, 210–12
"Chinese wall," 113, 117, 123–24
    Cromley v. Board of Education, 129
class action cases, 54–61, 68
client-centered lawyering, 217